EXISTENTIALISM AND CONTEMPORARY CINEMA

EXISTENTIALISM AND CONTEMPORARY CINEMA

A Beauvoirian Perspective

Edited by

Jean-Pierre Boulé and Ursula Tidd

berghahn
NEW YORK · OXFORD
www.berghahnbooks.com

First published in 2012 by

Berghahn Books

www.berghahnbooks.com

©2012, 2015 Jean-Pierre Boulé and Ursula Tidd
First paperback edition published in 2015

Library of Congress Cataloging-in-Publication Data

Existentialism and contemporary cinema: a Beauvoirian perspective / edited
by Jean-Pierre Boulé, and Ursula Tidd.
    p. cm.
Includes bibliographical references and index.
ISBN 978-0-85745-729-5 (hardback : alk. paper) -- ISBN 978-1-78238-
903-3 (paperback : alk. paper) -- ISBN 978-0-85745-730-1 (ebook)
    1. Existentialism in motion pictures. 2. Philosophy in motion pictures.
    3. Beauvoir, Simone de, 1908-1986--Philosophy. 4. Beauvoir, Simone
    de, 1908-1986—Influence. 5. Feminism and motion pictures. I. Boulé,
    Jean-Pierre. II. Tidd, Ursula.

PN1995.9.E945E93 2012
791.43'684--dc23

                                                             2012029452

British Library Cataloguing in Publication Data

A catalogue record for this book is available from the British Library

Printed on acid-free paper.

ISBN: 978-0-85745-729-5 hardback
ISBN: 978-1-78238-903-3 paperback
ISBN: 978-0-85745-730-1 ebook

In memory of Elizabeth Fallaize 1950–2009

[U.]

For Lya

[J.-P.]

CONTENTS

Acknowledgements

We would like to thank Lucille Cairns, Darren Waldron and the anonymous readers from Berghahn Books for their helpful suggestions and support, and Nick James for the index.

INTRODUCTION

Jean-Pierre Boulé and Ursula Tidd

In *Existentialism and Contemporary Cinema: A Beauvoirian Perspective* we aim to re-open a dialogue between Simone de Beauvoir's philosophy and film studies which she herself inaugurated. In so doing, we offer a range of new Beauvoirian perspectives on the study of contemporary cinema and demonstrate the relevance of her thought to cinematic culture. In the chapters that follow this Introduction, key Beauvoirian themes and ideas will thus be brought into sharper focus through their application in a variety of ways to the analyses of films and their stars.

Simone de Beauvoir (1908–86) is most well known as the author of *The Second Sex* (1949), widely acknowledged as the foundational text of second wave feminism, and as an existentialist philosopher and literary writer of the French post-war period. However, her work, until this present volume, has not readily or often been associated with film studies.[1] This is paradoxical when it is recognised that Beauvoir was the first feminist thinker to inaugurate the concept of the gendered 'othering' gaze – a *sine qua non* of subsequent second-wave Anglophone feminist film theory.[2] Moreover, other concepts associated with Beauvoirian existentialism such as ambiguity, gendered alienation, situated freedom, woman as absolute Other, and the synergistic nexus of embodiment, temporality and agency are highly suggestive for reading screen culture as evidenced by many of the essays in this volume.

Despite Beauvoir's frequently proclaimed faith in the value of literature, language and philosophy as a means to know and interpret the world, her philosophical and personal writings contain abundant references to her cinema-going and cinematic interests. Beauvoir was an avid but not uncritical fan of 'le septième art', as it is known in France. She explained this interest in a rather phenomenological and ironically somewhat psychoanalytical description of her own role as a film spectator in the fourth volume of her memoirs, *All Said and Done*:

> When I go into a cinema, I leave my actual self at the door; and although my past is certainly there behind me as I react to the film, it is not there as a conscious entity

and my only project is to watch the scenes that go by before my eyes. I accept them as true, and I am not allowed to intervene in anyway; my praxis is paralysed and in some cases this paralysis emphasises the unbearable nature of the pictures, while in others it makes them enchanting. **Sitting there in front of the screen, I surrender myself entirely, as I do in dreams; and in this case too, it is visual images that hold me captive – that is why cinema awakens dream-like echoes in each beholder.** If a film affects me deeply, it does so either because it stirs unformulated memories or because it brings unspoken hopes back to life.

(Beauvoir 1977: 195–96)

Beauvoir explains here the fascination cinema held for her by describing the immediate power of visual images to captivate and activate the viewer's imaginary life. Distinct from the process of reading books, watching films induces a powerful dream-like state in her because of its altered temporality and relationship to the imagination; it involves her instantly and entirely: affectively, somatically, intellectually, and psychically. Film spectatorship, as she describes it, activates unconscious psychic fragments of the past and mobilises them into present lived experience. As such, then, Beauvoir recognised the power and influence of cinema as it was emerging as the increasingly dominant cultural discourse of the post-war period.

Her interest in cinema dates back to her earliest cinema outings during her student years alone or with her cousin Jacques to see art-house and early Hollywood films at the Studio des Ursulines, the Vieux-Colombier and Ciné Latin in Paris (Beauvoir 1963: 241). Rejecting the contemporary bourgeois disdain for cinema in the 1920s as 'entertainment for housemaids', Beauvoir embraced the cinematic avant-garde (Beauvoir 1965: 48). She then 'discovered' popular cinema in the form of cowboy films and whodunits in 1929 with Jean-Paul Sartre and, with Paul Nizan, they even made and acted in short amateur films together. In the 1930s, Hollywood cinema dominated their viewing interests; first, because it was a means to know America and, second, because they found crime and gangster movies more intellectually engaging than the crude realism of much French cinema of the era. They deplored the 'flat dialogue, insipid photography and actors talking in artificial voices' in French films, with the exception of work by Prévert, Carné and Vigo (Beauvoir 1963: 323). They initially lamented the arrival of the 'talkies' yet welcomed Chaplin's non-realist use of sound in *Modern Times* – a film which would lend its name to *Les Temps Modernes*, the journal they would later set up in 1945. A new generation of film directors such as Delannoy, Daquin and L'Herbier then drew Beauvoir and Sartre back to French cinema in the early 1940s and world cinema remained an enduring source of theoretical reflection, cultural interest and entertainment for Beauvoir until the 1970s, and constituted a rich corpus of source material for her own writing and philosophy.

Before looking in more detail at the role of cinema among Beauvoir's theoretical interests, it is useful to note the broader influence of existentialism on cinema more generally.

Beauvoir and Sartre are of course synonymous with French atheistic existential phenomenology, one of the leading philosophies of the post-war period in continental Europe with diverse resonances across the world. In its heyday in the 1940s and 1950s, existentialism shares a rich cinematic tradition with classic French cinematic movements such as 'the new wave' and Hollywood genres such as '*film noir*' in the ways it influenced international directors and avant-garde filmmaking over the latter half of the twentieth century. The phenomenological focus of existentialism on temporally situated 'lived experience' and its recognition of the specular dynamic of self and other relationships are highly relevant to the study of cinema. As early as 1931, Sartre delivered a lecture on 'l'art cinématographique' to students in Le Havre which coincided with the period during which he began writing the first draft of *Nausea*, published in 1938. In the lecture, he argued that cinema reflected the spirit of the contemporary age and posed a challenge to the bourgeois hierarchies of theatre and its formal emphasis on the unity of action. Cinema was an authentic art form, in Sartre's view, because it constituted a visual manifestation of the irreversibility of time and an insight into the totalising process of human destiny. These proto-existentialist ideas were further developed in the existential philosophy that he and Beauvoir would later set out, according to which temporally situated existence precedes essence (Sartre 1970: 549). At its height in the 1940s and 1950s, existentialism influenced classic French cinematic movements such as 'the new wave' and Hollywood genres such as '*film noir*' and in turn shaped the work of international directors and avant-garde filmmaking throughout the latter half of the twentieth century.

In *Film Theory, An Introduction*, Robert Lapsley and Michael Westlake analyse the politics of film (2006: 1–31). They see the politics of gender becoming important from the late 1970s onwards, displacing the previous focus on the politics of class (Lapsley and Westlake 2006: 23). The original aim of this first wave of Anglophone feminist film criticism was to establish feminist methodologies for interpreting film culture. This was firstly achieved by denouncing the patriarchal ideology which underpinned the greater part of Hollywood's output, secondly by debating whether the few films which starred women protagonists perpetuated stereotypes or challenged them, contributing to a 'redefinition of femininity' (Lapsley and Westlake 2006: 24), and, thirdly, by recovering a lost history of women's filmmaking as 'writers, editors and above all directors' (ibid.). By then, cinema imperatively needed to 'break with received notions of femininity and depict women truthfully' (Lapsley and Westlake 2006: 24–25). If we substitute 'truthfully' for 'authentically', this could almost be the definition of Beauvoir's project in *The Second Sex*. Ensuing gender political debates in cinema then sought to address notions of female specificity and essence, adopting instead the notion of 'femininity as a construct' (Lapsley and Westlake 2006: 25). The gender political content of film was not the only realm to be investigated: the formal properties of film came under the spotlight. In this respect, Beauvoir proved to be a pioneer with her essay on 'Brigitte Bardot and the Lolita Syndrome', published in 1959, which critiqued form as well as content.[3] Subsequent Anglophone feminist film critics turned their attention to genre cinema. For instance, melodrama, which had often been seen to perpetuate stereotypes of women, could be read as subversive, as could *film noir*, as a means of signifying the return of the repressed (Harvey 1978: 33). Avant-garde filming practice was also encouraged as 'a truly progressive cinema would need to break with all existing modes of representation' (Lapsley and Westlake 2006: 29). Instead of suppressing gender difference in order not to sustain male dominance, there was a need for the 'delineation and specification of difference as liberating, as offering the only possibility of radical change' (Doane, Mellencamp and Williams 1984: 12).

In France, women filmmakers and screenplay writers such as Agnès Varda and Marguerite Duras were pioneers in their displacement of the male objectifying gaze and their gender political focus on the representation of women's experience in films such as Alain Resnais's *Hiroshima mon amour* (1959) and Varda's *Cléo de 5 à 7* (1962), even if feminist film theory originating within France has developed only recently and intermittently.[4] As French women's writing developed under the influence of second-wave feminism, the avant-garde practice of 'écriture féminine' would constitute a challenge to phallogocentric literature and further influence the theory and practice of women's filmmaking.[5]

Published only four years after the end of the Second World War, '*The Second Sex* was an act of Promethean audacity – a theft of Olympian fire – from which there was no turning back ... it marks the place in history where an enlightenment begins' (Thurman 2010). An aspect of this enlightenment was quite simply a new way of 'seeing gender'. Bhabha states the originality of Beauvoir's thought when he writes: 'The power of Beauvoir's thinking and feelings lies in her ability to articulate – with a certain ambiguity – the anxiety of the psychic landscape with the agency of the political terrain' (Bhabha 2010: 1). In *The Second Sex*, Beauvoir deploys key existentialist notions such as the interrelationship of freedom and facticity (or the 'given' features of our existence which we have not chosen); transcendence and immanence; being-for-others; existential ambiguity; alienation; authenticity; bad faith (or the denial of our radical freedom) to analyse how woman becomes the 'absolute Other' in western patriarchal society. *The Second Sex* is divided into two volumes: the first is entitled 'Facts and Myths'; the second, 'Lived Experience', reflecting Beauvoir's phenomenological approach to the question of women's oppression.[6] She demonstrates how femininity has been conceptualised and how women 'become' relative beings in a patriarchal society. Her main argument is that throughout history, man has assumed the position of universal subject, and woman is positioned as relative 'Other' or object of male consciousness. Patriarchal society is consequently structured to perpetuate these sexually differentiated roles which are detrimental to women leading autonomous and fulfilling lives on terms of equality with men. The persistence of patriarchal ideology throughout history has enabled men to assume that they have a right to maintain women in a subordinate state and women have internalised and adapted to this oppressed state. Beauvoir argues that both men and women perpetuate patriarchy, which is why it is able to continue. Sexual oppression continues because, according to Beauvoir, gender roles are learned from the very earliest age and reinforced perpetually. The famous phrase that opens the second volume of *The Second Sex* – 'One is not born but rather becomes a woman' –constitutes a rejection of the patriarchal notion that there is a female nature or essence. Here, Beauvoir applies existentialism's notion of 'existence precedes essence' to women's situation, arguing that fixed or determining male or female identities are a *product* not a cause of patriarchal society's organisation as a sexual apartheid or segregation, rooted in men's and women's different biological make-up and reproductive roles. This results in woman's reproductive capacity being valued more than her intellectual development or autonomy, so that society's laws, institutions, belief systems and cultures reflect this view of women's secondary role in society.

A common misreading of *The Second Sex* has been that Beauvoir does not recognise sexual difference and thinks that women should become like men in their quest for freedom. In fact, Beauvoir does recognise sexual difference but does not accept that the deterministic valuing of these differences between women and men should justify the oppression of women and their status as second-class citizens in patriarchal society. Beauvoir contends instead that gender identity (as any other aspect of identity) is ambiguous and never fixed. In patriarchal society, however, women learn to become alienated in their body and sexed identity and the 'gendered gaze' plays a key role in this process of alienation, as will be explained below. Marriage and motherhood are consequently deemed to be the most important roles for women in society and their professional roles and opportunities have been limited as a result. Throughout history, most women have adapted to this second-class status which has encouraged their 'inauthenticity' to a lesser or greater extent. Beauvoir argues that the way forward for women is to pursue economic autonomy through independent work and through a socialist organisation of society which (in the late 1940s) she believed would favour women's emancipation and autonomy.

In *The Second Sex*, there are several references to Hollywood stars and films which are used by Beauvoir to illustrate certain of her arguments concerning myth and patriarchal hegemony in practice. For example, in the 'Myths' section of Volume I, she highlights the negative stereotyping of the 'femme fatale' and 'the vamp' in Hollywood cinema as responsible for perpetuating the myth that free women are a danger to society (Beauvoir 2009: 213). Further examples to support her arguments about myth are drawn from Orson Welles's *Citizen Kane* (1941) and Edmund Goulding's *The Razor's Edge* (1946). These films are cited by Beauvoir as examples of 'the Cinderella myth' whereby a wealthy male benefactor 'rescues' a woman from danger and ensures her enslavement by constructing himself as her unique destiny (Beauvoir 2009: 207). In Volume II, in appraising the culture of female self-beautification, Beauvoir astutely notes that 'the Hollywood star triumphs over nature but she finds herself a passive object in the producer's hands', as she would later argue in relation to the depiction of women in French new wave films such as Bardot in Jean-Luc Godard's *Contempt* (1963) (Beauvoir 2009: 591). Indeed, it is in *The Second Sex* that Beauvoir can be said to inaugurate feminist film theory by (i) establishing a synthetic methodology which, combining concepts from Hegelianism, Marxism, phenomenology, psychoanalysis, anthropology, ontology and ethics, analyses how woman becomes the absolute Other in western patriarchal societies through an ideological privileging of the heterospecular patriarchal economy and (ii) citing cinema as one of several cultural means through which this oppression of women is embedded and perpetuated in society through institutional, mythological and individual practices.

A crucial feature of Beauvoir's inaugural contribution to feminist film theory is, as noted above, her concept of the gendered 'othering' gaze. In *The Second Sex*, Beauvoir gives a gender political twist to the Sartrean theory of the look which passes between self and other (itself adapted from the moment of 'recognition' in Hegel's master–slave dialectic). As Sartre observes in *Being and Nothingness*: 'The look of the other' is a fundamental aspect of existentialist philosophy; it is the way in which the other is immediately present to us as the transcendence of our transcendence (Sartre 1958: 252–302). The look is both a literal and metaphorical ideological phenomenon and in *The Second Sex* Beauvoir shows how woman's transcendence can be halted by the patriarchal gaze. She also draws on Jacques Lacan's highly influential account of the Mirror Stage, according to which the infant encounters its alter ego in the mirror, by looking at him- or herself and by the process of him- or herself being reflected back by the other's mirroring, identity-mediating gaze. Through a process of identification with the mirror image, the child's ego identity is formed, which provides an illusory sense of mastery over a fragmented bodily experience. Yet the ego is the result of misrecognition and an alienation that, according to Beauvoir, is experienced differently by boys and girls in patriarchal society, as Moi has discussed (Moi 2008: 176–184). Experiencing a perpetual tension between their transcendence and immanence, girls are acculturated towards passivity and immanence in order to comply with their status as absolute Other in patriarchal society: 'For woman there is, from the start, a conflict between her autonomous existence and her "being-other"; she is taught that to please, she must try to please, she must make herself an object; she must therefore renounce her autonomy. She is treated like a living doll and freedom is denied her' (Beauvoir 2009: 305).

Women do not enjoy the same physical freedoms as men: 'If they wander the streets, they are stared at, accosted … and they will be insulted or followed or approached' (Beauvoir 2009: 358). Women accordingly learn that 'she will not gain value in the eyes of males by increasing her human worth, but by modelling herself on their dreams' (Beauvoir 2009: 358). Hence in her theory of the gendered 'othering' gaze, Beauvoir adds the Hegelian moment of recognition between self and other (constituted by the look) to Lacan's concept of the founding of subjectivity in alienation and misrecognition in the Mirror

Stage and applies this synthesis to her theorisation of woman's subjectivity in patriarchal society as the absolute Other.

Objectified as man's 'Other', women are hence seen but their voices are unheard. Learning to internalise the patriarchal gaze and to become alienated in their bodies, Beauvoir shows how women learn to become narcissistic and to accept their secondary status in the eyes of the male other. Narcissism is an aspect of women's alienation whereby they take their self as an absolute end; the intersubjective possibilities of the gaze are in effect sacrificed to the delusory 'cult of self' through which woman's transcendence is turned away from the world and back upon itself. Hence, as Beauvoir explains in *The Second Sex*, women's alienated situation in patriarchal society is maintained by this complex specular economy, which has been a key focus for feminist film theory, to which we will now turn.

For students and scholars of feminist film studies, the notion of the 'gendered gaze' is more usually associated with the work of leading feminist film theorist Laura Mulvey and her contemporaries. In a more explicitly psychoanalytical discussion than Beauvoir's, Mulvey described the gendered gaze in her groundbreaking 1975 essay, 'Visual Pleasure and Narrative Cinema': 'In a world ordered by sexual imbalance, pleasure in looking has been split between active/male and passive/female ... in their traditional exhibitionist role women are simultaneously looked at and displayed, with their appearance coded for strong visual and erotic impact so that they can be said to connote *to-be-looked-at-ness*' (Mulvey 1975: 6–18).

Early Anglophone feminist film critics such as Mulvey and Claire Johnston drew on continental philosophy, psychoanalysis, anthropology, and political and linguistic theory as it was circulating in France in the 1970s. Their focus was to analyse the patriarchal codes and structures underpinning filmic representations of women. In *The Second Sex*, Beauvoir similarly drew on a complex synthesis of continental philosophy, social and political theory, as noted above. But her work was only partially taken up by Anglophone materialist feminism prior to the 1990s due to Beauvoir's methodology being rooted in Franco-Germanic existential phenomenology, and because *The Second Sex* was only available in an abridged and inaccurate translation which misrepresented its philosophical content and sophistication.[7] Moreover, *The Second Sex* has had a complex history of reception in the respective fields of French and Anglo-American feminist theory. At times, it has been seen as remote from post-1968 feminist debates in France and how those debates have subsequently circulated within Anglo-American feminism. These debates were viewed as being predominantly concerned with psychoanalytic and linguistic approaches to sexual difference and hence not concerned with the same kinds of questions as Beauvoir in *The Second Sex*, even though her work still bore strong affinities with French materialist feminism.[8]

Despite Beauvoir's important feminist critique of psychoanalysis in *The Second Sex* and her brief recourse to Lacan's work, her overall stance towards psychoanalysis is certainly ambivalent. This distanced her work from that of early Anglophone feminist film critics such as Mulvey. As Judith Mayne has argued in a review of the discipline of feminist film theory from 1975 to 1985, Mulvey 'postulate[d] psychoanalysis as a privileged mode of inquiry for feminism and cinema, a postulation based on the assumption that cinema is, in its very essence, a soul mate to psychoanalysis'.[9] As Beauvoir's methodology in her subsequent essay on Bardot showed, she did not share Mulvey's confidence in psychoanalysis as a useful theoretical tool for the feminist study of film.

A further point of neglected dialogue between Beauvoir and 1970s feminist film theorists was her pioneering use of her friend Lévi-Strauss's structuralist anthropology in *The Second Sex* to analyse myths of women prevalent in patriarchal society. Her interest in structuralist anthropology was nonetheless shared by Johnston and other feminist film scholars from the mid-1970s onwards. Johnston in particular is judged by Shohini Chaudhuri to have 'provided the groundwork for the feminist analysis of Woman as a "sign" signifying the myths of patriarchal discourse', despite Beauvoir's earlier work in this area.[10] Johnston and other feminist film theorists had turned not to Beauvoir but instead to Roland Barthes's later semiotic analysis of myths in popular culture to deconstruct the mythic qualities of film and its ideological investment in sexism. Writing of myths of women in cinema, Johnston wrote in 1973: 'Myth transmits and transforms that ideology of sexism and renders it invisible', strikingly echoing Beauvoir's analyses of myth in *The Second Sex* (Johnston 1973: 32).

Beauvoir's sole essay of film criticism is of particular interest to feminist film studies although it has not been as widely cited as it merits.[11] In 'Brigitte Bardot and the Lolita Syndrome', written originally for *Esquire* magazine, Beauvoir further developed her ideological interest in cinema, drawing on her work on women and myth in *The Second Sex*. In common with later feminist film theory, Beauvoir explicitly recognises in her essay on Bardot that film is as complicit as any other cultural discourse in positioning woman as absolute Other and yet she also identifies the subversive feminist potential of the star and film spectators in their respective processes of existential becoming. Published in 1959, Beauvoir's essay is pioneering because it critiques both cinematic form and content as well as analysing Bardot's particular brand of stardom. Already in *The Second Sex*, Beauvoir had noted how fashion could serve to deprive the female Hollywood star from embodied transcendence (Beauvoir 2009: 182). Yet she saw that it could also be used subversively to connote independence and rebellion as in the 1938 film, *Jezebel*, in which Bette Davis scandalised mid-nineteenth century Louisiana society by wearing a red dress to the most important ball of the season to revenge herself on her fiancé for his neglect (Beauvoir 2009: 588). In her essay on Bardot, Beauvoir analyses how the young Bardot inaugurates literally a new embodiment of the old myth of 'the eternal feminine' in Roger Vadim's *And Woman … Was Created* (1956). Set in St Tropez, it depicts Juliette (played by Bardot), a highly-sexualised 18-year-old, who is the focus of an older man's obsession. He acts as her protector, although he plans to marry her off to a man she does not love. The viewer is positioned to identify with the gaze of the older man that consumes and polices the body of Bardot, which is 'always there to be speculated', as Hayward notes (1993: 177). Bardot pouts and dances her way around St Tropez, and the film's 'highlight' for Bardot fans is the final sequence of mambo dancing which, shot in a bar in close-up from the waist down, seems to frame Bardot's body as an object to be consumed by an implied heterosexual male voyeur.

According to Beauvoir, Bardot's incarnation of the myth of 'the eternal feminine' was less successful in France than in America because American men were less threatened by Bardot's sexually liberated behaviour. Although Beauvoir does not mention it, it is also worth noting the impact of the Hays Code which censored what could be shown on US cinema screens from 1930 until 1968. The code was losing its force by the 1950s and hence Bardot's emancipated sexuality and exoticism must have appeared highly erotic to US audiences.[12] Indeed, although Bardot was a major success in the US and, as Beauvoir terms it, as important a French 'export' as Renault cars, Bardot was subjected to a volley of accusations of immorality levelled at her in the French press. In her essay, Beauvoir was interested in the disruptive erotic power of Bardot as a combination of 'femme fatale' and 'nymphette' who is not so much immoral as amoral. She was also intrigued by Bardot's liberated and sensual style of embodiment which contrasted with the restrained stance of other film actresses. This recalls her phenomenological analyses of the relationship between gendered embodiment and space in the second volume of *The Second Sex*. Although Vadim, director of *And Woman … Was Created*, positioned the spectator implicitly as a heterosexual male 'voyeur', Beauvoir reads Bardot both on and off screen as resistant to being positioned as the fetishised body-object of the heterosexual male gaze, leaving that category of spectator feeling cheated and vindictive. The male gaze is also frustrated by Vadim's analytical style which fails to render the story or characters at all convincing and heightens the effect of Bardot's 'aggressive' femininity which positions men as erotic objects. This is particularly evident in the well-known 'mambo' sequence in which Bardot dances herself into an erotic trance, intoxicated by her own pleasure in embodiment and oblivious to the reactions of the male onlookers around her. Beauvoir's focus here on Bardot's liberated style of embodiment chimes with her interest in dance as a potential form of embodied existential freedom for women, as evident in episodes from her fictional texts such as *She Came to Stay* (1943), *Les Mandarins* (1954) and *Les Belles Images* (1966).[13]

In this way Beauvoir argues that Bardot achieves erotic embodied agency within the film's diegesis at various points, even if it is an agency limited by Vadim's direction. In her essay, Beauvoir is acutely attentive to the politics of the gendered gaze in 1950s cinema and analyses Bardot's on-screen persona alongside the myth of Bardot in contemporary French society. She also establishes a clear feminist methodology for interpreting film culture by exposing patriarchal ideology in the form of myth and analysing how Bardot challenges female stereotypes in cinema. Both of these aims were common to early feminist film criticism of the 1970s.

To consider Beauvoir's importance for film studies in the contemporary period, much of her philosophy remains valuable. While the space limitations of this Introduction mean that we can only indicate some areas of relevance, we observe that her contribution to ethics and phenomenology resonates strongly with the focus on ethics, aesthetics and sense experience in film studies in recent years. The 'phenomenological turn' in film studies which has been taking place since the late 1990s, with its focus on embodied lived experience and the haptic, resonates strikingly with Beauvoirian philosophy, yet again references to her work as an inaugural feminist existential phenomenologist are few within this sub-field of contemporary film studies.[14] Then, the recent trend in French cinema for depicting graphic sexual violence and for rape revenge films made by both female and male directors, such as *La Squale* (2000), *Irréversible* (2002) and *Baise-moi* (2000), continue to offer fertile ground for the application of Beauvoir's ethics as well as her theory of the gendered gaze. Similarly, her work on ageing in *Old Age* (1970) is a key tool of analysis for film culture in the context of film being a cultural discourse which, necessarily centred on image, has tended to glorify youth and beauty, even if now it is finally turning its attention to the lived situation of the aged against the backdrop of demographically ageing societies across the world.

In the present collection of essays, whilst *The Second Sex* is inevitably a key theoretical resource for many of the contributors, there are also existentialist readings of contemporary films drawing on other works by Beauvoir such as *The Ethics of Ambiguity* (1947), the novels and memoirs, as well as *Old Age* (1970). Beauvoir's *The Ethics of Ambiguity* features prominently in this collection because, as Debra Bergoffen has argued, one sees in this essay Beauvoir's affinity with phenomenology 'as distinct from existentialism' and her explicitly ethical concerns expressed without reference to Jean-Paul Sartre's existential ontology as constituted by *Being and Nothingness* (Bergoffen 1997: 21).[15] William McBride has perhaps the final word on the debate surrounding the mutual influence of Beauvoir and Sartre when he concludes:

> Because of her breakthrough insight into the phenomenon of the 'second sex' and its overwhelming importance throughout history and into present times, it is not unthinkable to consider [Beauvoir] to have been even more original than [Sartre] and ultimately to have exerted even far greater influence not so much on Sartre, even though that was no doubt significant, but on the development of contemporary human thought itself in our ever more globalized world.
>
> (McBride 2009: 200–1)

By foregrounding the centrality of key themes such as the individual, the gendered gaze, 'situation', freedom, femininity, sexuality, 'ambiguity' and alienation, the chapters in this volume demonstrate the relevance of Beauvoirian existentialism (understood in its broadest sense) to film studies in the postmodern context.

The first three chapters deal with gender relations, from childhood to motherhood, as well as race relations. Emma Wilson investigates the implications of Beauvoir's account of childhood in passages from *The Ethics of Ambiguity*, *The Second Sex*, the first excised chapter from *She Came to Stay*, and the first section of *Memoirs of a Dutiful Daughter*. Taking Lucile Hadzihalilovic's *Innocence* (2004), a film about an imagined girls' school, as her object of enquiry, Wilson explores the ways in which this contemporary film about girlhood is illuminated by Beauvoir's thinking and yet also opens her ideas to further inquiry. The ethics of the representation of children within audiovisual media and of the positioning of the spectator are also explored. The second chapter by Ursula Tidd deploys Beauvoir's analyses of motherhood and female sexuality in *The Second Sex* and in her essay 'Must We Burn Sade?' to question whether Isabelle Huppert's recent and most unsettling roles offer a new understanding of the dynamics of the maternal bond or whether the mothers depicted are caught up in mere variants of traditional patriarchal roles circumscribed by political and sexual double-standards. The discussion focuses on Raúl Ruiz's *Comedy of Innocence* (2000), Michael Haneke's *The Piano Teacher* (2001) and Allessandro Capone's *Hidden Love* (2007). In the third chapter, using Claire Denis's *Chocolat* (1988), Jean-Pierre Boulé studies the interaction of three characters: Aimée, the white mother and wife of the colonial administrator; France, her daughter; and Protée, the black servant (called 'the boy'), guided by *The Second Sex*. Boulé's essay charts the relationship between each of these characters, including the *mise-en-scène*, movement and framing of the camera (the look, objectification, (in)visibility) in an attempt to enrich post-colonial readings of the film with an existential feminist reading.

The next four chapters all engage with ethical questions relating to the meaning of existence and its relationship to freedom and responsibility. In chapter four, Connie Mui and Julien Murphy focus on gender relations and a heterosexual couple's relationship in the context of an ethical interrogation of human freedom. They assess Beauvoir's early philosophy of freedom as an ambiguous dialectical interplay between individual choices and social conventions through a critical analysis of the film *Revolutionary Road*, directed by Sam Mendes (2008). They also demonstrate the relevance of Beauvoir's treatment of gender, marriage, love and independence in *The Second Sex* to the dilemmas faced by Frank and April Wheeler in the film. In chapter five, Linnell Secomb reflects on the relationship between Simone de Beauvoir's philosophy, as adumbrated in *The Ethics of Ambiguity* and *The Second Sex*, and melodrama. Focusing on Todd Haynes's postmodern melodrama *Far From Heaven* (2002) and on its intertext, Douglas Sirk's *All That Heaven Allows* (1955), the chapter analyses the differing depictions of the female experience of love in Beauvoir's *The Second Sex* and in these two films. Secomb also compares the melodramatic character formation evident within this text with that in the film melodramas. Finally, the questioning of, and recuperation of, transcendence that emerges in these divergent texts is traced, not only within the content and narrative but also within structure and *mise-en-scène*. In the next chapter, Claire Humphrey studies *La Petite Jérusalem* by Karin Albou (2005) in conjunction with Beauvoir's feminist phenomenology, as set out in *The Ethics of Ambiguity* and *The Second*

Sex, and haptic cinematography. Beauvoir's perspective highlights the connections between ambiguity, ideology and viewing positions in the experience of watching cinema, in a way which grounds discussion of individual narratives and film aesthetics within a particular social context. Subsequently, Bradley Stephens offers an existentialist analysis of *I* ♥ *Huckabees* (2004), directed and co-written by David O. Russell, which humorously explores what happens when we seek out a more authentic meaning to our world than consumerist culture offers. The film dramatises the kind of transformative logic that Beauvoir sets out in *The Ethics of Ambiguity*. Both the film and Beauvoir embrace ambiguity so as to dismantle supposedly unchanging and self-evident ways of being in favour of a more dynamic existence, pertinent to contemporary cultural and political concerns in the twenty-first century.

Chapters eight to ten address the field of gerontology. Michelle Royer opens a dialogue between Beauvoir's existentialist analysis of ageing femininity (*Old Age*) and the screen representation of older women in Yamina Benguigui's *Inch'Allah Sunday* (2001). The contrast between the generations and the break with tradition and imprisonment are translated by the cinematic aesthetics of the film – the music, the *mise-en-scène*, the use of close-up and long shots – providing visual representations of Beauvoir's existentialist concepts. Benguigui's film provides both support for and a critique of Beauvoir's perspective on old age. Oliver Davis then analyses the ageing of heroic American masculinity in Clint Eastwood's *Gran Torino* (2008) from the perspectives both of *Old Age* and *The Second Sex*, arguing that Beauvoir's ontology of ageing is premised on the inevitability of violence. Davis plots an exchange between the film, with its presentation of hegemonic masculinity as a learned performance, and Beauvoir's work on ageing and gender which he calls *farfelu* (as 'another queer mode of excess'). His conclusion is that Eastwood and the Beauvoir of *Old Age* stand strong together in unlikely agreement. Next Susan Bainbrigge explores the ways in which a number of Beauvoirian concerns (mid-life crisis, old age and death) are played out in *The Savages* (2007), written and directed by Tamara Jenkins, in terms of both form and content. She argues that the film has at its core universally-recognisable concerns – relationships, ageing and dying – and dramatises existential questions of 'embodied' living and dying that so concerned Simone de Beauvoir (drawing in particular on *Old Age, A Very Easy Death* and *The Woman Destroyed*), creating an existentialist framework in dialogue with gerontology and film studies.

In chapter eleven, Kate Ince foregrounds Beauvoir's contribution as a feminist phenomenologist, notably through her concept of the (historical) body as situation. Ince uses Beauvoir's 'Literature and Metaphysics', *The Ethics of Ambiguity* and *The Second Sex* to read Sally Potter's films *Orlando* (1992), *The Tango Lesson* (1997) and *Yes* (2005). She explores the suggestive connections between Beauvoir's work and contemporary women's filmmaking, and considers the contribution made by Potter's films – through their emphasis on women's bodily actions, movement, desire and historical experience – to the burgeoning discipline of feminist phenomenology. Thus all of the chapters in their various ways constitute what Alice Jardine calls in her homage to Beauvoir the exciting research now being undertaken in 'different epistemological directions … stepping off from the threshold of Beauvoir's work' (Jardine 2010: 69).

As such, then, the collection offers a rich set of resources for Beauvoirian readings of contemporary film and, in so doing, draws on a wide variety of filmic genres, namely: biography, comedy, drama, fiction, music, mystery, romance and thriller; spanning a roughly twenty-year period from 1988 until 2007.[16] We like to think that this plethora of genres would have amused Beauvoir who herself wrote in a variety of genres. The work of fourteen directors is represented: four American, four French, two British, one Danish-German, one Franco-Chilean, one German and one Italian, comprising eight male directors and six female directors.[17] As we write this introduction in late 2011 there are some grounds for optimism – at least within France – that women directors are continuing to shape the direction of cinema. An article appearing in *The Guardian* in March 2011 hailed 'France's female new wave' directors: Mia Hansen-Løve, Rebecca Zlotowski and Katell Quillévéré, with the latter declaring that cinema is a 'liberation process' (Poirier 2011). In this respect, Laura Gragg observes: 'These women film directors offer better and stronger parts to actresses, and their films have contributed to changing the way we consider women, not women as girls but women as individuals'.[18] Similarly, in opening a dialogue between Beauvoirian philosophy and contemporary film, as editors, we foreground not only Beauvoir's importance as the inaugural theorist of feminist film studies but also the continuing relevance of her thought to the liberatory potential of cinema.[19]

Notes

1. For example, among other survey works in the field, there is just one brief reference to Beauvoir's work on myth in relation to cinema in Thornham (1999: 10). Similarly Shohini Chaudhuri (2006) positions Beauvoir's *The Second Sex* as heralding second-wave feminism but she does not discuss Beauvoir's work on the gendered gaze, myth or stardom in cinema.
2. A feature of her analysis of woman's situation as 'absolute other' in patriarchal society, Beauvoir's theory of the gendered gaze is predominantly located in *The Second Sex* (1949) and also in *Brigitte Bardot and the Lolita Syndrome* (1959). It is also illustrated in her novels, especially *She Came to Stay* (1943) and *Les Belles Images* (1966).
3. For instance Beauvoir remarks upon the use of fake colours by Vadim which allows him to flash 'a number of "high spots" in which all the sensuality of the film is concentrated' and this discontinuity 'heightens the aggressive character of BB's femininity' (1960: 44). For Beauvoir, Vadim's abstract style places the spectator as a voyeur.
4. See for example Sellier (2005) and Burch and Sellier (2009).
5. 'Ecriture féminine' emerged in France during the post-1968 period of second-wave feminism and was a form of literary practice theorised by Hélène Cixous and associated with 'Psychanalyse et politique', a faction within the French feminist movement. Cixous sought to theorise the difference of female subjectivity beyond the constraints of phallogocentrism (a term, derived from Jacques Derrida, coined from 'phallocentrism' or privileging the phallus as dominant signifier and 'logocentrism' or privileging the word

as a means to full truth and presence). Phallogocentrism refers to the privileging of patriarchy through language and representation and acts as a means to maintain the political hegemony of patriarchy; see Cixous (1976) and Moi (1987).

6. For a more detailed overview of Beauvoir's *The Second Sex*, see 'Becoming Woman' in Tidd (2004), pp. 49–70.

7. For an overview of the issues concerning the two translations of *Le Deuxième Sexe*, see Simons (1999), Glazer (2004) and Moi (2010).

8. See, for example, French materialist feminist Christine Delphy's discussion of the ideological invention of 'French Feminism' by Anglophone scholars as being predominantly concerned with psychoanalytic and linguistic approaches to sexual difference (1995:190–221). In Toril Moi's 1987 anthology *French Feminist Thought*, she noted that the muted reception of French materialist feminism was the result of their work being 'less frequently translated and less well-known precisely because of their relative similarity: they have ... been perceived as lacking in exotic difference'. Indeed, Beauvoir's antipathy towards psychoanalysis as a theoretical base from which to think about gender, her rejection of poststructuralist concepts of the subject and her persistent focus on the material and phenomenological aspects of sexual oppression in *Le Deuxième Sexe* have only latterly been understood as a powerful alternative to what many Anglophone scholars perceived in the 1970s and 1980s as 'French feminist theory'.

9. See Mayne (1985: 82).

10. See Chaudhuri (2006: 29).

11. Leading feminist film critic Ginette Vincendeau is one of very few to have analysed Beauvoir's essay in this regard; see her forthcoming book on Brigitte Bardot.

12. Our thanks to Darren Waldron for this observation.

13. For a brief discussion of Beauvoir's interest in dance and embodiment, see Fishwick (2002: 253–63).

14. See for example Sobchack (1991, 2004), Marks (2000) and Barker (2009).

15. Although there is a common misconception that Beauvoir's *Ethics of Ambiguity* is 'the most likely formulation of an ethics one could draw from *Being and Nothingness*'; see Pamerleau (2009: 30).

16. Strictly speaking, it starts in 1955 with *All That Heaven Allows* but the main film under study in this essay is the 2002 postmodern melodrama from Todd Haynes, *Far From Heaven* (see chapter five).

17. The Cannes film festival attracted controversy as recently as 2010 for not shortlisting a single woman film director – see Shoard and Millward (2010) – although this is a different issue. This is about the critical establishment and whether they are prepared to acknowledge the women who have been working in cinema for a long time. The latter adds: 'There have been 212 films in competition in Cannes since 2000, and only 17 (by 14 women) have had a look in'.

18. Laura Gragg is an American production consultant living in Paris, former deputy head of ACE, a network of European producers.

19. A parallel volume on Sartre was published in 2011; see Boulé and McCaffrey (2011).

Bibliography

Barker, J. 2009. *The Tactile Eye: Touch and the Cinematic Experience*. Berkeley and Los Angeles: University of California Press.

Beauvoir, S. de. [1943] 1975. *L'Invitée (She Came to Stay)*, trans. Y. Moyse and R. Senhouse. Glasgow: William Collins.

———. [1947] 1976. *Pour une morale de l'ambiguïté (The Ethics of Ambiguity)*, trans. B. Frechtmann. New York: Citadel.

———. [1949] 2009. *Le Deuxième Sexe* (*The Second Sex*), trans. C. Borde and S. Malovany-Chevallier. London: Jonathan Cape.

———. [1954] 1957. *Les Mandarins* (*The Mandarins*), trans. L.M. Friedman. London : Collins.

———. [1958] 1963. *Mémoires d'une jeune fille rangée* (*Memoirs of a Dutiful Daughter*), trans. J. Kirkup. Harmondsworth: Penguin.

———. [1959] 1960. *Brigitte Bardot and The Lolita Syndrome*, trans. B. Fretchman, London: New English Library.

———. [1960] 1965. *La Force de l'âge* (*The Prime of Life*), trans, P. Green. Harmondsworth: Penguin.

———. [1966] 1968. *Les Belles Images* (*Les Belles Images*), trans. P. O'Brian. Glasgow: William Collins.

———. [1970] 1972. *La Vieillesse* (*Old Age*), trans. P. O'Brian. London: André Deutsch and Weidenfeld and Nicolson.

———. [1972] 1977. *Tout compte fait* (*All Said and Done*), trans. P. O'Brian. Harmondsworth: Penguin.

Bergoffen, D.B. 1997. *The Philosophy of Simone de Beauvoir, Gendered Phenomenologies, Erotic Generosities*. New York: State University of New York Press.

Bhabha, H. 2010. 'Introduction', *French Politics, Culture and Society* 28(2), Summer: 1–3.

Boulé, J.-P. and E. McCaffrey (eds). 2011. *Existentialism and Contemporary Cinema. A Sartrean Perspective*. Oxford: Berghahn Books.

Burch, N. and G. Sellier. 2009. *Le cinéma au prisme des rapports de sexe*. Paris: Vrin.

Chaudhuri, S. 2006. *Feminist Film Theorists, Laura Mulvey, Kaja Silverman, Teresa de Lauretis, Barbara Creed*. Abingdon: Routledge.

Cixous, Hélène. [1975] 1976. 'The Laugh of the Medusa', trans. K. Cohen and P. Cohen, *Signs* 1(4): 875–93.

Delphy, C. 1995. 'The Invention of French Feminism: An Essential Move', *Yale French Studies, Another Look, Another Woman: Retranslations of French Feminism* 87: 190–221.

Doane, M.A., P. Mellencamp and L.Williams. 1984. *Re-vision*. Los Angeles: American Film Institute.

Fishwick, S. 2002. *The Body in the Work of Simone de Beauvoir*. Oxford and Bern: Peter Lang.

Glazer, S. 2004. 'Lost in Translation', *New York Times*, 22 August. Retrieved 4 July 2011 from http://www.nytimes.com/2004/08/22/books/essay-lost-in-translation.html

Harvey, S. 1978. 'Women's Place: the Absent Family of Film Noir', in E.A. Kaplan (ed.), *Women and Film Noir*. London: British Film Institute.

Hayward, S. 1993. *French National Cinema*. London: Routledge.

Jardine, A. 2010. 'What Feminism?', *French Politics, Culture and Society* 28(2), Summer: 66–74.

Johnston, C. 1973. 'Women's Cinema as Counter-Cinema' reprinted in S. Thornham (ed.) *Feminist Film Theory: A Reader*. Edinburgh University Press, 1999, pp. 31–40.

Lapsley, R. and M. Westlake. [1998] 2006. *Film Theory, An Introduction*. Manchester: Manchester University Press.

Marks, L. 2000. *The Skin of the Film, Intercultural Cinema, Embodiment and the Senses*. Durham and London: Duke University Press.

Mayne, J. 1985. 'Feminist Film Theory and Criticism', *Signs* 11(1): 81–100.

McBride, W.L. 2009. 'Taking a Distance: Exploring Some Points of Divergence between Beauvoir and Sartre', in C. Daigle and J. Golomb (eds), *Beauvoir and*

Sartre. The Riddle of Influence. Bloomington and Indianapolis: Indiana University Press, pp. 189–202.

Moi, T. (ed.). 1987. *French Feminist Thought, A Reader*. New York and Oxford: Blackwell.

———. 2008. *Simone de Beauvoir, The Making of an Intellectual Woman*. Oxford: Oxford University Press.

———. 2011. 'The Adulteress Wife', *London Review of Books* 32(3), 11 February. Retrieved 4 July 2011 from http://www.lrb.co.uk/v32/n03/toril-moi/the-adulteress-wife

Mulvey, L. 1975. 'Visual Pleasure and Narrative Cinema', *Screen* 16(3): 6–18.

Pamerleau, W.C. 2009. *Existentialist Cinema*. London: Palgrave Macmillan.

Poirier, A. 2011. 'France's Female New Wave', *The Guardian*, 24 March, 8.

Sartre, J.-P. [1938] 1963. *La Nausée (Nausea)*, trans. R. Baldick. London: Penguin Classics.

———. [1943] 1958. *L'Etre et le néant (Being and Nothingness)*, trans. H. Barnes. London: Methuen.

———. 1970. 'L'art cinématographique', in M. Contat and M. Rybalka (eds), *Les Ecrits de Sartre*. Paris: Gallimard, pp. 546–52.

Sellier, G. 2005. *La Nouvelle Vague: un Cinéma au masculin singulier*. Paris: CNRS.

Shoard, C. and R. Millward. 2010. 'Does It Matter That There Are No Women Up for the Palme d'Or?, *The Observer*, 16 May. Retrieved 2 April 2011 from http://www.guardian.co.uk/theobserver/2010/may/16/cannesfilmfestival-women

Simons, M. 1999. 'The Silencing of Simone de Beauvoir: Guess What's Missing from *The Second Sex*', in *Beauvoir and The Second Sex: Feminism, Race and the Origins of Existentialism*. Lanham and Oxford: Rowman and Littlefield, pp. 61–71.

Sobchack, V. 1991. *The Address of the Eye: A Phenomenology of Film Experience*. New Jersey: Princeton University Press.

———. 2004. *Carnal Thoughts: Embodiment and Moving Image Culture*. Berkeley and Los Angeles: University of California Press.

Thornham, S. (ed.).1999. *Feminist Film Theory*. Edinburgh: Edinburgh University Press.

Thurman, J. 2010. 'Introduction to Simone de Beauvoir's "The Second Sex"', *New York Times*, 27 May.

Tidd, U. 2004. *Simone de Beauvoir*. London and New York: Routledge.

Filmography

Despentes, V., Coralie (dirs.). 2000. *Baise-moi (Rape Me)*. Canal +. Pan Européenne Production. Take One.

Gaspar, N (dir.). 2002. *Irréversible (Irreversible)*. 120 Films. Eskwad. Grandpierre.

Genestal, F (dir.). 2000. *La Squale (The Squale)*. Ciné Nominé. M6 Films.

Godard, J.-L. (dir.). 1963. *Le Mépris (Contempt)*. Les Films Concordia. Rome Paris Films.

Goulding, E. (dir.). 1946. *The Razor's Edge*. Twentieth Century Fox Film Corporation.

Resnais, A. (dir.). 1959. *Hiroshima mon amour*. Argos Films. Como Films. Daiei Studios.

Vadim, R. (dir.). 1956. *Et Dieu créa … la femme (And Woman … Was Created)*. Cocinor. Iéna Productions. UCIL.

Varda, A. (dir.). 1962. *Cléo de 5 à 7 (Cleo from 5 to 7)*. Ciné Tamaris. Rome Paris Films.

Welles, O. (dir.). 1941. *Citizen Kane*. Mercury Productions. RKO Radio Pictures.

1

BEAUVOIR'S CHILDREN: GIRLHOOD IN *INNOCENCE*

Emma Wilson

The door shut behind him and I could hear his footsteps growing fainter as he walked off down the hall. I lay there alone in bed, feeling the black shadow creeping up the underside of the world like a flood tide. Nothing held, nothing was left. The silver airplanes and the blue capes all dissolved and vanished, wiped away like the crude drawings of a child in colored chalk from the colossal blackboard of the dark.

(Plath 1977: 166)

Ursula Tidd has argued that 'Beauvoir's philosophical interest in the experience of childhood is a feature that distinguishes her work from Sartre's prior to 1950' (Tidd 1999: 25).[1] I suggest that Beauvoir offers invaluable resources for contemplating the child as subject and the specificity of subjectivity in childhood; for thinking about that subjectivity as at once embodied, gendered and acculturated; and for thinking about the meanings which attach to childhood once we leave it behind, meanings invoking questions about innocence and loss. These questions are the basis for Beauvoir's thinking about how one becomes a woman and assumes a position of alterity. They are also of interest in their own right as discussions of childhood, of child identities, and of the particular experiences of childhood known by young women. Contemporary women's filmmaking in France has also paid attention to girlhood, as well as womanhood, in its attempts to open imaginings of embodied female subjectivity at different ages and stages of life.[2] It is the conjunction of Beauvoir's interest in childhood, and the representations of young girls' experiences found in female-authored films, which inspires this chapter. Taking Lucile Hadzihalilovic's *Innocence* (2004), a film about an imagined girls' school, as my object of enquiry, I explore the ways in which this contemporary film about girlhood is illumined by Beauvoir's thinking and yet also opens her ideas to further questions.[3] This chapter looks at Beauvoir's account of childhood in passages from *The Ethics of Ambiguity*, *The Second Sex*, the first excised chapter from *She Came to Stay*, and the first section of *Memoirs of a Dutiful Daughter*. In *Innocence*, I look at the drama of the middle child, Alice (Lea Bridarolli), a sequence of nine minutes in length enfolded in the centre of the film.

As this volume testifies, there has as yet been little attention to the rich resources for film analysis of Beauvoir's work. Tarr and Rollet, naming their volume on French women filmmakers *Cinema and the Second Sex*, reference Beauvoir in thinking about the context of late twentieth-century France. They speak of the progress in the numbers of women entering the industry, and making films, yet note: 'despite the heritage of Beauvoir's work and the women's movement of the 1970s, French women directors characteristically disclaim their gender as a significant factor in their filmmaking and their films lack a critical engagement with feminism and feminist film theory as it has developed in Britain, Germany and the United States over the last twenty years' (2001: 1–2). While this is largely still the case ten years on, women filmmakers are finding the means through aesthetic choices, as well as alternative film narratives, to explore concerns about embodied subjectivity and, as discussed here, specifically about childhood that Beauvoir has foregrounded in her writing.

Childhood in Beauvoir's Thought

In *The Ethics of Ambiguity*, Beauvoir discusses the situation of the child, not distinguishing at this point between the lived experience of the boy and the girl. This initial lack of distinction is apt given her recognition in *The Second Sex* that boys and girls arrive in the world with no differentiation of their relation to situation and culture. She argues: 'The child's situation is character-ised by his finding himself cast into a universe which he has not helped to establish, which has been fashioned without him, and which appears to him as an absolute to which he can only submit' (Beauvoir 2009: 35). The child's situation is at once one of limit and of privilege. The child is effectively freed of the anguish of freedom and responsibility. Yet his or her relation to the world is in a certain way curtailed and contained. Beauvoir continues to explain:

> In his child's circle he feels that he can passionately pursue and joyfully attain goals which he has set up for himself. But if he fulfils this experience in all tranquillity, it is precisely because the domain open to his subjectivity seems insignificant and puerile in his own eyes. He feels himself happily irresponsible. The real world is that of adults where he is allowed only to respect and obey.
>
> (Beauvoir 2009: 35)

Tidd sums up Beauvoir's position: 'The child is happily irresponsible because the parents play the role of divine beings to which she or he is subject. Yet the child's world is metaphysically privileged because he or she escapes the anguish of freedom as a result of the existential unimportance of his or her actions' (1999: 25). This recognition of the child's world as metaphysically privileged has a particular bearing on the meanings ascribed to childhood in retrospect. Beauvoir is a perhaps surprising theorist of nostalgia for childhood. She does, however, see this nostalgia as a form of misfortune, writing: 'the misfortune which comes to man as a result of the fact that he was a child is that his freedom was first concealed from him'; 'all his life he will be nostalgic for the time when he did not know its exigencies' (Beauvoir 2009: 40).

Beauvoir proposes a view of childhood as protected, as, in an illusory way, existentially secure. Childhood protection is made the more precious and the more desirable by threats to metaphysical privilege, to secure existence in a world of unimpeachable adults. Beauvoir charts with extraordinary prescience the emotions and sensations attaching to the growing realisation that the tranquillity of childhood is an illusion. At first, an inkling of a flaw or dent is carefully denied:

> In his universe of definite and substantial things, beneath the sovereign eyes of grown-up persons, he [the child] thinks that he too has *being* in a definite and substantial way. ... If something deep inside him belies his conviction, he conceals this imperfection. He consoles himself for an inconsistency which he attributes to his young age by pinning his hopes on the future.
>
> (Beauvoir 2009: 36)

Yet such inconsistencies begin to be obtrusive. As soon as Beauvoir has established the security and tranquillity of childhood, she moves on to show the rupture of this intact world. She recognises: 'it is very rare for the infantile world to maintain itself beyond adolescence. From childhood on, flaws begin to be revealed in it' (2009: 38). Adolescence may be the time when, as Tidd puts it, 'one discovers one's own subjectivity and the subjectivity of others' (1999: 26), yet this discovery is also breaking into childhood:

> With astonishment, revolt and disrespect the child little by little asks himself, 'Why must I act that way? What good is it? And what will happen if I act in another way?'. He discovers his subjectivity; he discovers that of others. And when he arrives at the age of adolescence he begins to vacillate because he notices the contradictions among adults as well as their hesitations and weaknesses.
>
> (Beauvoir 2009: 38–39)

The recognition of flaws and questioning of absolutes begins in childhood in a manner which, arguably, makes childhood privileged as the era and age in which an intimation of loss and failure is first imagined, an era where blemishes and inequality are first seen to reign.

As we have seen, *The Ethics of Ambiguity* does not distinguish the experience of the boy and the girl. In her subsequent approaches to childhood, Beauvoir explores the further specificities of the situation of young girls who share the drama of concealment and loss described for all children, yet find this further complicated by the active construction and policing of their feminine identities. In *Memoirs of a Dutiful Daughter* Beauvoir writes about her own experience of childhood peace in terms reminiscent of *The Ethics of Ambiguity*: 'Few things could disturb my equanimity. I looked upon life as a happy adventure' (1959: 48). Gender difference does not trouble her tranquillity, though she acknowledges that this is not because it does not actually inflect or affect her life. She writes: 'I had no brother; there were no comparisons to make which would have revealed to me that certain liberties were not permitted me on the grounds of my sex; I attributed the restraints that were put upon me to my age. Being a child filled me with passionate resentment; my feminine gender, never' (1959: 55–56).

In the section on childhood in *The Second Sex*, Beauvoir lays emphasis immediately on the body and its relation to subjectivity: 'For girls and boys, the body is first the radiation of a subjectivity, the instrument that brings about the comprehension of the world: they apprehend the universe through their eyes and hands, and not through their sexual parts' (2009: 293). While the focus in this description is the lack of distinction between male and female, her vision of infant exploration is different from that in *The Ethics of Ambiguity* in its emphasis on this prehensile, sensory engagement with the world. The child may be protected but is always already seeking knowledge and apprehension. This search for knowledge through fleshy engagement brings with it an early sense of flaw and failure, dating right to separation and individuation rather than to puberty and adolescence: 'in a bodily form he discovers finitude, solitude and abandonment in an alien world' (2009: 294).

From this vision of symmetry between the girl and boy, Beauvoir moves quickly to explore the different treatment of female children. She writes:

> the little girl continues to be doted upon, she is allowed to hide behind her mother's skirts, her father takes her on his knees and pats her hair; she is dressed in dresses as lovely as kisses, her tears and whims are treated indulgently, her hair is done carefully, her expressions and affectations amuse: physical contact and complaisant looks protect her against the anxiety of solitude.
>
> (Beauvoir 2009: 296)

The description here interacts interestingly with the former comment on physical exploration and solitude. The female child is protected from her apprehension of solitude by being dressed up in compliments. Her masquerade of femininity distances her from awareness of the illusory tranquillity in which she exists. Given her emphasis on the flesh and subjectivity as embodied, Beauvoir's focus here on garments and dress is telling. In this first evocation of a cradled, protected girlhood, baby girls' clothes are seen as being as soft as kisses, their delicate and tactile fabrics almost confused with the parental affection, nurture, construction and approval they imply. Yet the guarantor of affection and security, the sensory fabric, becomes very quickly the constraining garb of femininity. The lovely fabrics impose different meanings: 'she is dressed in uncomfortable and fancy clothes that she has to take care of, her hair is done in complicated styles, posture is imposed on her' (2009: 306). The body, that instrument for discovering the word, is regulated in clothes of disarming fragility that require and impose particular codes of behaviour. Such garments further instantiate a constructed understanding of the meanings and capacities of the young girl's body. Beauvoir writes: 'The girl hates the idea that this body she identifies with may be perforated as one perforates leather, that it can be torn as one tears a piece of fabric. But the girl refuses more than the wound and the accompanying pain; she refuses that these be *inflicted*' (2009: 346). In addition to the confusion of body and subjectivity comes the confusion of the body with the garments that clothe it. The young girl's body is constructed as fragile through the fabrics that clothe it. The fabrics themselves are material manifestations of her parents' hopes and dreams for her femininity. They are part of the web of acculturating images, words, compliments, fantasies, fairy tales, mirror reflections through which she finds her femininity inscribed and with which she becomes complicit. In this way, the female child becomes trapped: 'She is treated like a living doll and freedom is denied her; thus a vicious circle is closed; for the less she exercises her freedom to understand, grasp and discover the world around her, the less she will dare to affirm herself as subject' (2009: 305). It is clear that her relation to subjectivity, to freedom and to the protection of childhood, is different from that of the male child and that protection itself becomes bound closely with policing and control.[4]

Aligning the construction of identity, symbolic and literal images of materiality, and actual material, Beauvoir writes of the little girl:

> She has to be white like an ermine, transparent like crystal, she is dressed in vaporous organdie, her room is decorated with candy-coloured hangings, people lower their voice when she approaches, she is prohibited from seeing indecent books; yet there is not one child on earth who does not relish 'abominable' images and desires.
>
> (Beauvoir 2009: 347)

This disparity is one Beauvoir consciously explores in the first chapter of *She Came to Stay*, one of the two early chapters of the novel Beauvoir was advised to excise.[5] The infant Françoise develops in stages that look forward to *The Ethics of Ambiguity* and *The Second Sex*. Her apprehension of the world is sensory and immediate, as she is seen feeling each movement in her hand, hearing the sounds around her, and responding to her environment. Her world is protected by sovereign parents who provide an identity for Françoise to take on: ' "She's a precocious child", her father said with satisfaction; and her mother replies: "She has a good character and is very straightforward. She tells me everything" ' (Beauvoir 1979: 277).[6] We see Françoise reflecting her parents' approbation: 'She was proud of her curls and of her good marks, and proud of being a precocious little girl with a good character' (1979: 277). It is a source of her self-construction, as she regards herself: 'This little girl was Françoise; she looked at her in the mirror with satisfaction, and she said to herself "That's me!" ' (1979: 277). Yet at exactly the same point in the text Beauvoir illustrates too the ways in which this perfect, reflecting world also knows its own fissures and flaws. This is witnessed in the treatment she gives to the development of Françoise's sexuality and her autoerotic pleasure. Beauvoir writes: 'It's a silly thing in bed at night to spend a long time tickling the place where the skin is all soft and sticky. Françoise told her mother everything, but silly things didn't exist, they were nothing and there weren't any words to speak about them' (1979: 277). The transparency and trust her mother praises are shown to be more complicated. Françoise, touching herself, knows enough not to reveal this secret pleasure to her mother. By designating this act a silly thing she can categorise it as beneath her mother's attention.[7] She can therefore continue to take pleasure and yet leave apparently pristine her mother's image of her as a pure, confiding child. This duplicity is shown as blithe. Beauvoir's use of *style indirect libre* here belies the child's happy self-justification (thus prefiguring Françoise's later nurture of her own self-image through the novel).[8] Beauvoir shows how the child may always already recognise, however secretly, his or her own autonomy. Flaws and dents may be hidden, yet the carefree protection of childhood is barely blemish-free. Beauvoir creates an Edenic image of Françoise, joyfully reared on *Bluebeard* and other fairy tales, making her way into the forest: 'She begins to run into the woods, her heart beating: in the shade of the tall pine trees she was going to find once more the joy and anguish that she never knew in the garden that lay stretched out in the daylight for everyone to see' (1979: 278). In her shady sylvan world, 'she pealed the bark off a little wood branch and gently rubbed the damp stick between her thighs' (1979: 279). Sexuality and knowledge are always already part of this green paradise of childhood.[9]

In *The Ethics of Ambiguity*, Beauvoir has sustained an image of a realm of freedom from the anguish of choice, and protection from agency. In *The Second Sex* and the first unpublished chapter of *She Came to Stay* she shows the situation for young girls to be somewhat more complicated as they are constrained by gender-specific parental aims and ideals. The section on 'Childhood' in *The Second Sex* comes to a close with strong imagery of the female child's social and cultural mutilation. Beauvoir evokes 'a mutilated and frozen existence' and ends with the lines 'She makes her way towards the future wounded, shamed, worried and guilty' (2009: 351). The imagery recalls the iconography of Eve cast out of the Garden of Eden. Yet what *The Second Sex* and *She Came to Stay* have led me to wonder is how far the little girl's experience has ever been one of the childhood paradise, and freedom from agency, for which adults become nostalgic later in life. Perhaps this paradise, indeed, is a retrospective illusion cast over the fractious, constrained time of little girlhood. This is a question raised too in *Innocence*.

Innocence

Hadzihalilovic's film, an adaptation of Wedekind's *Mine-Haha or On the Bodily Education of Young Girls*,[10] appears to be a film concerned with an ideal world of childhood innocence. The film depicts a girls' school lost in the forest, perpetuating the sylvan and Edenic imagery found in Beauvoir. Hadzihalilovic shows apparently pristine little girls in white school uniforms, their short skirts showing the lengths of their 'creamy legs' (Quinlivan 2009: 221). The iconography of the film partakes of the tradition of 'pictures of innocence' that overinvest childhood innocence and purity to the extent that it becomes an erotic ideal in itself.[11] We see the girls in woodland glades in the summer sunlight, dancing, skipping and turning somersaults. The aesthetic of the film is influenced by Peter Weir's *Picnic at Hanging Rock* (1975) which, while exploring female adolescence, rather than childhood itself, draws on the tropes of innocence and primal nature familiar in the Australian fascination with missing children.[12] While it resonates then with such strongly cathected and ethereal representations of innocence and childish beauty, the achievement of *Innocence* comes in its acute questioning of child subjectivity, agency and constraint. Its take on its own title may be revealed, in this respect, to be highly ironic.

The situation Hadzihalilovic explores is in one way different to that which Beauvoir analyses in her work on the *formation* of little girls. In *The Second Sex*, *She Came to Stay* and her *Memoirs of a Dutiful Daughter*, Beauvoir pays attention essentially to the bourgeois family and the situation of the child therein. References to education and to the early experience of the girls' school are scant in *The Second Sex*, though Beauvoir does refer to the experiences and feelings of the girls she herself taught in Sèvres, to films such as *Maidens in Uniform* (Leontine Sagan, 1931), and to a number of novels that focus on female education.[13] In *Innocence* the family has been left behind and the film focuses almost exclusively on the experiences of girls alone, in a world where boys are missing, and ageless teachers take on the sovereign roles of parents. In this confected world Hadzihalilovic looks at issues congruent with those raised by Beauvoir in her questioning of childhood.[14]

Innocence as a drama, and in particular in the filmic style and textures Hadzihalilovic adopts, is peculiarly apt for exemplifying the child's fleshy engagement with the world. As Davina Quinlivan describes beautifully, '[t]he sensuous rhythms of objects and matter invest the film with an enchanted resonance in which bodies and matter become interchangeable, performing a strange dance together' (2009: 220). In particular, Hadzihalilovic draws attention to the ways in which this enfleshed encounter with the world is productive of the child's subjectivity. The sequence I discuss below is bound up with the feelings, wishes and desires of Alice, a blue-ribboned child.[15] Mid-way through the narrative, Alice's drama effectively displaces that of Iris (Zoé Auclair), the newest child, who has been the focus and consciousness of the first parts of the film. We move on to a narrative of Alice's grave desire to be chosen as a dancer by the Headmistress (Corinne Marchand) on her annual visit to the school.

In the opening of the sequence, Alice is seen walking intently along a forest path, leading from her 'house' to the school. The camera follows her at exactly her height and pace, her face illumined, offering effectively her viewpoint on the world. Although the camera is tracking her, rather than literally showing what she sees, there is a sense that our angle of vision is fitted to the contours of her embodied living. The shots are tranquil and pictorial as we see sunlight reflecting off the wintery trees and glowing on the cream wool of her scarf. Her brilliant blue ribbons disrupt the frosted colours of the scene, signalling abruptly the sequencing of the girls' lives in the school (where different colour ribbons adorn the children of different ages). Only natural sound accompanies Alice's walk through the forest. We share the scene silently and privately with her, gauging her thoughts from her self-possessed and shimmering expression. There is lightness to her pace and expectant levity as she moves through this wooded world.

In the wood-panelled interior of the school, with its mirrored walls, Alice enters the competition room late. Four other small girls in white leotards with blue hair ribbons wait at the barre. Alice joins their ranks. Silence is replaced by dance music by Janacek (it has been heard before when we have seen Alice practising ballet). The intimacy with Alice established in the opening shots allows her to remain the emotional focus of the scene, this effect unobtrusively confirmed by the attention of the camera. When another child performs, we see Alice neatly posed in front of the barre with her mirrored reflection in pro-file beside her. The reflection allows us to notice that she is very slightly tipped forward, her stance revealing her expectancy and desire. Her profile is rimmed in light, leaving her face between determination and radiance. These shots of Alice show her slight tremors and her bodily control. The camera switches attention to the floor of the dance room just before she launches herself into her gymnastic dance. We see her in rapid motion, turning to the music so that again we see her from all sides, performing a cartwheel and moving through ballet poses with agility and grace. For this sequence, her moving body is the film's object of attention as she cuts through the spaces of the room, absorbed in her performance.

Once she has finished, her image is captured at the very edge of the frame, her face in half profile, confident, composed, as she watches the next girls perform. She seems breathless or nervous as her chest rises and falls after her performance. Such a sensory detail confirms that the film captures the rhythms of her embodied being. As the last girl performs, strikingly thinner and more elastic than the others, we watch Alice observing. Her pose is a little more controlled than that of the other children, but there is no particular sense at this point that the other dancing child poses a threat to Alice, to her autonomous positioning. When the dancing is over, Alice looks carefully towards the Headmistress.

In an extended sequence after the dancing, each child is examined by the Headmistress. They are asked to show the length of their necks, to turn this way and that, and to smile to show their teeth. The Headmistress's assistant (Sonia Petrovna) is firm and gentle with the children. The inspection reveals how their bodies are regulated and controlled by the adults, measured against a perfect ideal. The assistant's hands, with infinite composure, move and direct the children. We find a physical image of the moulding function of the regime in which they find themselves entrapped. As Alice comes forward to be examined, the assistant raises the handfuls of her long bunches and ribbons and allows her neck to be bared and observed. She raises Alice's arms and carefully turns her, as if she were a small marionette. As Alice looks upwards for approbation, she is gently moved on. As the fourth girl is examined, we can see

Alice's back in reflection in the mirror. Her back view seems a variation on the image of the child being examined, a reflection in a Surrealist mirror.

At the end of the sequence, both Alice and the thinner child are singled out. The assistant presents them, one on either side. What distinguishes them visually here is Alice's raised chin and expectant gaze. She is seen with light falling on her and we see the full glow of her desire, her steadiness, and her disquiet, as she is compared to the other child. There is a brief pause and then the other child (Grizelle Croset) is chosen. In a repeating gesture, Alice is again gently moved away from the circle of attention to return to the barre with the others. We see her move forward as if to protest, before restraining her body. We then hear her summoned by Mademoiselle Eva (Marion Cotillard) as she runs down the stairs to beg the judge to pick her too. We see the emotional urgency of Alice's appeal to the judge, her pose with outstretched arms suddenly frozen as Mademoiselle Eva reaches her at the bottom of the stairs. In shot/reverse shot editing between the adult and the child, with the camera matching the viewpoint of each, Alice accuses her teacher of promising that she would be picked. The teacher denies this, but we have witnessed her saying this very thing at the end of a New Year's dinner in a preceding scene. The film lends authenticity to the child in a mendacious world of adults. Alice collapses at the bottom of the stairs, the camera following the folding over of her body and accompanying her close-up, distorted gaze of her own hand on the floor carpet. We observe from close beside Alice herself. We view from her slant and her perspective, both spatially and mentally.

This congruence is marked by the gap in narrative where Alice is unconscious. The film cuts to a slightly blurred, inverted vision of Alice's bedroom as we share her perspective as she wakes up. We then see familiar shots of the children gathered around Alice's bed, as we have seen them previously gathered round the coffin in which Iris, the youngest child, arrived in the school. Here, as at the start, where the girls are together, adults are almost completely absent, so we see a child-orchestrated, child-centred world. Alice lies like an invalid as the eldest child, Bianca (Bérangère Haubruge), gives her some water to drink. Against shots of empty corridors and passageways we begin to hear the ghostly trace of the Janacek once more. It might be music overheard in the schoolhouse, but an extreme close-up of Alice's sleeping face, her closed eye, her hair brushed behind her ear, seems to intimate that we garner the music that accompanies her dreams, and that the film finds this aural clue to indicate the return of grief and rage as Alice lies apparently asleep. In a cut-away we learn that the viewer of this image of Alice sleeping is Mademoiselle Eva who now sits beside her in her bedroom. This music accompanies the drama between them. The teacher sits silently beside the apparently unconscious child.

In a following shot we see Alice turned away, huddled into herself in her white nightdress, her bare arm out of the covers against the whiteness of the sheet. Here, as in earlier swimming scenes and dressing scenes, *Innocence* shows a complete ease and lack of self-consciousness in its imaging of the corporeal presence of these children both dressed and undressed. While the scale of the shot and its textures point to the embodied reality of child life, its meanings from the child's perspective relate rather to the fierce emotions and feelings harboured by Alice. These are illustrated after her teacher has left, unspeaking. We now see a shot of Alice's face while she lies in the same huddled pose. This time her eyes are open and staring into the distance as she clenches her fists. The image is tranquil but full of wistfulness, gravity and grief. The scale of the shot and the film's attention to Alice's sorrow indicate its careful means of taking its child subject, her subjectivity, seriously as its object of attention.

We see the window of the bedroom directly from Alice's prone point of view. We seem to share her imagining as she watches the bare branches of the trees outside. Alice seems completely impassive and silent as she is then carefully washed in bed. The physical regulation we have seen in the earlier dance sequence is now replaced by a physical tending that is almost maternal, and reminiscent of washing scenes in paintings by Cassatt or Degas. Yet, Alice's face is turned away from the elderly woman who washes her. Her depression has stilled her body. She is subsumed by her disappointment and finds relief from it only in her bid to escape the school's regime.

The film cuts from her obdurate face to uncertain images of the school domain, snow-covered trees, a landing stage stretching out into the lake, a frog caught frozen and dead in the broken ice. It is not clear here whether we are seeing images that Alice imagines as she contemplates escape, or images that figure something of her own glacial stasis. Perhaps we see Alice imagining death by drowning. (In a preceding sequence, Laura – Olga Peytavi-Müller – the youngest child in another house, has drowned in the lake in a doomed attempt to escape from the school domain.) The corpse of the frog gently turns in the ice and water, its motion captured. The film returns us to Alice entranced on the bed, staring into space, her hands clasped around her knees. Her gaze is unwavering as her stillness and eerie calm create a thread running through this sequence of the film. Close-up images of brick walls and ivy cut into the film. The walls have been marked as the edge of the school grounds. Returning now, they prefigure Alice's escape. As it comes, we catch her moves in the cracked glass of the bedroom mirror.[16]

The film winds round itself in repetitions. We see Alice hastily on the stairs and then running through the frozen woodland. The structure of the external shots matches those of the opening of the sequence, but their affect and pace are altered. Alice reaches the outer limit of the school domain, the ivy-clad wall, and now she climbs the wall as we view her from above. Her gestures and laboured breathing emphasise the physical exertion of her escape. Her face is as pale as her cream coat and the snow in the landscape around. The duration of the climb is emphasised as it is caught in a long take. Standing at the top, Alice surveys the woodland world outside the school. A shot of her face and ribbons matches the early shots we have seen, but now her resolve leads her to leap to freedom beyond this boundary and to disappear into the far depths of the forest. We can hear hunting dogs in the distance and a gunshot. But the threat these imply is oblique. These aural triggers may have no connection to Alice as she disappears.

Alice does not return in the narrative and her history is suspended. Mademoiselle Edith (Hélène de Fougerolles) and Mademoiselle Eva gather the children together before an open fire and tell them that Alice 'has been very bad [*a commis une faute très grave*]' and that they will never mention her again. The film cuts away to an image of flowing water, signalling the arrival of spring. It is left unclear what Alice's crime has been, whether it is her refusal of the school's authority, her running away, or in still darker imaginings, the possibility that she has followed her despair and anger through to suicide. Her erasure from the film, without the answering of these questions, makes the viewer feel more fully the controlling force of the regime from which Alice has made her exit.

We may question whether Alice has existed as the secure, protected child of *The Ethics of Ambiguity*. Her initial self-involved trajectory marks out her perception of her place in the world and of its beauty and sense. Through the dance sequence, she submits to the authority of sovereign adults. The contest itself and the judging of the bodies of the tiny dancers offers a magnified image of child life regulated, and of the infant female body patrolled. Yet Alice has questioned the system earlier, saying that threats of punishment are false and that the children cannot be kept there eternally against their will. Until the dance sequence she has offered no actual protest, though, and she has respected the authority of the female guardians of power in the school. It is when she encounters what she perceives as inconsistency and failure that her protest comes.

The film leaves further ambiguities around Alice's belief that she will be the chosen one. While she protests at her own rejection, there is a sense too that she objects to the foundering of her teacher's authority and the failure of the fixed system of justice and virtue in which she has strived to compete and in which she has been assured of success. Alice finds herself in a system which controls her, but which does not bring the reassuring stability of values of which she has been confident. Further, in her relation to the child who is chosen, Alice finds a rival who undermines her sense of self and achievement. The young Simone may express with confidence in her memoirs that she always comes first, before her sister; the child Alice finds another child chosen in preference. From its opening, *Innocence* has been in some senses a drama of usurpation where the arrival of the tiniest child, Iris, initiates a ritual where the girls hand on their hair ribbons, acknowledging that they have each reached the next new stage in development.

Alice's grief is complicated further if we remember that she has stated that she wishes to be chosen by the Headmistress because this is a way to exit the school more quickly. Despite the sylvan idyll the film creates, all the children in different ways ache to leave the school behind. There is realism in the treatment of children's homesickness at boarding school and in their resistance to the regime of obedience they are slowly moulded to adopt. Yet if we read the world of *Innocence* as a material imagining of childhood itself, it is striking that the children are all deeply impelled to leave its bounds, to refuse the authority of the sovereign subjects around them, and to realise their own desires. This Alice chooses to do, come what may, after she has failed to secure her exit by the school's own established route. Childhood is perceived here as a time of waiting and latency, of passions not given their vent, and adults whose authority is aberrant.

Quinlivan notes with relation to the surreal coffin in which Iris arrives: 'the coffin underlines Hadzihalilovic's thematic interest in the end, and loss of, childhood and its innocent world. This coming to the end of childhood and, importantly, girlhood, is what Hadzihalilovic commemorates in her film' (2009: 216). Perhaps it is significant that the coffin is there at the very opening. Despite the film's luxuriance and its hypnotic images of performing children, it is not so much about the loss of innocence as it is about losing the notion of childhood as an innocent world. The children depicted are always already autonomous subjects, but more vulnerable, more hopeful, less knowing, than the adolescents and adults they will become. The work of the film is to stage the very gradual processes of gestation, the duration of waiting and entrapment, capturing the different emotions the children themselves attach to their own uncontrolled relation to the world.

Beauvoir's writing has shown a gradual opening to the notion that childhood experience is always already flawed, and that the absence of the anguish of freedom is short-lived at best. Early in *Memoirs of a Dutiful Daughter*, Beauvoir acknowledges that her view of a secure protected childhood, here associated with the dual comforts and constraints of bourgeois living, always already had something wrong: 'Sheltered, petted, and constantly entertained by the endless novelty of life, I was a madly gay little girl. Nevertheless, there must have been something wrong somewhere: I had fits of rage during which my face turned purple and I would fall to the ground in convulsions' (1959: 13). She leaves mysterious the specific nature of what is wrong, but her rages look forward to Alice's passions in *Innocence*.

Like *The Second Sex*, *Innocence* examines the childhood of future women, and the specific entrapment of *little girls* in a world of gendered acculturation. If the world of *Innocence* is exaggerated, timeless and surreal, the enhanced image of social education it offers reflects still on the processes of *formation* Beauvoir describes so closely in her volumes. The girls in *Innocence* follow a curriculum peculiarly limited to natural history and gymnastic dance. These subjects allow the film to elaborate on subjects close to Beauvoir's agenda in *The Second Sex*. The regimen of dance, as illustrated in the sequence discussed above, allows concerns with body formation and embodied identity to overlap with the questions about modelling ideal small female identities. The dancing is another illustration of the modes of being in the material world that require extreme physical control, bodily and psychological submission to an imposed ideal of diaphanous weightlessness and grace, where the girls are taught to aspire to be as delicate and pristine as the garments they wear.[17]

That the girls in *Innocence* also take classes in Natural History, watching butterflies and other insects and birds, and are themselves likened to future butterflies that will emerge from their chrysalis, further aligns the film's world with the gender programme that Beauvoir describes in *The Second Sex*. Beauvoir has recourse herself to insect imagery as she describes the changes wrought by the onset of adolescence: 'The metamorphosis of the caterpillar, through chrysalis and into butterfly brings about a deep uneasiness: is it still the same caterpillar after this long sleep? Does she recognise herself under these brilliant wings?' (2009: 329). Metamorphosis brings stages of non-self-identity and self-questioning as the rapidly growing child questions sensuously her relation to the world:

> And yet, the metamorphosis takes place. The little girl herself does not understand the meaning, but she realises that in her relations with the world and her own body something is changing subtly: she is sensitive to contacts, tastes and odours that prev-iously left her indifferent; baroque images pass through her head; she barely recog-nises herself in mirrors; she feels 'funny', things seem 'funny'.
>
> (Beauvoir 2009: 329)

In *The Second Sex*, as well as in her fiction and autobiographical writing, Beauvoir takes strongly into account the specificity and texture of girlhood feelings and emotions. By way of references to a series of literary evocations of girlhood, but also through an extraordinary act of recall or projection, and a style bordering on *style indirect libre* in its proximity to a girl's consciousness, Beauvoir charts the embodied experience of childhood. This is what I suggest Hadzihalilovic achieves too in her filmic capture of individual experiences of childhood. Despite its apparent timelessness, *Innocence*, in its opening into a contemporary context at its end, implies the persistence, for girls, of the process of acculturation that Beauvoir critiques. Yet what the film makes felt, in ways that come through only latterly in Beauvoir's writing on girlhood, is the way in which this acculturation is bound up with myths of childhood innocence sustained and policed by nostalgic adults.

Notes

1. Tidd references the discussion of childhood in Beauvoir pursued in Simons (1986).
2. See my articles (Wilson 2005, 2006 and 2007). These pieces look variously at *Mina Tannenbaum* (1994), *Y aura-t-il de la neige à Noël?* (1996), *Martha … Martha* (2001) and *Innocence* (2004). Other female-authored French films which, in one way or another, explore girlhood include *Coup de foudre* (1983), *Chocolat* (1988), *Récréations* (1998), *La vie ne me fait pas peur* (1999), *Saint-Cyr* (2000), *Tout est pardonné* (2007), *Les Plages d'Agnès* (2009), *Barbe Bleue* (2009). See Tarr and Rollet (2001: 25–53) for further discussion of the representation of girlhood. See also Jean-Pierre Boulé, 'Claire Denis's *Chocolat* and the Politics of Desire', in this volume.
3. Lucile Hadzihalilovic graduated from the ESEC film school in 1982. She has made two short films, *La Bouche de Jean-Pierre* (1996) and *Good Boys Use Condoms* (1998), and wrote

the screenplay for Gaspar Noé's *Enter the Void* (2009). She has also worked as an editor on Noé's films. *Innocence* is her first feature film.

4. A question *The Second Sex* leaves unanswered is whether Beauvoir continues to believe that women as well as men retain nostalgia for childhood tranquillity.

5. For further discussion of these chapters see Fishwick (2002: 174–75).

6. All translations from this text are mine.

7. This contrasts with Françoise's later stance in relation to Pierre where she feels she has to relate everything to him in order for it to exist.

8. As Tidd points out: 'For Beauvoir, unsurprisingly, the child does not contain the future adult, although it is always on the basis of the past that an adult makes choices regarding future behaviour' (1999: 26).

9. See Lury (2010: 126) for discussion of the forest in films about children.

10. *Innocence* borrows many of its motifs and the details of its setting and scenarios from the text. The film shows greater attention to its protagonists Iris, Alice and Bianca, however, and moves to bring us closer to their subjective experience. This is particularly the case with Alice who does not appear directly as a character in *Mine-Haha* and whose direct experience of the ritual of dancing for the Headmistress is not represented. *Mine-Haha* refers rather to a series of dancing selections in which the girls are judged. In keeping with the more explicit sexualisation of the girls' school in the text, the girls are first stripped naked to be judged physically. Although it pays attention to the girls' sensuality, where we see small girls pass a daisy over Iris's skin and we see Bianca caress her own thighs with a kid glove she has found, *Innocence* seems more engaged than *Mine-Haha* in showing embodied activities as they are experienced by children, rather than displaying its child cast more voyeuristically.

11. See Higonnet (1998).

12. See Pierce (1999) on the Australian fascination with missing children.

13. Toril Moi offers discussion of female education in Beauvoir's era (see Moi 1994: 38–47).

14. Vicky Lebeau offers a different, and compelling, reading, arguing: 'drawing on both the legacy of cinema's fetishization of the young girl *and* a contemporary pressure towards ever more vigilant, ever more sexually self-conscious, looking at children, *Innocence* creates a remarkably suspenseful depiction of a boarding school for girls' (2008: 119).

15. The children are arranged in five 'houses', each with a series of girls of different ages. *Innocence* focuses on three girls from House 3, where Iris is the youngest, Bianca the eldest, and Alice is in between.

16. The glass was broken close to the start of the film by the next to youngest child protesting at the arrival of Iris.

17. See Fishwick (2002: 253–64) for discussion of Beauvoir's interest in dance and gender.

Bibliography

Beauvoir, S. de. [1948] 1967. *The Ethics of Ambiguity*, trans. B. Frechtman. New York: The Citadel Press.

———. [1949] 2009. *The Second Sex*, trans. C. Borde and S. Malovany-Chevalier. London: Jonathan Cape.

———. [1958] 1959. *Memoirs of A Dutiful Daughter*, trans. J. Kirkup. London: André Deutsch and Weidenfeld and Nicolson.

———. 1979. 'Deux chapitres inédits de *L'Invitée*', in C. Francis and F. Gontier. *Les Ecrits de Simone de Beauvoir*. Paris: Gallimard, pp. 275–316.

Fishwick, S. 2002. *The Body in the Work of Simone de Beauvoir*. Bern: Peter Lang.

Francis, C. and F. Gontier. 1979. *Les Ecrits de Simone de Beauvoir*. Paris: Gallimard.

Higonnet, A. 1998. *Pictures of Innocence: The History and Crisis of Ideal Childhood*. London: Thames and Hudson, 1998.

Lebeau, V. 2008. *Childhood and Cinema*. London: Reaktion Books.

Lury, K. 2010. *The Child in Film: Tears, Fears and Fairy Tales*. London: I.B. Tauris.

Moi, T. 1994. *Simone de Beauvoir: The Making of an Intellectual Woman*. Oxford: Blackwell.

Pierce, P. 1999. *The Country of Lost Children: An Australian Anxiety*. Cambridge: Cambridge University Press.

Plath, S. 1977. 'Superman and Paula Brown's New Snowsuit', in *Johnny Panic and the Bible of Dreams*. London: Faber and Faber, pp. 160–166.

Quinlivan, D. 2009. 'Material Hauntings: The Kinaesthesia of Sound in *Innocence* (Hadzihalilovic, 2004)', *Studies in French Cinema* 9(3): 215–224.

Simons. M.A. 1986. 'Beauvoir and Sartre: The Philosophical Relationship', 'Simone de Beauvoir: Witness to a Century', *Yale French Studies* 72: 165–179.

Tarr, C. and B. Rollet. 2001. *Cinema and the Second Sex: Women's Filmmaking in France in the 1980s and 1990s*. New York and London: Continuum.

Tidd, U. 1999. *Simone de Beauvoir: Gender and Testimony*. Cambridge: Cambridge University Press.

Wedekind, F. [1903] 2010. *Mine-Haha or On the Bodily Education of Young Girls*, trans. P. Ward. London: Hesperus Press.

Wilson, E. 2005. 'Children, Emotion and Viewing in Contemporary European Film', *Screen* 46(3), Autumn: 329–40.

———. 2006. 'Women Filming Children', *Nottingham French Studies* 45(3), Autumn: 105–18.

———. 2007. 'Miniature Lives, Intrusion and Innocence: Women Filming Children (2)', *French Cultural Studies* 18(2), June: 169–83.

Filmography

Breillat, C. (dir.). 2009. *Barbe Bleue*. Flach Film.

Denis, C. (dir.). 1988. *Chocolat*. Caroline Productions.

Dugowson, M. (dir.). 1994. *Mina Tannenbaum*. Studio Canal.

Hadzihalilovic, L. (dir.). 2004. *Innocence*. Ex nihilo.

Hansen-Løve, M. (dir.). 2007. *Tout est pardonné*. Les Films Pelléas.

Kurys, D. (dir.). 1983. *Coup de foudre*. Studio Canal.

Lvovsky, N. (dir.). 1999. *La vie ne me fait pas peur*. Canal +.

Mazuy, P. (dir.). 2000. *Saint-Cyr*. Canal +.

Simon, C. (dir.). 1998. *Récréations*. Les Films d'ici.

Varda, A. (dir.). 2009. *Les Plages d'Agnès*. Ciné Tamaris.

Veysset, S. (dir.). 1996. *Y aura-t-il de la neige à Noël?* Canal +.

———. 2001. *Martha … Martha*. Canal +.

2

'DEVENIR MÈRE': TRAJECTORIES OF THE MATERNAL BOND IN RECENT FILMS STARRING ISABELLE HUPPERT

Ursula Tidd

Isabelle Huppert has long occupied iconic status as one of France's major film actresses. Playing complex and transgressive roles which frequently combine masochism, sadism and exhibitionism, Huppert incarnates the existential ambiguity of women's situation in post-war western patriarchy as a twisting path between freedom and responsibility, transgression and convention. Huppert's star persona combines a cerebral detachment with an edgy yet melancholic vulnerability which can provoke strong reactions of disquiet and fascination in her audience. Director Michael Haneke observes: '[Huppert] has such professionalism, the way she is able to represent suffering. At one end you have the extreme of her suffering and then you have her icy intellectualism. No other actor can combine the two.'[1]

In many of Huppert's recent roles, the erotic charge and suffering of mothering are foregrounded in ways which illustrate and develop Simone de Beauvoir's controversial analyses of the mother's situation and women's experience of sexuality in *The Second Sex* (1949).[2] Here, *inter alia*, Beauvoir argues that a maternal instinct does not exist and that women experience a variety of responses to the existential situations of motherhood and sexuality. Huppert's choice in recent years to act in films in which the mother–child bond is explored in its inevitable dysfunctionality is underpinned by her recognition, shared both by Beauvoir and many theories of child psycho-affective development, that a necessary rupture must occur between mother and child to facilitate the child's autonomous subjectivity.[3] For Huppert has observed that 'however loving a mother might be, she will necessarily be a threat to her child, who demands an unconditional love. All of the child's learning process will entail living in the shadow of an inevitable rupture' (Gianorio 2001: 1).

In this chapter, three of Huppert's recent films which explore this 'threat' and 'inevitable rupture' at the heart of the mother–child bond will be discussed in the context of Beauvoir's analyses of motherhood and female sexuality in *The Second Sex* and in her essay 'Must We Burn Sade?'. The chapter's aim is to analyse how some of Huppert's recent and most unsettling roles can offer fresh insights into the dynamics of the mother–child bond in the contemporary era in which women seek to reconcile the demands of motherhood with their complex professional and private lives. The discussion will focus on *Comédie de l'Innocence*, *La Pianiste*, and *L'Amour caché*. The latter two films deal with mother–daughter relationships, whereas *Comédie de l'Innocence* focuses on a mother–son relationship, although the pedagogical relationship and age difference between Erika Kohut (Isabelle Huppert) and Walter Klemmer (Benoît Magimel) in *La Pianiste* suggest an additional eroticised mother–son dynamic in that film. All three films foreground mothering as a site of violent attachment and loss and, consonant with Beauvoir's analyses in *The Second Sex*, challenge the patriarchal myth that the mother–child bond is an idyll of maternal fulfilment and protective, unconditional nurture.

The first film, *Comédie de l'Innocence*, mobilises ghost story, thriller and fantasy tropes in a disquieting tale based on a 1929 novel by Massimo Bontempelli, an Italian magical realist writer of fascist sympathies.[4] Raúl Ruiz, the film's Chilean director, is highly prolific – his best-known film is perhaps his 1999 filmic adaptation of Marcel Proust's *Le Temps retrouvé* – and his reputation as a director of 'intellectual' films is founded on his explorations of schizoid identity, memory, and the alterity of the everyday in labyrinthine films which fuse imagination and reality. Ruiz deploys a complex visual language which entails swirling camera movements of close-up and point-of-view shots which can destabilise the viewer's perception of 'reality'. He has described *Comédie de l'Innocence* as 'a movie about Don Juan's childhood' – an apt description insofar as the film explores maternal loss and bereavement in relation to the child's phantasy of being able to choose his/her mother. At a more general level, however, the film fundamentally questions the parameters of motherhood, as was noted in the French press on its release.[5]

In the ironically titled *Comédie de l'Innocence*, Camille (Nils Hugon), who is celebrating his ninth birthday, rejects Ariane D'Orville (Huppert), his biological mother who works as a theatre designer and artist, and asks to be reunited with his 'real' mother Isabella (Jeanne Balibar). The latter, a violin teacher, is a recently bereaved mother and is herself 'motherless'. Camille claims to be Isabella's son, Paul, who was born on the same day but drowned in the Seine two years earlier. Camille says that he has been living with Isabella in a rented apartment in Belleville, an historically left-wing working class and immigrant district on the north-east side of Paris.[6] The film is set in a bleached, wintry Paris with much of the action taking place in or near the mansion where Ariane lives with Pierre, her husband, and Camille. Two other members of the family also live there: Ariane's psychiatrist brother, Serge (Charles Berling), an emotionally volatile figure who is fiercely attached to his childhood toys with which he still plays, and Hélène (Laure de Clermont-Tonnerre), who (somewhat improbably) is an avid student of probability theory. She is also Serge's secret lover and, as au pair to the family, fulfils the role of a (rather unreliable) maternal surrogate to Camille. The action centres on the psycho-affective struggle between Ariane and Isabella for possession of Camille, who spends his time recording the world on a camcorder, thereby multiplying the layers of phantasy within the film, and talking to his mysterious friend Alexandre. The film raises unsettling questions about familial relationships because it invites the audience to reflect on the mother–child relationship as a site of phantasy and loss and because it questions the extent of familial rights and responsibilities.[7]

Indications of the troubled subconscious reality underpinning the veneer of bourgeois family life are provided by the marginal character of Isabella's too-knowing and unnerving, predatory neighbour (Edith Scob) and by the psychiatric sub-plot which pits Serge against Isabella which leads the viewer to question who is the most mentally unbalanced. Highly suggestive mythological and cultural references are provided by the family's artworks, such as the print of 'The Judgement of Solomon', which is referred to as 'too relevant' in the current maternal crisis and is mysteriously defaced during the film.[8] The white neo-classical busts and contemporary art of Ariane's family home are also set against the 'primitive' large dark African statuary of Isabella's flat, which suggests a psycho-affective conflict between the ostensibly civilised and the primal. Moreover, Ariane's name alludes to Ariadne of classical myth with the associated wordplay in French of 'fils' (son) and 'fils' (threads),[9] and the story of *Tom Thumb* is also cited and re-told by Camille.[10] As the film builds to its fragile resolution, it becomes apparent that it is Camille who has primarily orchestrated the attempt to leave his biological mother (rather than being the victim of manipulation by Isabella) and, with the return of Pierre, his father, at the end of the film, a precarious patriarchal order is restored.

The second, and probably most controversial, of Huppert's recent films, *La Pianiste*, directed by Michael Haneke, has been selected here for its powerful exploration of female sexuality in the context of a dysfunctional mother–daughter relationship. The film is based on Elfriede Jelinek's 1983 eponymous novel and depicts two intense sado-masochistic relationships in the life of Erika Kohut, a distinguished pianist and Schubert scholar at the Vienna Conservatory. The first of these relationships is with her widowed (and unnamed) mother (Annie Girardot) with whom she lives in a claustrophobic intimacy; the second is with Walter Klemmer, her music student and a local Don Juan figure, with whom she embarks on a relationship. Before meeting Walter, Erika is portrayed as soothing herself by self-mutilation and engaging in solipsistic and voyeuristic sexual pleasure. Kept under constant surveillance by her mother, she struggles to express her needs and desires. In her professional life, Erika is an exacting teacher and frequently teaches young women who, like her, are compelled by their mothers to sacrifice themselves for the sake of musical accomplishment and bourgeois social advancement. Yet Erika is easily threatened and, needing to maintain control, cannot allow these young women to surpass her: in one instance, she places broken glass in the coat pocket of a stage-frightened female student who is being tutored supportively by Walter, which sabotages the student's ability to participate in a recital.

Erika shares her passion and identification with Schubert with Walter – specifically her identification with the period of Schubert's 'twilight of the mind' in which self-dispossession precedes abandonment. As Haneke astutely comments, 'there is a great sense of mourning in Schubert that is very much part of the film. Someone with the tremendous problems borne by Erika may well project them onto an artist of Schubert's very complex sensibility'.[11] Schubert's *Winterreise* song cycle features throughout the film and its focus on alienation and unrequited love is heightened for Erika, as Wheatley notes, by the fact that Erika can only play the accompanying music to the male singer's words.[12] Indeed, it is Erika's inability to answer the question articulated in the *Winterreise* – 'What is this foolish desire driving me into the wilderness?' – that prevents her from seeing that Walter only alights on her identification with Schubert to seduce rather than to love her. When Walter is unable to comply with Erika's masochistic fantasies or to 'read' her suffering, he stages a violent exit from the relationship by means of rape. In the final scene, Erika stabs herself in the chest in the foyer of the Vienna opera house as she is due to deliver a recital of the *Winterreise*, attended by her mother, Walter, other students and their parents. As she leaves the opera house without performing the recital, her fate is uncertain.

The third film for consideration here is *L'Amour caché*, directed by Alessandro Capone, which depicts the reciprocal hatred between Danielle Girard (Huppert) and her daughter, Sophie (Mélanie Laurent), as recounted in present-day monologue and flashback to Dr Madeleine Nielsen (Greta Scacchi) in the psychiatric hospital where Danielle is being treated. The central dysfunctional mother–daughter relationship is offset by Sophie's apparently happy relationship with her own daughter, Dominique, and Dr Nielsen's recognition that she is (like Isabella in *Comédie de l'Innocence*) a 'motherless child'. Via medical and psychotherapeutic detours from Danielle's auto-biographical monologue and with a more sustained focus on dysfunctional mothering than that of *La Pianiste*, *L'Amour caché* stages the mother–daughter bond as a hellish life-or-death struggle.[13] Mother and daughter each view the other as the obstacle to their individual transcendence and happiness. Simultaneously, Dr Madeleine Nielsen, herself childless, becomes increasingly emotionally conflicted as she finds herself psychologically contaminated by the mother–daughter struggle that she is witnessing. The film draws to a close with Sophie committing suicide and Danielle resenting her daughter for having ended her life before she could take her own. She observes poignantly: 'a bad mother and a small heap of bones – that's all that will remain of our story'. However, a certain affective recuperation does occur in Sophie's spectral voice-over entrusting her daughter to Danielle. In the film's final frame, which is shot as a high angle long shot, we see Danielle walking away contentedly across the sand dunes affectionately chattering to her grand-daughter.

In all three films the mother–child bond is represented as powerful, painful and the result of compulsory and compulsive attachment rather than of free choice. As such, the mother–child bond is staged as an existential conundrum and a '*huis clos*' from which, as in Jean-Paul Sartre's 1944 eponymous play, there is no exit – a dire but not inevitable predicament for mother, child and society at large which Beauvoir was keen to expose in *The Second Sex*.

Beauvoir's own 'lived experience' of the mother–daughter relationship, told and re-told in several of her autobiographical and fictional texts, first awakened her to the potency of this primal and primary relationship. With characteristic clarity, Beauvoir set out in *The Second Sex* to challenge patriarchal society's simultaneous idealisation and denigration of motherhood at a time when abortion and contraception were illegal in France. Alert to the ways in which motherhood has been institutionalised and functions as a dense site of power relations steeped in patriarchal mythology, Beauvoir argues that women's experience of motherhood varies according to the particularities of their 'situation'. This means that motherhood, like any other aspect of lived experience, is both the result of freedom and facticity (the latter being those aspects of existence which are 'given' and hence not chosen by human consciousness). In patriarchal society, however, girls and women are inculcated with the myth of motherhood as their ideal destiny: at a young age, girls are encouraged to care for dolls as prototype infants and become alienated in this nurturing role and in this passive object when no ready outlet is available for their emerging desire for autonomy and subjecthood. In *Comédie de l'Innocence*, for example, Ariane chides the au pair Hélène for playing with her doll (which Ariane claims to use in her work as a theatre designer) in a scene which acts as a *mise-en-abyme* for Ariane's continuing battle with Isabella over possession of Camille. No reason is given for Hélène's attachment to the doll which stands in ironic counterpoint to her casual supervision of Camille as he wanders about the Champ de Mars talking to strangers. In fact, her reluctant child minding parallels instances of Ariane's maternal truancy when she arrives very late to meet Camille for a walk on the Champ de Mars on his birthday. It seems that both Ariane and Hélène experience an easier attachment to the passive doll than the real, pro-active child, Camille.

His idealisation of motherhood and his disappointment when Ariane inevitably fails him leads him to find a fantasy solution to his quest for an ideal mother in his adoption of the recently bereaved Isabella and in his re-telling of the *Tom Thumb* story. Significantly, Camille tells the story to Isabella as an abandonment narrative: Tom Thumb set off one day on a quest to find his mother (who had gone to the theatre and not returned) because he was fed up of living alone in an empty house. This articulates Camille's perception of his situation: that his mother, Ariane, has abandoned him in favour of her work. It is also the predicament described by Freud in the 'fort-da' game in *Beyond the Pleasure Principle* (1920), whereby the baby invents a linguistic reparation to manage his anxiety resulting from his perceived abandonment by his mother.[14] Isabella reminds Camille that he tells the tale differently – sometimes Tom has a mother and sometimes he does not – which corresponds to Camille's perception of Ariane's intermittent presence. Already Camille appears to have made powerful value judgements about what constitutes 'good' and 'bad' mothering and is intent on getting his needs met by turning mothering into a quest in such a way that will ensure that he captures his mother's attention.

Without the device of the quest, Ariane's suffering as a mother would be considerably less 'readable'. For in *Comédie de l'Innocence*, as in *L'Amour caché* and *La Pianiste*, as John Champagne notes in relation to the latter film, much of the viewer's work consists in reading Huppert's 'always ambiguous face'.[15] As will be argued below, it is the lingering close-up shots of Huppert in these films which express the conflicts inherent in patriarchal motherhood and femininity, experienced as alienation and traumatic loss.

Desire, Alienation and the Gaze

'Becoming a woman' in patriarchal society is an alienating process, according to Beauvoir, and one which is highly detrimental to girls and women.[16] Although, as LaCapra argues in a rather different context, all human beings are alienated to some extent and hence experience a 'structural' trauma in relation to their coming into being as a subject in the world, Beauvoir argues that girls are raised to alienate themselves in their image and anatomy and to accept a secondary status as Other in relation to an ideal of transcendental masculinity (Beauvoir 2009: 59).[17] As Beauvoir shows in *The Second Sex*, this is an historicised process for there is nothing 'natural' or inevitable about girls' or women's secondary status in patriarchal society. Hence it can be argued that girls experience a gendered alienation and an historical trauma in addition to the 'generalised' alienation and structural trauma to which everyone is subjected. Unlike boys, girls do not reintegrate their alienated image of themselves back into their own subjectivity; they are alienated in their whole body. Beauvoir argues that this is due to the (different values attached to) anatomical difference between girls and boys: boys project their transcendence into the penis which both is and is not co-extensive with their identity. Due to this ambiguity, boys are able to recover their alienated transcendence because the penis acts as a talisman or totem facilitating male subjectivity and authenticity. An extreme example of just such a recovery is Walter Klemmer's sexual violation of Erika at the end of *La Pianiste*: his masculine transcendence is destabilised by her list of sexual demands and, unable to subordinate her 'masculine' desires to his, Walter (coded for much of the film as a dominant white male) wrests back control of both his penis and the phallus. In so doing, he undermines Erika's attempt to control her life, to achieve agency, to love and to be loved.[18]

Moi has argued that Beauvoir's analyses of female alienation in *The Second Sex* risks idealising and normatising masculinity and that she fails to integrate sufficiently the biological with the psycho-social: that the child's alienation in the gaze of the other needs to be integrated with the process of somatic alienation that is also underway (Moi 1994: 163–64). In the present context, it is important to note that the process of somatic alienation and recognition is usually regulated by the maternal gaze – the receipt of which may not, in reality, be a benevolent or unequivocally positive experience for the child, as all three films illustrate.

In *Comédie de l'Innocence*, Camille's attempt to escape his biological mother suggest his failure to register her gaze of loving possession and his rejection of her maternal role. Like his fellow *Don Juan*, Walter Klemmer in *La Pianiste*, Camille's seduction of Isabella is, as Ruiz has observed, a false emancipation because it entails a flight from self-elaboration and the Real into the vertiginous spiral of seduction (Tranchant 2000: 1). Moreover, the dominance of Camille's own gaze is established at the beginning of the film with point-of-view shots panning across objects as he films his domestic environment. When his mother plaintively asks: 'Camille, could you tell us what we're looking at?', he lists them ('ashtray, shells, alarm clock, plants, hibiscus'), and ends with 'nothing, nothing, nothing'. Then, as Ariane enquires: 'What do you mean, nothing?' the camera cuts to water images which can be interpreted retrospectively as a reference to Paul's death by drowning. The 'nothingness' or alienated desire of the male gaze is equated here with death when it fails to commands its specular environment, although it is a phantasised rather than an actual death as far as Camille is concerned.

In *L'Amour caché*, the catastrophic alienation between mother Danielle and daughter Sophie is pithily expressed early in the film when Sophie exclaims to her that 'I am the monster incarnating your worst failings!'. Sophie's internalisation of her mother's gaze as unloving and rejecting will lead her ultimately to suicide. However, in *Comédie de l'Innocence*, Camille orchestrates both a maternal surrogate and a death surrogate for himself when he replaces his 'undesirable' mother with Isabella and staves off his own feared annihilation by acting as a surrogate for Paul. In that sense, unlike Sophie in *L'Amour caché*, Camille refuses to internalise Ariane's gaze as unloving and rejecting and develops artful means to ensure that it is more loving and vigilant in the future by turning 'good' mothering into a quest.

In *La Pianiste*, surveillance of Erika by her mother leads Erika to ever more extreme sado-masochistic fantasies and enactments in order both to elude and experience the censoring maternal gaze. The all-pervasiveness of this gaze is apparent throughout the film, evident in Erika's mother's domineering presence overseeing her career, her daily professional schedule and domestic situation. In such a claustrophobic situation (evident, too, in *L'Amour caché*), it is hardly surprising that violence and ambiguity are deeply imbricated in the mother–child bond.

Violence and Ambiguity in the Mother–Child Bond

Although there is only one reference to the psychoanalytic work of Melanie Klein in *The Second Sex* (in the context of the young girl's fear of menstruation), Beauvoir and Klein were both interested in the violence and ambiguity of the mother–child relationship. Both, despite their different approaches, sought to reinscribe maternal subjectivity within the mother–child dyad. Although no feminist, Klein played a leading role in developing a mother-centred psychoanalysis in her work on play analysis and the pre-Oedipal psyche. Klein focused primarily on the infant's phantasies of the mother and the developing ego's strategies of defence in response to the conflict between the life and death drives. She formulated the two key concepts of the depressive and paranoid-schizoid positions which function as mental structures in both the child and adult psyche (Doane and Hodges 1992; Klein 1988a, Klein 1988b). The paranoid-schizoid position explores the child's early relationships to part-objects such as the maternal breast. This position is dominated by anxiety, projection, introjection, splitting and persecution in which the nascent self attempts to order its psychic life by separating off good and bad parts and identifying the maternal body with its projected parts. In the depressive position, the self has evolved to see the mother as a whole rather than a part-object and recognises that its feelings of hatred and love are in fact directed at the same person. This may cause the child to feel guilt, anxiety and loss and a desire to make reparation for its earlier violence and hatred. The depressive position allowed Klein to explore women's pre-Oedipal relationship with the mother, offering a viable alternative to the masculinism of Freud's Oedipus complex, as Beauvoir similarly sought to theorise in *The Second Sex*. However, Beauvoir's lack of detailed engagement with Klein's psychoanalysis can be explained by various factors: Klein's inheritance of the Freudian vocabulary of instincts and drives and her focus on the child's phantasy life conflict with Beauvoir's trenchant feminist existentialist criticisms of the deterministic and universalising tendencies of classical psychoanalysis. Moreover, Beauvoir's analyses of the mother–child bond in *The Second Sex* emphasise the diversity of women's *lived experience* of motherhood, that is, as it unfolds in the social as well as the psychic sphere. This phenomenological focus on the diversity of mothering is highly original and sets Beauvoir's account apart from that of Klein and other psychoanalytic and object-relations theorists, such as Nancy Chodorow and, more recently, Julia Kristeva. Most importantly, Klein had no interest in the patriarchal societal structures that produce women's subordination and structure the mother–child relationship, which is clearly a fundamental focus for Beauvoir in *The Second Sex*. Noting these significant differences between them, Kleinian theory nonetheless offers a useful adjunct to Beauvoirian theory in this discussion's focus on trajectories of mothering in the three films, specifically the troubling aspects of women's psychosexual behaviour such as aggression, sadomasochism, depression and paranoia as they are manifest in the mother–child relationship.

In *Comédie de l'Innocence*, *La Pianiste* and *L'Amour caché*, many of these behavioural patterns are evident. In *Comédie de l'Innocence*, Camille 'splits' the mother in what can be characterised as evidence of Klein's paranoid-schizoid position and seeks to annihilate the 'bad mother' symbolically by leaving the family home and attaching himself to another 'better' mother. His filming, as a '*mise-en-scène*' of his own life, like his re-telling of the *Tom Thumb* tale, further allows him to order his life by separating off the 'bad' parts of it. In *La Pianiste* and *L'Amour caché*, the relationship of the female protagonists to their mothers is more complex and passive: they appear to have less power to separate from the 'bad' mother figure and, in both films, the mother–daughter relationships entail verbal and physical violence, self-harm, depression and paranoia.

In Beauvoir's account of motherhood in *The Second Sex*, as distinct from Klein's, the relative success or failure of the mother–child bond is highly dependent on the mother's overall 'situation' as the locus of her existential freedom and facticity. In her analyses of motherhood in patriarchal society, she notes that the mother can form an exclusive bond with her child and yet, despite this exclusivity, 'she will only devote herself joyously to a newborn if a man devotes himself to her' (Beauvoir 2009: 550). The father's attitude towards the mother and to the child often shapes the mother's attitude to the child, in Beauvoir's account. Over sixty years on, family structures have diversified to include single-sex couples and single parents; however, the attitudes of the biological parents towards the child remain key: in many of Huppert's films in which motherhood plays a central if dysfunctional role (including the three under discussion here), the biological father is either dead or largely absent. In *Comédie de l'Innocence*, the father is absent on a business trip for most of the film and is 'replaced' by Serge, Ariane's psychiatrist brother. She appears considerably closer to Serge than to her husband and she largely delegates to him the responsibility to slay the metaphorical minotaur, that is, to unravel the mystery of Camille's attachment to Isabella. Professionally, Serge would seem the best suited for this task although as a proto-Theseus, he reveals himself to be insufficiently psychologically stable to complete the task.

In *La Pianiste*, the father is similarly absent although to a more confusing extent. Erika's mother tells her that father has just died insane in the nearby Steinhof asylum on the outskirts of Vienna, yet Erika also claims that her father has been dead for some years. This ambiguity suggests that Erika *perceives* her father as having been long absent in her life. In Jelinek's eponymous book (from which the film is adapted), Erika visits her father in the asylum and his psychiatric illness is said to have been caused by his marriage, implying that Erika's unnamed mother is a psychologically threatening companion and at least partially responsible for Erika's 'perverse' behaviour (Jelinek 1989: 13).

In *L'Amour caché*, Danielle's partner, Michel, is eleven years older and a cameo figure evoked only in recollection. Danielle relates to Dr Nielsen that she felt such physical disgust for Michel that she took contraception secretly in order to avoid falling pregnant by him. Hence it is implied that the subsequent mother–daughter conflict that ensues between Danielle and Sophie might be related to Danielle's physical rejection of Michel. We see here that Beauvoir's emphasis on the overall existential situation of the mother is valuable in providing a fuller explanation for the breakdown in the mother–daughter relationship.

In *Comédie de l'Innocence*, the father's distance and absence facilitates Camille's attachment to another mother, as he seeks to escape a familial context which is already coded in the film as incestuous and pathological. However, in *La Pianiste* and *L'Amour caché*, the father's absence coincides with a deeper bonding between mother and daughter which becomes violent, possessive and claustrophobic with strong overtones of gendered trauma and depression. In *L'Amour caché*, Danielle is eerily silent in the film's opening frames as if she were frozen in the melancholia of motherhood. Close-up shots reveal Danielle's blank, unmade-up face – a blankness which is familiar to viewers of Huppert's cinema, some of whom, as Beauvoir argued in relation to Brigitte Bardot, may be frustrated by the star's ability to elude the patriarchal spectatorial gaze (Beauvoir 1960: 30). Danielle is gradually cajoled into relating her life story by Dr Nielsen who tells her: 'Don't be afraid of your voice. Not talking doesn't mean not existing. It's like existing disarmed, with no shape, no power.' Danielle begins by furiously writing brief fragments about her life, each on a separate page. Surrounded by empty space, these isolated paragraphs on separate single pages evoke the trauma of maternal suffering and alienation. Referring to her experience of mothering as 'a trail of blood and irresponsibility', Danielle describes an unhappy marriage and her intense guilt and resentment at having had to assume maternal responsibility. For, as Beauvoir observes in *The Second Sex*, after the initial elation of birth, mothers can rapidly feel overwhelmed by the tyranny of the baby's needs and can retaliate with hostility: '[the baby] is like a tyrant; she feels hostility for this little individual who threatens her flesh, her freedom, her whole self' (Beauvoir 2009: 565). Most mothers, aware of their duties towards the dependent child, manage to overcome this hostility but feel remorse and anxiety, as Klein has also shown. But the fact that mothers experience such hostility at all towards their babies endorses one of the most often-cited sections of *The Second Sex* in which Beauvoir argues that 'there is no such thing as maternal "instinct": the word does not in any case apply to the human species. The mother's attitude is defined by her total situation and by the way she accepts it' (Beauvoir 2009: 567).

What is striking in all three films is the lack of explicit context provided concerning these mothers' situations. Characteristic of many of Huppert's recent roles, here she plays mothers and daughters who are alienated by their gendered suffering – to the point of extreme psycho-affective disturbance in *La Pianiste* and *L'Amour caché*. Without more information on these women's existential situations, the viewer is literally faced with the riddle of Huppert's blank melancholic face and left wondering how the mother–child relationship could have gone so wrong. Yet, as Beauvoir argues in *The Second Sex*, the mother–daughter relationship experienced within patriarchal society is especially set up to fail. The mother feels necessary to the child but it is a non-reciprocated relationship in that the child cannot confer value upon her or fulfil her needs. The mother–child bond can be highly erotic, according to Beauvoir, yet it can also be the locus of violence, as already noted, because the mother can exploit her child to vent her own frustrations over her situation as it is circumscribed by patriarchy:

> A mother who beats her child does not only beat the child; in a way, she does not beat him at all: she is taking vengeance on a man, on the world, or on herself; but it is certainly the child who receives the blows.
>
> (Beauvoir 2009: 570)

In *La Pianiste*, we witness a violent dispute between Erika and her mother at the start of the film concerning Erika's late return home and her mother's discovery of a skimpy dress which Erika has bought. She condemns Erika for wearing make-up and for spending money on the dress rather than saving it towards getting a larger apartment for them both. The conflict places Erika's sexuality in opposition to her mother's desire for domestic comfort and symbiosis with her daughter. It escalates into physical violence which, in terms of what is shown on-screen, reverses Beauvoir's point concerning the child cited above – for it is Erika who is physically violent towards her mother.

But here, as in *L'Amour caché*, this violence must be set within the emotional vocabulary of the relationship. The violence is part of a generalised physical intimacy between Erika and her mother which is shown to be far more powerful than Erika's failed intimacy with Walter, albeit unusual between a mother and an adult daughter. In a subsequent scene early in the film which further develops this dynamic of psychic and physical intimacy, mother and daughter are invited to the Klemmer family apartment to attend a drinks reception and recital. On entering the lift, they deliberately close the lift, thereby shutting out a young man (who turns out to be Walter) and obliging him to walk up several flights of stairs to the apartment. This scene will be counter-balanced towards the end of the film when Erika is barricaded into her bedroom by Walter and she reads a list of her masochistic fantasies to him. But Walter's inability to interpret Erika's suffering, to respond to her demands and to love her is expressed in his patriarchal labelling of her as sick and deviant before he leaves in disgust. Henceforth, the primacy of the mother–daughter bond is restored. In an immediately subsequent scene, we see Erika revert to habitual pre-Oedipal intimacy with her mother: as they lie in bed together, Erika gets on top of her, kisses her and tells her that she loves her. Her mother pushes her away and tells her that she is crazy. In the ensuing struggle, Erika pulls up her mother's nightdress to reveal her mother's pubis. The viewer may be tempted to read this encounter as an incest scenario given the graphic presentation of sexuality in the film. However, Huppert has described this scene as an attempt by Erika to return to the site of her own origin and to explore the mystery of her mother as a desiring subject.[19] For Huppert, Erika is 'someone who isn't yet born, who would like to live and for whom everything is confused and merged' (Tranchant 2001: 1). In a frightening world with which she finds it difficult to engage and which has proved resistant to satisfying her desires or relieving her suffering, it seems entirely plausible that Erika should wish to return to the reassuring physicality of the maternal body. In so doing, she can recover a space of childlike safety and intimacy with her mother by witnessing the genital site of adult female sexuality.

This scene from *La Pianiste* recalls a similar encounter with the maternal body in Beauvoir's *A Very Easy Death* in which Beauvoir depicts the final month of her mother's life and death from intestinal cancer. Recalling a visit to her mother in hospital, Beauvoir relates her shock at the sight of Françoise de Beauvoir's naked abdomen and pubis as a physiotherapist conducts a pelvic examination:

> The sight of my mother's nakedness had jarred me. No body existed less for me: none existed more. As a child I had loved it dearly; as an adolescent it had filled me with an uneasy repulsion: all this was perfectly in the ordinary course of things and it seemed reasonable to me that her body should retain its dual nature, that it should be both repugnant and holy – a taboo.[20]

In *Comédie de l'Innocence*, Camille also seeks a return to his origins, albeit narratively rather than somatically. At the start of the film, as if trying to ascertain her role, he asks Ariane if she remembers what time he was born and whether she was there at his birth. She reassures him of her presence and describes him as 'a veritable apparition' and as 'an angel' being held out to her by the medical staff. As in the re-told *Tom Thumb* story, it is the quality of Ariane's presence in his life which Camille finds unsatisfactory and which will propel his search for another mother.

In *L'Amour caché*, the violence and hatred depicted at the heart of the mother–daughter bond co-exist with a passionate love which struggles to find expression. Sophie describes her mother to Dr Nielsen as 'an incredible actress with no heart' and as 'destructive' but immediately exclaims 'don't you think that I might after all love her?'

Such co-existing but mutually contradictory feelings characterise the ambiguity and violence of the mother–daughter bond. As Beauvoir notes, the mother projects the ambiguity of her relationship with herself into her relationship with her daughter so that the daughter's self-affirmation and independence is experienced as a betrayal by the mother (Beauvoir 2009: 575). Mother–son relationships, however, unfold differently according to Beauvoir's analyses, as evidenced in *Comédie de l'Innocence*.

Mothers and Sons

In *The Second Sex*, Beauvoir argues that in patriarchal society the mother–son relationship operates differently to the mother–daughter relationship because the mother aims to direct a being who is free and who will define himself by a necessary rebellion. The son can be contemptuous of his mother's 'feminine' world as he assumes his masculine prerogatives (Beauvoir 2009: 574). Although boys are more difficult to bring up, the mother usually gets along better with her son than her daughter. This is because of the prestige that women accord to men and the practical advantages men hold in a patriarchal society which privileges them. Her son mediates the world: 'Through him she will possess the world but on condition that she possesses her son' (Beauvoir 2009: 574). In *Comédie de l'Innocence*, Ariane is a professional woman and her world is not mediated by Camille in this way; nonetheless, the question of maternal possession is at the very heart of the film. As Beauvoir argues, the mother's total situation will shape her attitude towards her son: if she has been thwarted in life she will seek to dominate or even humiliate him, even though she realises that this is ultimately futile. In her powerlessness, she may resort to playing the role of a *mater dolorosa* or exhibit an ambivalent pride.

In *Comédie de l'Innocence*, as noted earlier, Camille's gender dominance is established at the start of the film in his rejection of his mother Ariane and his adoption of Isabella which sets up the mystery at the heart of the narrative. Why would a son do this to his mother? What kind of mother is he trying to escape? Is it fantasy or reality? In his control of the prowling video camera, replicating Raul Rúiz's directorial use of the camera, Camille further destabilises the 'reality' of his bourgeois family and torments his mother at times by circling her and filming her against her wishes. As one reviewer has commented, Huppert seems trapped in these circular camera movements as Camille imposes his fantasy reality upon the adults (Mulon 2001: 1). Like Ariane who is 'doubled' by Isabella, he also has a 'double' in his friend, Alexandre, with whom he has clandestine meetings. When Camille disappears, Alexandre delivers his videotapes to Ariane in a parodic performance of a secret agent whose 'mission is now accomplished'. In fact, Camille's videotapes (as an evocation of his phantasy life) prove to be his own deliberate undoing because they reveal by the film's end that it is Camille who has pursued and attached himself to Isabella, despite her protestations. In one of the last shots of the film, Camille is told by a triumphant Ariane that his father is arriving home tomorrow. The film ends with Camille filming his mother preening herself in the mirror, suggesting that she now controls the maternal double which as *imago* has been restored to Camille's phantasy life.[21] So, in the context of Beauvoir's analyses, at one level, *Comédie de l'Innocence* is concerned with Ariane's quest to tame Camille's patriarchal gaze and to regain control of him so that he can come to accept the necessary failure of maternal love. Yet his power in the film is considerable insofar as it is his initial rejection of his mother that drives the film and causes Isabella to be detained at an open psychiatric hospital for 'observation' while Ariane's confident demeanour disintegrates during the film. As Camille's fantasy quest for the ideal mother itself unravels (for such a being does not exist), Ariane and Serge 'rescue' him from Isabella and the barge moored on the Seine from which Paul fell. Camille has nonetheless learned the efficacy of the patriarchal gaze and will not 'fall back' into the watery pre-Oedipal world of the feminine because Ariane has responded to his quest.[22] Moreover, his safe passage to patriarchal masculinity is assured by his father's return at the end of the film which, as *deus ex machina* device, suggests that the Law of the Father has been restored.

Mothers, Daughters and Sado-Masochism

In *La Pianiste* and *L'Amour caché*, however, there is no such patriarchal saviour figure to resolve the intense self–other conflict between mother and daughter. As Beauvoir argues, within patriarchal society the mother–daughter bond is played out as an intense drama in which the mother seeks her double and projects all the ambiguity of her relationship with herself into her relationship with her daughter (Beauvoir 2009: 575). When the daughter asserts her independence and alterity, the mother experiences it as a betrayal by this alter ego. As Beauvoir argues and as *La Pianiste* demonstrates, a mother's tyrannical devotion to her daughter causes her to be timid and frightened of responsibilities because she has been too sheltered (Beauvoir 2009: 575). Both *La Pianiste* and *L'Amour caché* depict the self-mutilation of daughters, exemplified in Erika's self-cutting and Sophie's suicide.[23] In *The Second Sex*, Beauvoir discusses female masochism in several chapters, namely those on 'Childhood', 'the Girl', 'Sexual Initiation', 'the Mother', 'the Woman in Love' and 'the Independent Woman' which span the four main sections of the second volume ('Formation'; 'Education'; 'Justifications'; 'Towards Liberation'). From early childhood, girls are encouraged to play the martyr (316) and to indulge in narcissism which is closely linked to masochism (372): 'the girl is susceptible to [masochism] since she is easily narcissistic and narcissism consists in alienating oneself in one's ego' (425). And, as Erika's self-mutilation and sexual masochism in *La Pianiste* illustrate: 'in masochism, she will wildly enslave herself to the male ... she will wish to be humiliated, beaten; she will alienate herself more and more deeply out of fury for having agreed to the alienation' (425). Beauvoir concludes by noting that 'masochism is part of juvenile perversion ... it is not an authentic solution to the conflict created by woman's sexual destiny, but a way of avoiding it by wallowing in it. In no way does it constitute the normal and healthy blossoming of feminine eroticism' (426). In this, Huppert appears to agree with Beauvoir in her description of Erika's sado-masochistic relationships as 'a metaphor for [her] suffering and hence her ability to cause suffering' (Tranchant 2000: 1).

As Beauvoir argues in her essay, 'Must We Burn Sade?', although the existence of sado-masochism enables us to reflect on the limits and possibilities of human sexuality, power, transgression and embodiment, sado-masochism per se is rooted in narcissism and, as such, is ultimately an ethical failure. In her discussion of Sade, Beauvoir notes how he 'posed the problem of the *other* in its most extreme terms; in his excesses, man-as-transcendence and man-as-object achieve a dramatic confrontation' (Beauvoir 1968: 255). She interprets Sade's unconventional extreme sexual preferences as attempting to compensate for being unable to experience emotional intoxication in sexual love (Beauvoir 1953: 33) Sade is simply unable to 'lose himself' in the erotic encounter with the Other, as is Erika in *La Pianiste*, albeit with different consequences. As Beauvoir argues, 'the state of emotional intoxication allows one to grasp existence in one's self and in the other, as both subjectivity and passivity. The two partners merge in this ambiguous unity; each one is freed of his own presence and achieves immediate communication with the other' (33). For Beauvoir, sexual desire and exchange involve a reciprocal encounter between embodied consciousnesses who are ethically implicated with each other so that the erotic relation acts as an ethical building block of a broader social and ethical relation. In the theatre of the erotic, Beauvoir contends that Sade demonstrated how the interests of master and slave can be irreconcilable and, in so doing, he foresaw the class struggle.

In this respect, Wood has argued in relation to *La Pianiste* that sado-masochism can be viewed as replicating the power structures of capitalist culture by transposing the sensations of power-wielding and powerlessness into the realm of the erotic (Wood 2002: 2). Additionally, Erika's sado-masochistic encounters with Walter are circumscribed by the patriarchal roots of this capitalist culture. Erika's cardinal error in this regard is to seek to play both roles: to perform 'female masculinity' as well as patriarchal femininity.[24] Wheatley observes that 'Haneke's film leads us thus to ask … who the real masochist is? Is it Erika, whose desire for brutality and violence from her lover corresponds to pornographic designations of the term masochism? Or Walter, whose desire for Erika, fuelled by her apparent unattainability, conforms to the traditional, literary and cinematic conception of masochism?' (Wheatley 2006: 122). Yet, as noted above, Beauvoir has argued that female masochism is a response to women's conflicted and oppressed situation in patriarchal society in a way that heterosexual male masochism is not. Hence the masochist here is Erika insofar as she has enlisted the Other to help enact the violence of her own alienated situation upon her. Erika's mother has groomed her from an early age to service the cultural aspirations of the Viennese patriarchal bourge-oisie, as is implied by the utilitarian resonance of the film's title. However, Erika goes further in seeking to stage her subjectivity by sharing her Schubertian melancholia and suffering with Walter. In the ambiguous closing scene of the film, Erika's self-wounding and solitary departure from the opera house does not suggest any clear triumph (even though she does leave her mother behind). Her last glimpse of Walter, by contrast, suggests that he has confidently reprised his role as a popular Don Juan figure in Viennese society, which must only confirm her fears that her trust was misplaced. Huppert has described Erika as 'a little like Madame Bovary', and this is evidenced by Erika's tragedy and her tenacity to become a desiring subject in the face of a hostile patriarchal bourgeois society. Erika and Emma Bovary both want to be a woman and a man but they both put their trust in Don Juan figures who fail them. Both women, as their botched suicide and self-injuries indicate, fail to achieve agency even if, in Erika's case, the outcome of her final self-wounding is ambiguous.

As Beauvoir argued over sixty years ago, motherhood is a complex and dynamic synthesis of freedom and facticity which is experienced according to woman's existential situation in patriarchal society. Further, as these three recent films demonstrate, mother–daughter and mother–son relationships continue to be structured differently in the contemporary era, according to the persistence of maternal alienation and the child's burgeoning perception of enduring patriarchal power relations within the family nexus and in wider society. At the heart of the mother–child bond, a necessary rupture must occur for the child to achieve adult autonomy: as Beauvoir argued in *The Second Sex* and, as *La Pianiste* and *L'Amour caché* show, where mothers cannot or do not facilitate their daughters' autonomy, the consequences can be violent and existentially catastrophic for both parties. However, the outcome is not necessarily more favourable for Ariane and Camille in *Comédie de l'Innocence*: her triumphant recovery of her 'lost' son in pursuit of the 'good' mother risks only reinscribing her within patriarchal norms of maternal behaviour given that the patriarchal familial situation of traumatic dysfunction has not been worked through or worked out. In that respect, Camille's patriarchal quest for the 'good' mother risks being the real triumph. Sixty years on, Beauvoir's critique of patriarchy's mystification and mythologizing of motherhood continues to provide a powerful ideological analysis of how women become mothers in the contemporary era.

Notes

1. http://www.guardian.co.uk/film/2001/oct/28/londonfilmfestival2001.features. Retrieved September 2010.
2. See for example, *La Cérémonie* (1995); *Comédie de l'Innocence* (*Comedy of Innocence*, 2000); *La Pianiste* (*The Piano Teacher*, 2001); *Ma Mère* (2005); *L'Amour caché* (*Hidden Love*, 2007); *Nue Propriété* (*Private Property*, 2008).
3. Doane and Hodges observe, for example, that 'in all [classical] psychoanalytical accounts, the child's development is constructed as a move away from the mother and toward the father' (Doane and Hodges 1992: 11). Notwithstanding the reinstating of the mother's subjectivity into this developmental process by Beauvoir, Melanie Klein and subsequent feminist psychoanalytic accounts of child development, the need for the child to separate from the mother remains if 'good enough' development is to occur.
4. The story's theme of a struggle between a birth mother and another woman for possession of a child is also the focus of *The Circle of Chalk*, a classical Chinese play from the Yuan dynasty (1259–1368) by Li Xingdao, which formed the basis of Bertolt Brecht's play, *The Caucasian Chalk Circle* (1944).
5. See Jacques Morice's review of *Comédie de l'Innocence* in *Télérama*, 28 February 2001, p. 2.
6. The district is diametrically opposed (geographically, politically and socio-economically) to the D'Orville mansion located in the rue Daniel Stern in the exclusive fifteenth *arrondissement* on the left bank, near the Champ de Mars, site of the Eiffel Tower. Rue Daniel Stern is not without a certain symbolism: 'Daniel Stern' was the pen name of Marie D'Agoult (1805–1876), intellectual, novelist and historian of the French revolution and lover of Liszt; in the twentieth century, Daniel Stern is an influential psychoanalyst of infantile development.
7. Pathology and loss within the D'Orville family are indicated in various ways: the mansion is coded as a site of repressed familial suffering by references to the early death of Ariane's grandmother who, according to Ariane, died from distress relating to an incest experience. Ariane's parents are also dead, having been outlived by her recently deceased artist grandfather, nicknamed 'the Eternal Father'. Most of the family's possessions, including

those of the grandmother, are stored in the cellar so that much of the action of the film literally 'stands upon' this buried familial past.

8. In the Hebrew bible, Solomon was required to adjudicate between two mothers who each claimed they were the mother of a child. One of the women claimed that the other woman had killed her own child and had exchanged the two children, claiming that the living one was hers. Solomon decided the case by proclaiming he would cut the child in half. When one of the women agreed to this, the second woman protested and asked Solomon to give the child to the other woman. Solomon then decreed that her defence of the child's life demonstrated that she was the true mother of the child.

9. In classical mythology, Ariadne, daughter of King Minos, helped Athenian hero Theseus navigate the Cretan labyrinth and slay the minotaur at its centre by giving him a ball of red thread and a sword. She was thereafter either abandoned or slain, according to different versions of the myth.

10. Tom Thumb was a thumb-sized boy with magical powers born miraculously (by Merlin's intervention) to a childless couple. His minuscule size caused him to have many life-threatening adventures, including his ultimate demise by being bitten by a poisonous spider.

11. Sharrett (2004).

12. The *Winterreise* is one of Schubert's two major song cycles, the text of which constitutes a lengthy monologue on unrequited love and a descent into alienation.

13. *L'Amour caché* has strong resonances with Beauvoir's short story, 'Monologue', the second story of *The Woman Destroyed* [1968], with its similar focus on a highly dysfunctional mother–daughter relationship and filial suicide, portrayed via a mentally unstable maternal narrator; see Tidd (2002).

14. Freud observed his grandson playing the 'fort-da game' in which the boy would throw a cotton reel over the edge of his cot, so that it disappeared. He would pull it back, repeating this action many times. As he did this, Freud understood him to be saying '*Fort*' and '*Da*' (German: '*gone*' and '*there*'). Freud viewed the game of disappearance and return as a symbolising strategy which allowed the boy to manage his anxiety in relation to his perception of maternal abandonment. In human psychological development, symbolism coincides with the emergence of language or the child's entry into the Symbolic Order. Language allows us to present or re-present people, ideas, events, and feelings and recover the past, or restore what is absent. See Freud (2003: 43–102).

15. Champagne (2002). For a further discussion of Huppert's face, see Jeffries (2001).

16. I am indebted here to Toril Moi's clear exposition of Beauvoir's theory of alienation (1994: 156–64).

17. For a more detailed explanation of the distinction between 'structural' and 'historical' trauma, see Dominick LaCapra (1999: 696–727).

18. Birchall (2005: 13–14).

19. Interview with Isabelle Huppert, *La Pianiste* DVD (Artificial Eye, 2001).

20. Beauvoir (1969: 18).

21. The psychoanalytical term 'maternal imago' is used here to refer to Camille's unconscious representation of his mother. The maternal imago is inaugurated in the process of separation between mother and child (see Note 14 above).

22. Beauvoir argues in *The Second Sex* that the patriarchal imaginary connotes femininity negatively with the fluid elements of nature, such as water (see, for example, Beauvoir 2009: 167–70, 195, 409). Luce Irigaray has shown that this connotation is rooted in patriarchal disavowal of its own productive processes (see, for example, Irigaray 1980 and 1982). As Whitford notes: 'the elements allow Irigaray to speak of the female body, of its morphology, and of the erotic, while avoiding the sexual metaphoricity which is scopic and organised around the male gaze' (Whitford 1991: 62).

23. For a sensitive discussion of women's self-mutilation, see 'Cutting' in Christopher Bollas (1993: 137–43).

24. The term 'female masculinity' is used here with acknowledgement to Judith Halberstam's eponymous 1998 study. Here, *inter alia*, she argues that masculinity cannot and should not be conflated with the male body and its effects and that masculinity has been historically produced and performed by girls and women just as femininity has been produced and performed by boys and men. But not all masculinities are equal in a traditionally patriarchal society so that performances of alternative masculinities such as the tomboy, the invert, the lesbian butch, the drag king are deemed inauthentic and melancholic, 'the rejected scraps of a dominant masculinity in order that male masculinity may appear to be the real thing'; see Halberstam (1998: 1).

Bibliography

Beauvoir, S. de. [1949] 2009. *The Second Sex*, trans. C. Borde and S. Malovany-Chevallier. London: Jonathan Cape.

———. [1953]. *Must We Burn Sade?*, trans. A. Michelson. London: Peter Neville.

———. [1960]. *Brigitte Bardot and the Lolita Syndrome*, trans. B. Frechtmann. London: Deutsch/Weidenfeld and Nicolson.

———. [1963] (1968). *Force of Circumstance*, trans. R. Howard. Harmondsworth: Penguin.

———. [1964] (1969). *A Very Easy Death*, trans. P. O'Brian. Harmondsworth: Penguin.

Birchall, B. 2005. 'From Nude to metteuse-en-scène: Isabelle Huppert, Image and Desire in *La Dentellière* (Goretta, 1977) and *La Pianiste* (Haneke, 2001)', *Studies in French Cinema* 5(1): 13–14.

Bollas, C. 1993. *Being a Character: Psychoanalysis and Self Experience*. London and New York: Routledge.

Champagne, J. 2002. 'Undoing Oedipus: Feminism and Michael Haneke's *The Piano Teacher*'. Retrieved September 2010 from http://www.brightlightsfilm.com/36/pianoteacher1.html

Doane, J. and D. Hodges. 1992. *From Klein to Kristeva: Psychoanalytic Feminism and the Search for the 'Good Enough' Mother*. Ann Arbor: University of Michigan.

Flaubert, G. [1857]. *Madame Bovary*. Paris: Gallimard, Folio.

Freud, S. [1920] 2003. *Beyond the Pleasure Principle and Other Writings*. London: Penguin.

Gianorio, R. 2001. 'Ne jetons pas le cinéma d'auteur', *France-Soir*, 1 March, p. 1.

Halberstam, J. 1998. *Female Masculinity*. Durham and London: Duke University Press.

Irigaray, L. 1980. *Amante Marine: de Friedrich Nietzsche*. Paris: Les Editions de Minuit.

———. 1982. *Passions Elémentaires*. Paris: Les Editions de Minuit.

Jeffries, S. 'Just Don't Ask Her to Play Cute'. Retrieved September 2010 from http://www.guardian.co.uk/film/2001/oct/28/londonfilmfestival2001.features

Jelinek, E. 1989. *The Piano Teacher*, trans. J. Neugroschel. London: Serpent's Tail.

Klein, M. 1988a. *Love, Guilt and Reparation and Other Works 1921–1945*. London: Virago.

———. 1988b. *Envy and Gratitude and Other Works 1946–1963*. London: Virago.

LaCapra, D. 1999. 'Trauma, Absence and Loss', *Critical Inquiry* 25(4): 696–727.

Moi, T. 1994. *Simone de Beauvoir, The Making of an Intellectual Woman*. Oxford: Blackwell.

Mulon, J. 2001. 'Raúl Ruiz, Salomon entre deux mères', *La Croix*, 28 February, p. 1.

Sharrett, C. 2004. 'The World That is Known: Michael Haneke Interviewed', *Kinoeye* 4: 1. Retrieved September 2010 from http://www.kinoeye.org/04/01interview01.php

Tidd, U. 2002. 'Gendering Depersonalization: Simone de Beauvoir's 'Monologue' and R.D. Laing', *French Studies* LVI(3): 359–69.

Tranchant, M.-N. 2001. 'Isabelle Huppert, la note noire', *Le Figaro*, 14 May, p. 1.

Wheatley, C. 2006. 'The Masochistic Fantasy Made Flesh: Michael Haneke's *La Pianiste* as Melodrama', *Studies in French Cinema* 6(2): 117–27.

Whitford, M. 1991. *Luce Irigaray: Philosophy in the Feminine*. London: Routledge.

Wood, R. 2002. 'Do I Disgust You? Or, Tirez pas sur *La Pianiste*', *Filmhäftet* 121(3). Retrieved September 2010 from http://www.filmint.nu/pdf/121/doidisgustyou.pdf

Filmography

Capone, A. (dir.). 2007. *L'Amour caché* (*Hidden Love*). Parkland Pictures.

Chabrol, C. (dir.). 1995. *La Cérémonie*. France 3 cinema. MK2 productions.

Haneke, M. (dir.). 2001. *La Pianiste* (*The Piano Teacher*). Les Films Alain Sarde and Wega. Film Arte. France Cinema.

Honoré, C. (dir.). 2005. *Ma Mère*. Revolver Entertainment.

Lafosse, J. (dir.). 2008. *Nue Propriété* (*Private Property*). Tarantula. MACT Productions. RTBF.

Ruiz, R. (dir.). 2000. *Comédie de l'Innocence* (*Comedy of Innocence*). Canal+. CNC.

3

CLAIRE DENIS'S *CHOCOLAT* AND THE POLITICS OF DESIRE

Jean-Pierre Boulé

Chocolat by Claire Denis is the story of France (Cécile Ducasse) who, as a young adult (Mireille Perrier), goes back to Cameroon post-independence in the 1980s in search of her past. Most of the film is a flashback to her childhood in the 1950s. As France accepts a lift from Mungo Park (Emmet Judson Williamson), the main part of the film starts with a tracking shot of the passing countryside which transports France right back to her childhood. The countryside is often filmed in long sweeping panoramic shots with close-ups of a mountain called 'Mindif's Tooth' in order to take in large areas of the land-scape, which appears to be lovingly filmed; generally, the camera is kept at a distance. The young France lived in Cameroon with her mother, Aimée (Giulia Boschi), her father Marc (François Cluzet) who was a colonial administrator and district officer with military powers, and in close proximity to their black servant, Protée (Isaach de Bankolé), referred to as '*le boy*'. At the end of the film, we return to the frame and to France and Mungo in 1980s Cameroon.

Denis is considered one of the most influential filmmakers in France today. She worked as an assistant-director for Rivette, Costa-Gavras, Jarmusch and Wenders[1] before her first feature, *Chocolat*. Looking (critically) at the relationship between France and its colonies is a thematic that Denis has also explored in films such as *Beau travail* (*Good Work*, 2000) and her most recent film *White Material* (2009). Whilst this film resonates with Denis's own life experience (she grew up in Africa, the daughter of a colonial official), she asserts that it should not be read autobiographically and that the film is about a collection of received ideas and more than an individual story between a 'boy' and a 'white girl' as she terms it; 'a large-scale collective memory of the settlers' (Gili 1988: 15). One critic, Frédéric Strauss, has argued that Denis's work is part of the 'féminin colonial' (Strauss 1990: 29) because it does not glorify the colonial past but evokes instead 'the anti-colonial consciousness'.[2] Denis has not worked exclusively on decolonisation, having looked critically at contemporary society in films like *S'en fout la mort* (*No Fear, No Die*) (1990) and *J'ai pas sommeil* (*I Can't Sleep*) (1994).[3] According to Beugnet, Denis has long explored 'the functioning of the cinematic gaze, to question the conventions of *mise en scène* [sic] and characterisation, and the discourse of differentiation and categorisation – by race, by gender, by class – that they contribute to create' (2004: 34). I am proposing to combine this approach with a dialogue with Simone de Beauvoir's *The Second Sex* ([1949] 2009), *the* seminal work in the history of feminism which denounces the oppression of women.

Chocolat has received a lot of critical attention, mostly in debates around post-colonial cinema (see for instance Kaplan 1997) as one of the film's main themes is dealing with the colonial past. In *Chocolat* the story is centred on the story of the female protagonist, a child (France) and a black servant (Protée). In *The Second Sex* Beauvoir speaks of other oppressed groups such as black or Jewish people: 'Jews are the "others" for anti-Semites, blacks for racist Americans, indigenous people for the settlers ... "The eternal feminine" corresponds to "the black soul" or "the Jewish character"' (12; translation modified: *les colons*)[4]; Beauvoir specifically attributes similarities between black people and women (ibid.). Beugnet draws a parallel between feminist film theory, which denounces the female figure as being objectified, and post-colonial film theory, where strategies of the racial Other against which white western identity was asserted as the norm were also denounced (2004: 58). It is in this double-context that the politics of desire between the three characters Aimée, France and Protée will be explored in this chapter.

The action in the aforementioned long flashback, the main part of the film, is triggered by Marc leaving or by visitors to the household – each showing their disdain for the Africans – such as Jonathan Boothby (Kenneth Cranham), and especially after a plane crash when a coffee planter and his black mistress, the two pilots, a young couple, and later on Luc Segalen (Jean-Claude Adelin), an ex-seminarian, all enter the narrative. The focal point of the film is the colonial house and its surroundings, including the servants' quarters. The film relies more on the visual than on the verbal to communicate and to show desire but also race relations, with the difference between public and private space, laughter and silence, bright colours and lively music in the frames, a limited range of colours during the flashback resembling 'the old sepia photograph' (Beugnet 2004: 49), and chiaroscuro shots (contrasting light and dark). According to Neroni, 'the majority of [Denis's] shots are not simply descriptive or omniscient views; rather, each moment seems to be staged specifically for the gaze of one of the characters' (2007). These characters do not appear to represent dominant discourses of patriarchal masculinities but are peripheral to the colonial project, and contribute to what Beugnet refers to as 'the film's economy of gaze' (2004: 58). Mayne talks about 'relationships of vision' between France/Protée and France/Mungo, but also 'between the camera and the scene, and the spectator and the screen' (Mayne 2005: 37). Evidently, Denis's is a cinema of the senses.

France and the Child's Situation

France appears to be around seven years old during the main part of the film. We are therefore invited to look at colonialism through the eyes of a child who, in her relative innocence, is unaware of the power relations in play. France says very few words 'relayed by fixed frames and medium to long shots which evoke a child's neutral stance' (Beugnet 2004: 59) and even her innocence (ibid.: 61).[5] She is dressed as a pretty little girl, at times wearing the colonial hat, but she does not smile. She spends most of her time with Protée and he does not treat her as a 'living doll' (*Second Sex*, 305). Their relationship transgresses boundaries between two different cultures: 'Through their rituals, France and Protée perform a bonding beyond words, language and discourse that challenges colonial order, law and the Name of the Father' (Kaplan 1997: 165). He initiates her to his culture by means of riddles, he teaches her some words in his language, and he offers her local specialities such as an ant sandwich. Left to her own devices by her parents, she often sneaks into the kitchen, the boiler house, or the servants' quarters; for example, they all play *pétanque* with rotten apples. By standing in the space of the colonised, she can look into the coloniser's situation without fully adhering to it. She is positioned and, in turn, positions us viewers at a critical distance. She respects Protée whereas according to Beauvoir, 'for the daughter of a colonial officer, the native is not a man' (700). However, at times, France conforms to existing power relationships with Protée, for instance when she forces him to try some food first by spoon-feeding him. This is reinforced by the framing of the scene which cuts Protée's body so that all we see is his torso and his hands, not his face: he is objectified down to the body parts which serve his masters. Since the camera is fixed, the only way Protée's face can enter the frame is by kneeling down in front of the table, which he does. At other times, whilst he is getting help from the school teacher with a letter, France tells him in front of the whole school that they have to go back home. Although she is too young to understand what colonial power is, France is still exercising it by *mimicking* her parents (see Bhabha 1990).

Aimée does not spend much time with France so she does not impose her own patriarchally gendered destiny on to her daughter (306): 'Women brought up by a man escape many of the defects of femininity' (305). Aimée appears to be unhappy, or at least withdrawn. In the film, there is little communication between mother and daughter. This would confirm Beauvoir's view that children are only a source of joy in happy marriages and 'for the neglected, jealous wife they become a thankless burden' (520). According to Beauvoir's analysis, it is women who have the richest personal life who give the most to their children (582–83). France spends most of the time with her surrogate father, Protée (Hayward will even claim that he is 'France's maternal body', Hayward 2002: 41) who has a strong maternal influence on her. France is always looking out to the outdoor space where the black servants live, and where laughter can often be heard, in contrast with the obscurity and silence of her house. She is not only the link between coloniser and colonised but between Aimée and Protée.

Protée and the Black Man's Situation

Protée is 'the boy'; emasculated by this very appellation. He is a manservant for Aimée and for France, holding the role of a traditional maid. Very often, he is left to play outside with France when Aimée goes to visit other people. As she leaves, the 'children' are called: 'Aimée, Protée! We are leaving now'. Beauvoir addresses specifically this question in *The Second Sex*: '[Woman is condemned] to remaining "an eternal child"; it has also been said of workers, black slaves, and colonised natives that they were "big children" ' (654).[6] Protée is equally invisible when the colonisers talk about the insurrection of the natives even as he is standing behind them serving their food, eyes down. At times, the camera shows scenes from his point of view 'in a very important reversal of the regular mode of representing in Hollywood films about colonialism' (Kaplan 1997: 162–63). When he is naked taking his shower outside, we contemplate a medium-long shot of Protée on the right of the frame as he suddenly sees Aimée and France to the left of the frame. They are back from a shopping trip and France turns round slightly, facing his naked body. It is one of the rare moments when he shows his frustration by smashing his elbow against the concrete wall and crying, his nakedness compounding his vulnerability. As spectators, we are compelled to share Protée's pain and not to follow the women entering the house. If the colonisers cannot see Protée's pain, the spectators of the film can, although Denis forbids herself from claiming that she could, as a white European filmmaker, give us the point of view of a black colonised servant (Mayne 2005: 36).

Protée's patience and frustration will be tested to the full by the last visitor to enter the household, Luc. He is an *agent provocateur* who does not live by the conventions of the colonisers. Thus he sleeps in between the whites' house and the black quarters. Luc believes that Protée loses his dignity and his self-respect by being so docile. This is what Bergoffen speaks of, analysing Beauvoir, as 'the oppressed's complicity in their oppression' (1997: 107). Luc provokes Protée and Aimée in one key scene, which other critics like Beugnet have analysed as Luc having a 'jealous, cynical outburst' (47). First of all, his provocation of Protée. Not only has he showered in the boy's outside shower which Protée pointed out; he is eating outside with the servants. He tells Protée that the latter sulks: he wants to hear Protée say that it bothers him that he is sitting out there. Secondly, he provokes both Aimée and Protée when he tells Aimée who is observing them from her porch that she would like to be in his place rubbing against Protée. Luc acts 'like a mirror for the actual fields of power and desire that exist between the groups' (Neroni 2007). Neroni pinpoints the *mise-en-scène* as the element which really brings attention to the fields of desire. The scene is set up through a shot/counter-shot that goes back and forth between

Aimée in the colonial house surroundings, stood immobile and surrounded by semi-darkness and Luc sitting amongst the servants: 'The reverse shot of Luc, Protée and the others is a tighter one, emphasising the group warmly lit by the fire' (ibid.). But Neroni also points out that the field of desire between Aimée and Protée is in 'the field of the visible, which is intimately tied to representations of colonial power'. As he is preparing to bed down for the night on the very porch where Aimée was standing moments before, Luc pushes Protée to the limit by insulting him ('Beat it! … You son of a bitch … Go and lick the boots of your bosses … You are worse than the priests who raised you!'). Beauvoir remarks that in the south of the United States in the late 1940s, a black man cannot use violence against a white man, and his behaviour is based on the passivity to which he is condemned (354–55). But Protée, having had enough of being passive, lunges at Luc, wrestling him until he is able to throw him to the ground. Luc has acted as a catalyst; he is the Pied Piper. He will disappear that same night never to be seen again. He has accomplished his task and managed to get Protée to fight back and to regain his dignity.

Aimée and Women's Situation

A scene near the beginning of the film encapsulates Aimée's situation. Marc is leaving for an expedition; Aimée asks if he wants her to order him some books from Paris. He ignores his wife in order to give orders to one of his servants before turning back to Aimée querying what it was she was asking, to which she replies: '*Moi, rien*'. The sub-titles read: 'Never mind' but in French, this sentence could also mean: 'Me, I am nothing'. In existentialist terms, this could be interpreted as Aimée being objectified in her role as spouse of a coloniser – indeed Aimée is referred to as '*Mme La Commandante*' (Mrs Governor) showing that she derives her social status and power by being defined by her husband's social situation – and therefore she is not a free consciousness. Beauvoir would argue that she is economically dependent and deriving her status in life and economic stability thanks to her marriage and her role as a mother (11–12). In her situation, women are forced to put their whole selves into their marriage. They have no profession, no skills, and no personal relations: 'She is nothing but her husband's "other half" ' (518). This small exchange with her husband seems to put her in touch with some frustration of her own as he has to remind her to kiss him before he leaves. This first impression is compounded by Marc confiding Aimée and France to Protée. Despite the black servant being considered less than a white man, in the masculinist pecking order his status is above that of the woman and of her young daughter.

As Marc leaves for a ten-day trip exploring the country, Aimée is not allowed to come with him, seeming to confirm Beauvoir's analysis: 'Traditional marriage does not invite woman to transcend herself with him; it confines her to immanence' (481).[7] Instead she is confined to the home, as wife, mother and mistress of the house, and it is in marriage that her life's meaning lies. Her experience of the world and of limitless time is mediated through her husband's direct experience. Marc is a doer: in a key scene when he is with Protée having a toilet stop, the framing of the camera lulls us into a false sense of equity between them until the dialogue starts. As they are relieving themselves and contemplating the road, Marc exclaims: 'Next year, I will get this road widened' ('The male vocation is action', 481; 'Man's truth is in ... the forests he clears', 685). Aimée does not have the choice to be or not to be an adventurer; she is first and foremost *the wife of* an adventurer.

Aimée is left to run the household. Although she does not cook or clean, she likes to keep control of these activities. According to Beauvoir, a bourgeois woman will still insist on doing things herself. As the domestic domain has been thrust upon her as the only context in which she has any role, she is trying to assert the control that she is not allowed elsewhere in her life, if only by 'watching over, controlling and criticising, she endeavours to make her servants' results her own' (484). This Aimée attempts, but it soon appears that she is not able to assert her authority. In a key scene she confronts the cook, arguing that he does not listen to her.[8] She ends up insulting him and he walks away from his job, leaving Protée and the young black woman observing the scene in fits of laughter, which attracts the following comment from Aimée: 'As soon as the master is away, you all take advantage!'. Beauvoir believes that in such a case, whilst the mistress believes that the servants do not respect her will, 'the truth is that she has neither will nor particular ideas [*ni volonté, ni idées particulières*]' (602). Beauvoir argues that in any case this task brings no respite to women from their immanence and does not allow them to assert themselves individually [*une affirmation singulière*] (484), hence Aimée's apparent permanent frustration. Meanwhile, whilst men marry to anchor themselves in immanence, they do not confine themselves to this state of being: they want a home but they also want to escape from it. They want to settle down but they often remain a vagabond in their heart (496), which reflects Marc's situation.

With her husband away, Aimée does not have much contact with other adults, even though there are black women around the house but according to Beauvoir: 'As white women, they [women] are more in solidarity with white men and not with black women' (9). But Aimée is isolated from other women. She spends her days in solitude; her marriage has taken her away from her parents' home and the friends of her youth (598). There is one scene when she is with other colonial 'wives' and, interestingly, their gaze is on Protée as one of them exclaims to Aimée: 'He is handsome, your boy!'. This is the only illustration of what Beauvoir calls women's 'immanent complicity' (598), but one where women assume a traditionally masculine attitude of objectification.

From the outset, Aimée is respectful towards Protée. She accepts him as a protector and a carer for her daughter.[9] There are rules of engagement. He does not speak unless spoken to, he uses the formal *vous* form of address with her whilst she uses the familiar *tu* with him, and she does not look at him either. Aimée and Protée live intimately without being intimate. He serves her at the table from morning to night, makes her bed and even tidies her underwear in her bedroom. At times, Aimée can be disagreeable as when she remonstrates, seeing him handling her underwear: 'I don't want anyone nosing around my bedroom: get out!'. But according to Kaplan's analysis, her rejection carries an obvious repressed sexual desire and she cannot bear Protée 'that close to her body through her underwear' (1997: 169). Despite these colonial rules, one senses a growing respect and trust between them in the little dialogue they exchange but first and foremost in the silences they share, including the perception that they both feel uncomfortable with the power relations.

Aimée's monotonous life is interrupted when Boothby visits and stays overnight. Aimée adheres to all the protocols.[10] Boothby puts on a tuxedo for the evening so Aimée has to wear her evening gown. Beauvoir believes that these uncomfortable gowns change women into living dolls ['*poupées de chair*': literally: 'fleshy dolls']: 'the woman displays her shoulders, back, bosom' (589). When they dance, Protée is literally a couple of metres away, enduring the spectacle of her body contact with the old English gentleman. Afterwards, when she talks with her guest, Aimée leans against a pillar on the porch so that Protée and herself can observe each other, whilst she gives Boothby the illusion she is in conversation with him. As she watches Protée, she is allowing him to look at her and, in couching this scene in those terms, I am seeking to draw attention to the power relations at play. Protée does look at Aimée but he also gets on with his duties whilst her gaze lingers onto him. Beauvoir believes that, for the married woman, her husband's too mundane gaze no longer nurtures her image: 'She needs eyes still full of mystery to discover her as mystery … she is only desirable, lovable, if she is desired, loved' (606). Beauvoir is not talking specifically about interracial attraction. This is important because one of the fundamental questions in the relationship between Aimée and Protée, and in post-colonial criticism of the film, is whether Aimée is perpetuating colonial power relations by 'helping herself' to Protée whom she owns in some ways, or if she is authentically reaching out towards another oppressed consciousness. Is her attraction that of a woman for a man, rather than that of a white woman for a black man servant, or a mix of identification and attraction? I believe that Beauvoir can help us to answer these questions and show a fresh perspective on *Chocolat* rather than simply denouncing the film as 'Europe's impotence in productively dealing with its colonialist past' (Ang 1992: 25).

The Politics of Desire

Visitors to the house precipitate the fields of desire. The first uninvited guest is a 'hyena' heard around the compound in the night. Her husband being away, Aimée calls Protée, who at first does not come. We remember that the last frame we saw of Protée was when he was talking to the young black woman who lives in the servants' quarters and he comes out of a hut half-dressed, the implication being that he was being intimate with the aforementioned woman. It appears that Aimée believes this too as she shouts irritated: 'I have been calling you for ages!', which is not true. Is she possibly jealous? This scene is important because, perhaps for the first time, she sees Protée as a sexual being, although she has previously allowed him to look at her. He has not had time to button up his shirt, and she looks up at his athletic torso from a crouching position as she is searching in a drawer to look for the rifle. Nor has he done up his belt; both will remain undone throughout the scene. This is compounded by Aimée wearing a long white nightdress, and it is only when she gets into bed later on that she will put a dressing gown on top of her nightdress. Dresses and clothes are an important sub-plot in the film. After this episode, Aimée is often dressed rather seductively. For example, she has breakfast in a low-cut sleeveless dress, as if she is enticing Protée to lust after her body. Beauvoir believes that the woman who suffers from not *doing* anything thinks she is expressing her *being* through her dress (584). If we cast our mind back to the rifle scene, Aimée invites Protée to protect them and, in a trusting gesture, she gives him not only the rifle but also the ammunition which he requested.[11] He suggests taking a look around the house but she asks him to sit in their bedroom whilst she gets back into bed with France who has joined her in her double-bed, to dissipate some of the sexual tension by reinforcing her maternal role. That night marks a watershed; a taboo has been broken and, from then on, desire will be growing between Aimée and Protée.

The party in honour of the second visitor, Boothby, serves a useful purpose for the politics of desire. Aimée could not zip up the back of her evening gown so she calls Protée into her bedroom to do so, telling him to stand closer. A priori, this was not unusual, as the colonised did not 'exist' as human beings; the very same night, Boothby requests a servant to help undress him. But for Aimée, it is different. She allows Protée to touch her body as they are framed together by the camera positioned behind Protée. We see their reflection in a mirror as they gaze at each other in silence, each measuring the other's desire, and also weighed down by the considerable taboo in front of them. My contention is that Protée looks at Aimée as a desiring woman and not as his mistress and she looks at him as a desiring man: Aimée is the first one to avert her gaze, betraying her respect for Protée who 'should' normally always lower his gaze before his mistress's gaze, let alone look at her. It is as though, for a few seconds, power relations have been reversed; their desire is mutual.

Desire will reach its climax just after Protée has thrown Luc out. The whole scene is shot in fixed frame and in one take (Petrie 1992: 67), there is no dialogue, and it is in semi-darkness. Protée enters the house to draw the curtains and appears unaware that Aimée is crouched down on the floor (like the first time she really *looked* at him when she was searching for their rifle). However, when she touches his calf, he does not seem surprised. She slowly caresses him until she reaches his knee. Aimée transgresses all taboos and all the values imposed on her by patriarchal society when, as a married woman, with her husband in the house talking to their daughter in her bedroom, she tries to have this type of physical contact with Protée, naming her desire. Equality between them still does not exist. Whilst she is on the floor, traditionally the position of a slave, she still has power, as Protée is not really in a position to fend off her advances: he knows it would cost him at least his job. Before relating the end of this scene and Protée's reaction, it is worth freezing the frame at this point and concentrating on Aimée's gesture. Can desire exist in these circumstances and stand outside of colonial power-relations? I will be arguing that, with the aforementioned reservations, it can be constructed as a liberating action on Aimée's part and that a feminist/anti-colonialist consciousness may be possible within inter-racial desire.

Aimée transgresses patriarchal patterns of love on at least three counts. The first one is in terms of gender inequality. It has always been acceptable for a man to indulge in this type of behaviour ('Ancillary loves have always been tolerated … Nothing forbids the male from acting the master, from taking inferior creatures', 397) but if a bourgeois woman 'gives herself to a chauffeur or a gardener', she is socially degraded. The second count adds a racial dimension. Beauvoir reminds her readers that fiercely racist white men have always been permitted by custom to sleep with black women; one thinks of Joseph Delpich (Jacques Denis) and his black maid; if a white woman had relations with a black man in the time of slavery she would have been put to death and, at the time Beauvoir wrote *The Second Sex*, she claims that she would be lynched in parts of the USA (397). The last count is a direct comment on the institution of marriage. Beauvoir believes that it is disappointment that turns women into the arms of a lover and that marriage 'denies them the freedom and individuality of their feelings, drives them to adultery by way of a necessary and ironic dialectic' (607). For Beauvoir, there is an element of freedom in taking a lover since to marry was a constraint but to take a lover is a luxury: 'She is sure, if not of his love, at least of his desire' (608). Whilst Beauvoir depicts the married woman as passive ('it is because he has solicited her that the woman yields to him', ibid.), Aimée makes an active choice to authenticate her desire as we will see below.

Aside from transgressing patriarchal patterns of love, Aimée's decision is a particular form of liberation from the imperialist gaze, and as such it partly exonerates her for some critics. Aimée chooses the silent touch, echoing Bergoffen's analysis of Beauvoir's erotic generosities:

> Beauvoir discovers the erotic and the revelatory powers of touch … for if sight serves the illusions of autonomy and self-identity and empowers the desires of the imperialist other, the erotic touch shatters these illusions and undermines these desires. The sensuous touch discovers the polymorphous body. It discovers the ambiguity of the human condition.
>
> (Bergoffen 1997: 34)

For Bergoffen, the erotic is a key concept in Beauvoir: 'The erotic is the moment in which I recognise myself in the other without reducing the other to my double or dissolving myself in their otherness' (120). Aimée's gesture could be interpreted thus: 'As your lover I risk my subjectivity … by asking you to accept the gift of my vulnerability as you recognise me as your other' (161).

What is Protée's reaction? Initially, he carries on drawing the curtains. He then crouches down on the floor in order to be level with Aimée's eyes (so that there is no 'inequality' between them) before putting a hand on her shoulder, but they are not facing each other as yet. This is only the second time he has touched her in the whole film (the first time being when he zipped up her dress). She turns towards him and their faces are very close to each other when he very firmly gets a hold of her and jerks her into standing up (the forcefulness of the action showing his frustration), in a gesture which appears to be aimed at giving Aimée her dignity back, before holding her hips for a few seconds and walking away. Denis has stressed in interviews that, despite the producers' insistence that the film should turn into some kind of romance between Aimée and Protée, Protée's refusal of Aimée was the whole purpose of the film (Petrie 1992: 67). This is underlined by Hall: 'What is powerful about *Chocolat* is not what happens but what doesn't' (Hall 1992: 50). Is Protée's gesture to be categorised as Hall claims as a 'sweet symbolic moment of colonial revenge' (Hall 1992: 50)? Once more, by turning to a Beauvoir scholar and to the philosophy of existentialism, we can enrich this interpretation.

It is undeniable that, because of the material conditions of his situation, Protée cannot be reached as a free subject. But Aimée's transgression can be seen as posing a philosophical dilemma. As Moi analyses,[12] whatever [the man] decides to do *after* [her] gesture 'will be nothing but a response to a situation defined by the [woman]. But to define oneself simply as the negation or affirmation of somebody else's project is precisely not to assume one's existential freedom'. The [woman] represents the [man's] situation, whereas he is not [hers] and 'the lack of reciprocity in the situation flies in the face of the existentialist belief in the necessity of respecting the fundamental freedom of every consciousness' (1997: 117). By refusing something he appears to desire, Protée could be denying his existential freedom and be self-punishing. Sartre calls this fundamental freedom 'ontological'. Ontological freedom is freedom within each human being. Even a slave, Sartre will argue, is ontologically free; it is a freedom born with each consciousness. Sartre distinguishes this type of freedom from freedom within a situation (and within the situation, Protée is clearly not free). In the example she discusses, Moi, like Beauvoir earlier, is *not* talking about inter-racial relations. For all intents and purposes, the man and the woman are white. So we can conclude that his refusal carries the added dimension of Protée respecting his individual existential freedom as well as being a symbolic moment of colonial revenge.

This scene will prove cataclysmic. Looking troubled and sad, Aimée tells Marc the next morning at breakfast that she no longer wants Protée to work as 'the boy' and Marc relegates him to the boiler house. Is Protée being punished by the woman whose advances he has rejected, as some critics have claimed?[13] In other words, are we still following the trajectory of colonial power relations? It seems not. Rather, Aimée's request betrays an impossible situation: she can no longer have Protée used as 'the boy', and yet because she has articulated her desire so unequivocally, he cannot be anything else. It is partly in acknowledgement of her feelings and respect for him, having treated him as an equal, that Aimée asks that he should no longer serve her. 'Being cruel to be kind' comes to mind. But it could also be because she is afraid of herself when she is around him, and perhaps she does not trust her sense of control. One presumes that she will initially go back to acting the loyal wife to Marc but the experience has changed her forever as the medium shot of her lying down on the sofa resting on her husband's knees shows; they are together and yet not together and she turns away from him to hide her apparent sorrow.

This decision will also change someone else forever. France has heard her mother telling Marc that she no longer wanted Protée to work in the house. At night, she goes into the boiler room where Protée is. She asks, looking at the pipes: 'Does it burn?' and silently Protée puts his hand around the hot tube, scarring his flesh, which emphasises the earlier interpretation of self-punishment. France, trusting him, does the same and withdraws her hand in shock as she too is burnt; they are both branded permanently, she cannot ever forget his condition. We see a close-up of her burnt hand, and then of Protée's face who has tears in his eyes but remains silent before clenching the fist of his injured hand, increasing his pain. France and Protée slowly back away into opposite dark corners of the boiler house before Protée leaves. France will never see Protée again in the film.[14] This action has been analysed in a number of ways such as Protée taking revenge ('France burns her hand out of trust ... in this one case misplaced to punish her for being part of colonialism', Kaplan 1997: 162), or Protée's gesture being 'a powerful ... non-verbal comment upon the effects of colonial repression and the attempted erasure of his culture, history and memory' (Hayward 2002: 42), or Protée sharing the pain of his situation with France (Streiter 2008: 57). Aside from this colonised revenge narrative, it could equally be interpreted as a sign of love. Protée breaks up violently his relationship with France because, just like his relationship with Aimée, it is impossible, and their closeness cannot carry on without hurting France, and him. By hurting her, Protée liberates her from their friendship ('Being cruel to be kind' comes to mind again) and he gives France her freedom back (metonymically, France knows what it must do: leave Africa). Finally, combining both a post-colonial reading and a gender reading, Hayward gives the following powerful analysis:

> Protée ... can desire without desiring (Aimée, whom he can reject); he can nurture without nurturing (France, whom he can burn); he can occupy a double-gendered position that frees him from the tyranny of the masculine (the phallus, be it white or black) and the enslavement of the feminine.
>
> (Hayward 2002: 44–45)

The scarring of the hand is the link between the end of the flashback and the final frame between France and Mungo.

France as a Young Woman

Having asked to read France's palm to tell her if she should go and see the house where she lived as a child, Mungo sees her seared hand. He cannot make out any lines and concludes that she has no past and no future. France suggests to Mungo that they should go for a drink but he gently refuses. Could something have happened between them? It is only half-suggested, and it is France who takes the initiative but Mungo brushes her aside (in a repeat of Aimée/Protée). In any case, the suggestion made by France may have been more of a desire for connection, evoking 'a personal history of intimacy and loss in relationship to Protée' (Mayne 2005: 42), than flirtation. As Kaplan remarks, there was more closeness between France and Protée during colonialism than between France and Mungo in the 1980s independent Cameroon (Kaplan 1997: 162).

The film ends with France going to a hotel near the airport and then looking out of the window. We then see three porters loading art objects onto a plane before a rain storm; they appear to be joyous. I do not share Ang's view that the ending is disturbing as it shows France's powerlessness in articulating her post-colonial identity, and therefore European self-interrogation, concluding that the film is a Eurocentric film (Ang 1992: 29). France seems lost and somewhat confused. But is France's confusion rather not an illustration of the *ambiguity* of the colonial relationship in Beauvoir's terms and of Bhabha's notion of 'creative hybridity' and the *ambivalence* of the colonial relationship (see Bhabha 1994)? As Hall argues, *Chocolat* is an attempt to say something about Europe from its margins (1992: 36). I would agree with Portuges that the film problematises the impossible desire for reconciliation between coloniser and colonised, without any resolution (1996: 95). The film does not provide closure, and in this way, *Chocolat* is characteristic of Denis's films as belonging to the postmodern 'insofar as their denial of the comfort of the progressive unfolding and of the "logical" ending seems to echo the contemporary fading of the belief in safe, "grand narratives" ' (Beugnet 2004: 43).

My interpretation in this chapter has attempted to enrich post-colonial readings with an existential feminist reading. But this is not to refute the importance of denouncing the colonial system as Beauvoir herself states clearly in *The Second Sex*. For most of the film, Aimée (and Marc) have treated Protée with 'respect', despite their colonial power relations and in contract to the other Europeans. But as Beauvoir reminds us, there can be no justice within injustice and a colonial administrator cannot conduct herself/himself well with the indigenous population. The only solution is not to be a colonialist (775). '*Etre Chocolat*' means to be had, to be cheated, like black people in relation to the discourse of the coloniser but also, following Beauvoir, when two human beings cannot treat each other as two subjects and when one of them is 'the Other'. The ultimate goal for Beauvoir's *Second Sex* is 'to make the reign of freedom prevail' (782) and to recognise the other's freedom.

Notes

1. See Mayne (2005: 14) and Beugnet (2004: Introduction).
2. Strauss includes also Pisier (1990) and Roüan (1990).
3. For other films by Denis, see Beugnet (2004: Introduction).
4. All references to the 2009 translation of *The Second Sex* will be inserted in the text in parentheses with the page number only.
5. For more on this, see Beugnet (2004: 59), who explains that the shot/counter-shot is rarely used in the film as no explanations are given and the spectator is asked to engage their critical attention.
6. For an analysis of the situation of black people in the U.S. written by Beauvoir during her 1947 trip, see Beauvoir (1954: 230ff.).
7. Briefly, immanence is being stuck in one's situation and stagnating in it; transcendence is being able to change one's situation through the exercise of one's freedom.
8. See Cruickshank (2006) for a study of consumption in *Chocolat*.
9. Critics have pointed out the significance of Proteus, the old man of the sea, who metamorphoses into different roles and speaks many languages; see Hayward (2002: 39).
10. See Beauvoir's chapter 'Social Life', especially 585–86, and 596.
11. Bearing in mind that there is already some unrest for independence, and political meetings in the local school at night, Protée must be one of the few colonised to be armed by a coloniser; his body language as he walks outside with the rifle betrays this.
12. Moi discusses freedom and flirtation in Sartre and Beauvoir and her analysis applies to the woman (in my case I am using it for Protée) rather than to the man in Sartre's example of seduction in *Being and Nothingness*.
13. For instance, Mayne talks of an 'obvious punishment for humiliating the mistress of the house' (2005: 39).
14. At the end of the film, it appears that France is watching three porters at the airport. In fact, Protée is one of the three porters, though never shot in close-up but from the back or in profile. Denis said that Isaach de Bankolé always wanted to play one of the three porters (Mayne 2005: 47) but the way the scene is shot, and the film is cut, not too much significance should be attached to this casting role. I would like to thank Lya Lesport and Zoé for their comments and useful ideas on *Chocolat*.

Bibliography

Ang, I. 1992. 'Nostalgia and the Ideology of the Impossible in European Cinema', in D. Petrie (ed.), *Screening Europe*. London: Routledge, pp. 21–31.

Beauvoir, S. de. [1949] 2009. *Le deuxième Sexe* (*The Second Sex*), trans. C. Borde and S. Malovany-Chevallier. London: Jonathan Cape.

———. 1954. *L'Amérique au jour le jour* (*America Day by Day*). Paris: Gallimard.

Bergoffen, D. B. 1997. *The Philosophy of Simone de Beauvoir, Gendered Phenomenologies, Erotic Generosities*. New York: State University of New York Press.

Beugnet, M. 2004. *Claire Denis*. Manchester: Manchester University Press.

Bhabha, H. 1990. *Nation and Narration*. London: Routledge, esp. 'DissemiNation', pp. 291–322.

———. 1994. *The Location of Culture*. London: Routledge.

Cruickshank, R. 2006. 'Colonial, postcolonial and global economies: Questions of consumption in Claire Denis's *Chocolat*', *Studies in European Cinema*, 3 (1): 55–66.

Fourny, J.-F. and C.D. Minahen (eds). 1997. *Situating Sartre in Twentieth-Century Thought and Culture*. New York: St Martin's Press.

Gili, J. 1988. 'Entretien avec Claire Denis sur *Chocolat*', *Positif*, 328, June: 14–16.

Hall, S. 1992. 'European Cinema on the Verge of a Nervous Breakdown', in D. Petrie (ed.), *Screening Europe*. London: Routledge, pp. 45–53.

Hayward, S. 2002. 'Claire Denis's "Post-colonial" Films and Desiring Bodies', *L'Esprit créateur* XLII(3), Fall: 39–48.

Kaplan, A.E. 1997. *Feminism, Film and the Imperial Gaze*. London: Routledge.

Mayne, J. 2005. *Claire Denis*. Champaign: University of Illinois Press.

Moi, T. 1997. 'Freedom and Flirtation: Bad Faith in Sartre and Beauvoir', in J.-F. Fourny and C.D. Minahen (eds), *Situating Sartre in Twentieth-Century Thought and Culture*. New York: St Martin's Press, pp. 111–28.

Neroni, H. 2007. 'Lost in Fields of Interracial Desire', *Kinoeye*. Retrieved 7 September 2010 from http://www.kinoeye.org/03/07/neroni07.php

Petrie, D. (ed.). 1992. *Screening Europe*. London: Routledge, pp. 63–71.

Portuges, C. 1996. '*Le Colonial Féminin*: Women Directors Interrogate French Cinema', in D. Sherzer (ed.), *Cinema, Colonialism, Postcolonialism: Perspectives from the French and Francophone Worlds*. Austin: University of Texas Press, pp. 80–102.

Sherzer, D. (ed.). 1996. *Cinema, Colonialism, Postcolonialism: Perspectives from the French and Francophone Worlds*. Austin: University of Texas Press.

Strauss, F. 1990. 'Féminin colonial', *Les Cahiers du Cinéma* 434: 28–33.

Streiter, A. 2008. 'The Community According to Jean-Luc Nancy and Claire Denis', *Film-Philosophy* 12(1): 49–62. Retrieved 7 September 2010 from http://www.film-philosophy.com/2008v12n1/streiter.pdf

Filmography

Denis, C. (dir.). 1988. *Chocolat*. Caroline Productions.

———. 1990. *S'en fout la mort* (*No Fear, No Die*). Cinéa. NEF diffusion.

———. 1994. *J'ai pas sommeil* (*I Can't Sleep*). Agora Films S.A. France 3 Cinéma.

———. 1999. *Beau travail* (*Good Work*). La Sept-Arte. SM films.

———. 2009. *White Material*. Why Not Productions. Wild Bunch. France 3 Cinéma.

Pisier, M.-F. (dir.). 1990. *Le Bal du Gouverneur*. Les Films de L'Estrade.

Roüan, B. (dir.). 1990. *Outremer*. Paradise and films Lira.

4

Revolutionary Road and *The Second Sex*

Constance Mui and Julien Murphy

Revolutionary Road, a 2008 film directed by Sam Mendes, brings to the screen Richard Yates's 1961 novel of the same title. It is a realist novel about a young couple, Frank and April Wheeler (Leonardo DiCaprio and Kate Winslet), who are frustrated by the trappings of life in the suburbs in post-war America. Because of its stark portrayal of the Wheelers' mundane existence, it is easy to view *Revolutionary Road* as an existentialist commentary on the plight of human existence, especially women's existence, even though Yates was neither an existentialist nor a feminist, and there is no evidence, whether from his biographer or from his work, that Yates had read the works of Jean-Paul Sartre or Simone de Beauvoir. Indeed, the Wheelers' desperate search for meaning, so faithfully captured in Justin Haythe's screenplay, lends itself to existential and feminist readings that are reminiscent of Beauvoir's *The Second Sex*. With its stern critique of traditional gender roles in marriage and motherhood, *The Second Sex* provides a useful roadmap to both the novel and the film.

Curiously, *Revolutionary Road* was set in 1955, just two years after the first English translation of *The Second Sex*. In both the novel and the screenplay, Yates and Haythe use a series of flashbacks to the couple falling in love in the late 1940s, a time when Beauvoir first travelled to the United States, met with American writers, and began her lengthy romance with the Chicago writer, Nelson Algren. Some have suggested that it was Beauvoir's conversations with American women during this visit that shaped her analysis of woman's situation in *The Second Sex*, which was completed shortly after the publication of *America Day by Day* (Ascher 1981; Le Doeuff 2004; Seymour-Jones 2009). Just as Beauvoir was eager to experience post-war America, Frank Wheeler, who was in Paris as a young GI, longs to return to France, a place that has become for him the centre of vitality, meaning and authenticity. This is supported in the film by a photograph of Frank in uniform, standing gallantly in front of the Eiffel Tower in the aftermath of Liberation. The dream of returning to Paris is the hope that sustains, for a time, the Wheelers' marriage. In fact, France was restorative to Yates himself as well. He travelled there as a young writer in the early 1950s to launch his career by writing short stories.

In spite of Yates's stay in Paris at the height of the French existentialist movement in the 1950s, he alludes to existentialism only by placing Sartre's early novel, *Nausea*, in a stack of books in the Wheelers' home. One reviewer, F.J. Warnke, wrote in the *Yale Review* that the novel 'is really about the inadequacy of human beings to their own aspirations, and its target is not America but existence' (Bailey 2003: 229). If so, it should be noted that Yates is not offering a Sartrean-Beauvoirian existential approach to existence, one that is compatible with the account of human freedom made famous in Beauvoir's works, particularly in her *Ethics of Ambiguity*, or in her companion Jean-Paul Sartre's works, most notably, *Being and Nothingness*. Whereas Beauvoir and Sartre affirm the possibility of human authenticity, Frank Wheeler, Yates's anti-hero, has no clue as to what he wants for his own life. Frank wants to go back to Paris to pursue self-fulfilment. But when his wife April asks what he would accomplish there, he knows only that he needs his freedom, with no specific details as to how he plans to achieve it. This suggests that, while Yates is critical of social convention in circumventing human freedom, he does not have a comprehensive theory of human freedom against which to launch his critique. In writing a Parisian theme into the novel and exposing the crisis of meaning that plagued the 1950s, Yates's realism offers neither liberation nor authenticity for any of his characters. Whereas Sartre and Beauvoir refuse to see the search for meaning as an inevitably doomed or impossible endeavour, Yates offers only a dark view of the human condition, so much so that early plans for the film version by Samuel Goldwyn Jr. at Columbia Pictures were quickly shelved. As Yates himself observed, people were 'not ready for a story of such unrelieved tragedy, for so relentless a probing of the sources of pain' (Bailey 2003: 229). Forty years later, we finally have had the chance to see Mendes's cinematic adaptation of *Revolutionary Road*, and some of Yates's own assessment of American audiences may account for the film's mixed reviews.

Sam Mendes began his career in the London theatre where he directed numerous plays and won awards *for The Cherry Orchard* (1989), *The Glass Menagerie* (1995) and *Company* (1995) before turning to film. His first film, *American Beauty* (1999), won five Academy Awards, including Best Picture and Best Director. *Revolutionary Road* is his fourth film, preceded by *Road to Perdition* (2002) which he also directed and produced, and *Jarhead* (2005). While *Revolutionary Road* did not match the success of *American Beauty*, it was nominated for three Oscars and won a Golden Globe Award. After *Revolutionary Road*, Mendes directed *Away We Go* (2009). In *Revolutionary Road*, as in *American Beauty*, Mendes set the peaceful order of suburbia in stark relief against the loneliness of characters haunted by their unmet desires.

In applying an existentialist-feminist reading based on *The Second Sex* to *Revolutionary Road*, we believe the former can offer a valuable framework in which to examine the Wheelers' complex situation. It is a framework that consists not only of an ontology of human freedom, but also of an ethics derived from that freedom. This framework paints an indispensable picture of the human condition that underlies our experiences, including our values, choices and judgements. After all, conventional married life, as depicted in the Wheelers' relationship, can be experienced as stultifying and oppressive only for a free being, as opposed to a non-conscious being such as a rock, whose very freedom it compromises. The Beauvoirian framework further allows us to understand the characters' struggles against an oppressive situation as an attempt to turn away from alienation toward authenticity as a possibility. Reviewing *Revolutionary Road* in light of Beauvoir's work thus affords us a deeper and richer understanding of the critical choices made at various junctures of the Wheelers' lives. These choices include a conventional life in the suburbs, their extramarital affairs, their doomed plan to seek fulfillment in Paris, April's fatal abortion and Frank's ultimate resignation to the life he once rejected. Adopting Beauvoir's existentialist-feminist framework enables us to analyse the Wheelers' actions in terms of the human endeavour to transcend the given, bad faith versus authenticity, and the existential costs of people's choices. It will also shed light on the important role that gender plays both in shaping the Wheelers' situation and in presenting different sets of choices to April and Frank.

By Beauvoir's own admission, *The Second Sex* was a difficult and challenging endeavour.[1] We get a sense of her ambivalence in the very first line of the text, where she openly confesses, 'I hesitated a long time before writing a book on woman' (Beauvoir 2009: 3). This hesitation was brought on by Beauvoir's own scepticism over the growing body of literature on women that invariably uses women's happiness to justify their prescribed role as homemakers at the onset of the baby boom era. Dismissing such writings as 'volumes of idiocies', Beauvoir offers instead a perspective based on 'existential morality', an ethics that examines human meaning and value in terms of our efforts to strive toward authenticity in a world that often confines us to prescribed roles and fixed identities (16). Beauvoir argues that, to exist authentically, the human subject must strive to assert her essential freedom against 'a situation that constitutes her as inessential' (17). Beauvoir further casts this idea of existential morality in the more familiar language of Sartrean ontology, which analyses freedom in terms of temporality as a uniquely human feature. As she explains, 'every subject posits itself as a transcendence concretely through projects; there is no other justification for present existence than its expansion toward an indefinitely open future' (16). As such, the person exists by incorporating the past as facticity only to transcend it toward the future as possibility. To be human is to exist as a struggle, a dialectical stretching-out, between the essential (i.e. one's freedom) and the inessential (i.e. one's facticity, such as woman's restrictive role). Bad faith is precisely the inauthentic attitude behind any attempt to give up the struggle, which would result in a collapse of the essential into the inessential. This is often the case with women who resign themselves to a life of domestic slavery. They choose to identify with pure immanence by giving up on any possibility of transcending beyond the given toward a more open future.

In this way, Beauvoir maintains that what matters ethically is the choice people make in the face of the inessential, whether they actively resist it or willingly surrender themselves to it. As Beauvoir concludes, 'every time transcendence lapses into immanence, there is degradation of existence into "in-itself," [i.e. non-conscious being] or freedom into facticity; this fall is a moral fault if the subject consents to it' (16).

Re-examining *Revolutionary Road* in light of this ontology can shed light on the Wheelers' choices, ones that ultimately lead to the story's tragic ending. Any attempt to evaluate the authenticity of the Wheelers' actions must bring to bear the demands of their situation. As free beings, we choose, but only in situations that open up for us certain options while precluding others. The situation also determines the existential cost associated with particular choices. As Sartre has so famously claimed, 'I could have done otherwise, but at what price?' (1984: 454). An action has greater or lesser existential cost relative to one's situation, as well as one's project or choice of being vis-à-vis that situation. In the Wheelers' case, the situation that envelops their whole existence is the middle-class world of the 1950s in America, where marriage, the nuclear family, and a house in the suburbs were the norm, and where people fell unreflectively into assigned gender roles that were deemed natural. Personal fulfilment was to be attained through marriage and a stable family life. And yet Beauvoir offers a disparaging view of marriage as an inherently alienating institution in *The Second Sex*. In the chapter on the married woman, she exposes the failure of conventional married life to meet the needs of individuals. Beauvoir defines marriage as 'conjugal slavery' and cautions against the 'chains of marriage' that offer few escapes for people (527). In her view, authentic heterosexual relationships are possible, but not common in the current patriarchal arrangement of the marriage institution in our society.

Like Beauvoir, Yates does not paint a hopeful picture of marriage in *Revolutionary Road*, as much of the story revolves around the Wheelers' struggles of being torn between individuality and family life, between their dreams and the prohibitive situation that comprises their reality. As Alfred Kazin remarks on the back cover of the first edition of the book, 'This excellent novel is a powerful commentary on the way we live now. It locates the new American Tragedy squarely on the field of marriage.' But what is this new American Tragedy? It is that the very conventional forms of adult life – marriage, parenthood, a respectable job, home ownership in a quiet cul-de-sac, friends in same social circle – are the barriers, not the means, to self-fulfilment. Marriage, work and parenthood often present incompatible and impossible expectations and responsibilities. The Wheelers find themselves in this common tragedy. Add to this the social reality of the 1950s – almost two decades before second-wave feminism, and the baby boom era where divorce is uncommon, abortion illegal, and oral contraception unavailable – and we get a much more salient picture of the Wheelers' world. Despite Mendes's camera flashbacks to a rosier time in the 1940s, showing Frank and April as a young couple falling in love in a Greenwich Village apartment, their marriage is not easy. Mendes also captures the anguish they experience over the crushing of their potential by the weight of daily life. April and Frank are prone to fits of rage as they rail against their life and everything it stands for: security, respectability, orderliness and efficiency. Perhaps more poignantly, they are railing against their own feeble, half-hearted attempts throughout their young marriage at resisting the very situation that they have taken part in creating for themselves.

Assessing the Wheelers' anguish from an existentialist perspective, we see that every fit of rage they experience reveals a subjective confrontation with their own freedom. This confrontation involves a simultaneous reflection and projection: through reflection, the Wheelers unveil their present situation as oppressive and unbearable; through projection, they attempt to move beyond the unbearable by envisioning the possibility of a better, more bearable future. Their anguish thus serves, at least momentarily, as a defence against bad faith, against the temptation of succumbing to what is while losing sight of what could be. Ultimately, what matters ethically is the way in which these two characters choose themselves in the face of a situation that works against what it means to be an authentic human subject.

At this point, however, Beauvoir would be quick to point out to critics of *Revolutionary Road* that it is grossly misleading to refer to the Wheelers' situation as a single, monolithic setting that issues the same demands and determines the same options for both spouses. In Beauvoir's view, the institution of marriage is oppressive to women and men in vastly different ways and to significantly different degrees. Under the typical gender division of labour in the nuclear family, a woman's situation as wife and mother differs fundamentally and indeed radically from a man's situation as husband and father. Consider the woman's role as homemaker. In *The Second Sex*, Beauvoir offers a rare, original and remarkably insightful phenomenology of homemaking that describes not merely the drudgery of housework, but the corresponding consciousness or mindset it often produces in the homemaker. Beauvoir explores this consciousness with a critical eye, employing such familiar ontological categories as immanence and facticity on the one hand, and transcendence and freedom on the other. This phenomenology would anticipate what is dubbed 'the problem with no name' in 1963, the numbing condition experienced by many white, middle-class suburban women, whose interviews with Betty Friedan formed the basis of her book, *The Feminine Mystique*. Indeed, Beauvoir's phenomenology provides the indispensable context against which to analyse April Wheeler's existence as situated freedom in a patriarchal world.

Beauvoir begins by observing that woman's traditional role in the home is marked by the inessential, one that grants her no autonomy and confines her to a life of immanence. 'Woman's drama,' Beauvoir writes, 'lies in this conflict between the fundamental claim of every subject, which always posits itself as essential, and the demands of a situation that constitutes her as inessential'(17). Woman's married role is one that can be carried out only with utmost and uncompromising altruism. Just as April Wheeler must give up her acting career to raise a family, a woman exists not for herself, but for others. The homemaker justifies her existence through her husband and children, and in so doing, 'she is no more an inessential mediation in their lives' (484). This portrait of the married woman's immanence aptly depicts the mundane existence of April Wheeler, not to mention an entire generation of women who were similarly caught in this 'American Tragedy', the name Kazin has, albeit inadvertently, attributed to the problem with no name.

But Beauvoir goes further to assert that marriage does not merely deny a woman her career, her ambitions and other choices that come under the category of concrete or ontic freedom. More than that, marriage directly negates the woman's existence as freedom on the *ontological* level, where freedom is built into the very structure of human existence as moving beyond facticity toward possibility, as a negation of fixed identity. Calling to mind the crucial place that temporality occupies in Beauvoir's ontology, a free being posits itself as freedom by integrating the past as facticity and transcending it toward the future as possibility. But in marriage, a woman's relation to her past and her future is severely disrupted. Beauvoir argues that, as her husband's vassal, a woman 'takes his name … integrates into his class, his world, she belongs to his family. She follows him where his work calls him. [All told,] she breaks with her past more or less brutally, [and] is annexed to her husband's universe' (442). Through it all, the married woman's relation to her past takes on the form of a rupture.[2]

Severed from her connection to the past, the homemaker also loses her grip on the future. She has no significant hold on the future in as much as her life's vocation is essentially nothing more than to 'ensure the even rhythm of the day and the permanence of the home' (443). By contrast, the husband's role allows him actively to 'go beyond himself toward the totality of the universe and the infinity of the future' (468). Even for someone as downtrodden as Frank Wheeler, who sees his position at Knox Computers as a meaningless job, there is the prospect of a promotion on the horizon with new responsibilities and greater prestige. And yet the traditional wife's whole world is enclosed behind the picket fence of her home where there is no escape. Destined to repeat her mother's and grandmother's familiar journey, she sees everything that lies in front of her in a single frame. She faces an empty future, and 'has no choice but to build a stable life, where the present, prolonging the past, escapes the threats of tomorrow' (468–69). Indeed, the only happiness that marriage could promise the wife is not a life of transcendence but 'the peaceful equilibrium within immanence and repetition' (468). Severed from her connections to her past and future, the woman stands still in time, suspended in a state of inertia like a static thing. This point is made more explicit in Beauvoir's bleak comparison of the homemaker's life to Sisyphus's torment. Woman's work, says Beauvoir, consists of an endlessly repetitive, mind-numbing routine that does not open onto the future but serves only to perpetuate the present. The homemaker is not called upon to build the world; her work does not change history. Housework is useful for life but it confers no special meaning on life. The wife wakes up every morning only to find herself in the same place facing the same monotonous chores. In the film, Mendes offers glimpses of this haunting reality through the eerie stillness and orderliness of the Wheelers' home in the middle of the day, when Frank and the children are away at work and school. This life of repetition and immanence inevitably takes its toll on woman by altering her relation to time, wherein she grasps only its negative aspect. Even under the most efficient time management, her days are filled with long, tedious blocks of waiting – i.e. the empty minutes and hours it takes for the cake to bake, the floor to dry, the washer to complete its cycle. Her work becomes merely an 'inessential intermediary' between the present and the future. From the homemaker's vantage point, 'every day looks like the previous one; the present is eternal, useless, and hopeless' (475). This inauthentic relation to time could only produce an alienated consciousness. The married woman comes to identify with her passivity and otherness. In resignation, she *becomes* the docile and submissive housewife, with the usual depression and hysteria identified in modern science, simply by internalising her dependence and helplessness. A loss of freedom indeed entails a loss of identity.

This discussion brings out the basis of Beauvoir's moral condemnation of the woman's role as homemaker. For her, housework is oppressive, but not merely for the reasons that most people give, as compelling as they may be. In a manner that echoes Marx's attack on capitalism, Beauvoir finds women's role inherently dehumanizing because it works against the kind of existence that we, as free subjects, are meant to lead. Just as Marx's critique of capitalism is predicated on his view of human nature, Beauvoir's critique of woman's station in life is likewise predicated on her ontology of human freedom.[3] This critique provides a valuable philosophical framework and vocabulary to assess April Wheeler's choices. Like many women of her generation and social class, April lives under the crushing weight of an institution that gives her no hold on either her past or her future. An aspiring actress, her dream came to an end when she got married. Yates holds out no hope for this dream, as the novel begins with the words, 'The final dying sounds of their dress rehearsal', which invokes the death of April's acting career and foreshadows the tragic end that awaits her. While it is true that April could have continued to pursue her career by rejecting marriage and motherhood, the existential cost of such unconventional choices would have been far too great given her own romantic investment in Frank, as well as the socio-economic reality of the period.

In consenting to marry and settle down, April becomes the docile homemaker. She dabbles in community theatre, only to endure the humiliation of a polite audience's lukewarm applause. She tries to walk out on Frank during their fights, only to return to him moments later because of her economic dependence and emotional ties to her family. She takes the bold step to plan a new life in Paris for the entire family, only to have the plan scuttled by an unexpected pregnancy. Beauvoir's framework invites us to reexamine these choices in a different light. It allows us to see, for example, April's participation in an amateur theatre group, not as an idle hobby to kill time, but as a desperate way of establishing continuity with her past, under a prohibitive setting that has all but ruled out a serious acting career as a viable option. Indeed, by playing various roles on stage, the theatre provides April with a temporary escape into the imaginary. Similarly, April's plan to move the family to Paris could hardly be dismissed as a spontaneous diversion to combat boredom. Recalling the homemaker's warped relationship with time, April's action could be construed as a decisive project to restore an infinite future to a life that has merely been repeating the present. April's choices are attempts to dig herself out of alienation and inertia by embarking on a radical leap toward a possibility guided by her bold vision of a role reversal with Frank. In a situation where options are either limited or undesirable, and where the temptation to live in bad faith is ever-present, April's actions mark her struggle, feeble and futile as it may be, to live more authentically by regaining a hold on her past and future.

Like April's choices, Frank's choices are also shaped by his restrictive gender role. For starters, Frank's role as breadwinner affords him the possibility of maintaining a different, less alienating, relation to time. As Beauvoir points out, while woman is destined to a life of immanence, man is able to live a life of transcendence by pursuing productive and creative activities outside the home. Family life provides the breadwinner with a perfect balance of transcendence and immanence, one that enables him to project toward an open future with his feet firmed planted in the past.

But while the husband is able to enjoy many privileges at the wife's expense, marriage and fatherhood present man with his own crises. We see this in Frank Wheeler's angry outbursts over his frustrations and disappointments. The sad irony of patriarchy is that, in constructing a society to their advantage, men have created a completely docile feminine ideal that works against both sexes. Beauvoir develops this point by applying the master/slave dialectic and the maxim, 'In oppressing, one becomes oppressed' (522). As master, the husband is pressured daily to prove himself worthy of his station. Enslaved by his own sovereignty, his family's survival is placed squarely upon his shoulders. Frank Wheeler knows this burden all too well. Every day, he commutes to a job he hates. Mendes dramatises Frank's alienation with scenes of men at Grand Central Station who, like Frank, are dressed in suits and hats, with newspapers and briefcases in tow, as they travel in anonymous crowds to jobs in cubicles that obscure their individuality. Like woman's work in the home, man's paid labour is similarly regulated by the same cultural values of efficiency and organization.

Franks feels inadequate as a man, frustrated in a job for which he thinks he is overqualified, but a job to which he feels hopelessly chained nonetheless. His frustration soon turns into resentment and becomes an escalating source of conflict in the Wheelers' marriage. As April cries out about their 'ridiculous illusion' in a dramatic scene in the film, 'I think it's unrealistic for a man with a fine mind to go out working like a dog year after year at a job he can't stand, coming home to a place he can't stand, to a wife who's equally unable to stand the same things' (Haythe 2008: 28). Indeed, this pronouncement drives home Beauvoir's claim that married couples are caught in an oppressive institution they did not create. Having no other outlet, the Wheelers have resorted to extramarital affairs, only to discover that they are poor substitutes for freedom. They blame each other for their own unhappiness, each holding the other responsible for a dream that has turned into a bitter disappointment. All this, to be sure, is not lost on the Wheelers themselves, as April mutters in a soul-searching moment, 'We've been punishing each other for it!' (Haythe 2008: 28).

This recognition becomes a turning point in the Wheelers' life. Confronting their profound alienation in this way forces them to acknowledge, to themselves and to each other, that their whole life is meaningless and unbearable. They realize that they can no longer live in bad faith, and must act decisively to deliver themselves from this crisis. There simply is no going home again. April persuades Frank that they should move their family to Paris for a new beginning. In this vibrant city of dreams and opportunities, April will work for a government agency, and Frank will have leisure time to figure out what he really wants to do. Frank is happy to embrace this plan because it offers an escape to a new life, presumably one filled with meaning given his romantic notions of Paris from his GI days. On a deeper level, he is also drawn to the idea of a role reversal. Recalling here the master/slave dialectic which exposes the master's own enslavement, Frank can free himself only by freeing April, i.e. by supporting her in her productive endeavours as a way of lessening her dependence upon him.

And yet, Mendes tortures the viewer by dangling freedom in front of the Wheelers, only to snatch it away when it comes close within their reach. Empowered by the prospect of reversing roles with Frank, April takes charge of the practical arrangements for the trip. In the end, however, these efforts are for naught, as the Wheelers watch their plan fall through before their steamer even leaves the dock. April discovers that she is pregnant with their third child, while Frank is offered a promotion at company headquarters. These developments are seen through two very different lenses by the two spouses. From Frank's perspective, this sudden turn of events – the lure of a more prestigious and lucrative job; the anticipation of a new child – holds the promise of a new beginning, not the one they had planned, but one that could bring new meaning and hope all the same. His boss's words of advice struck a chord with him: 'A man only gets a couple chances in life. If he doesn't grab 'em, it won't be long before he find himself ... wondering how he got to be second rate' (Haythe 2008: 56). Forgoing the dream to live in Paris, Frank is on his way toward launching a promising future with his company, doing what a man is supposed to do. Besides, as his boss tells him, building his future with the company where his father had worked would be a fine tribute to his father. In continuing his father's legacy, Frank could now project toward an open future by integrating the past. Whereas the promotion showers him with pride, the pregnancy surprisingly brings him relief. Suddenly the pressure of taking his whole family to a foreign place to face the unknown is lifted, as his life has 'come mercifully back to normal' (Yates 2000: 207). Like Beauvoir's docile homemaker, Frank also wants to escape the threats of tomorrow.

From April's perspective, the pregnancy and promotion are nothing but cruel obstacles that stand in the way of a future she has been working earnestly to bring about, and, understandably, one that she is refusing to give up. Moving to Paris has been April's plan of escape from a mundane life in the home, the collective destiny that society forces upon woman. Now her plan is threatened by a destiny imposed from within: April's own reproductive biology, one that women experienced as much more burdensome before the availability of reliable contraception. Beauvoir describes woman's reproductive role as a crisis that enslaves her in repetition and immanence. It keeps woman from relating to her body authentically as for-itself, that is, as something to be transcended toward her project at hand. All told, 'Woman *is* her body as man *is* his, but her body is something other than herself' (41). If pregnancy is an ordeal for woman even under the most conducive circumstances, we could only imagine the profound alienation brought on by an unwanted pregnancy. For April, having another child would again condemn her to a life of immanence.

But as Beauvoir tells us, to exist as freedom is to exist by defying our bodily restrictions (48). As free subjects, it is up to us to transcend our body toward our chosen projects. And yet Beauvoir cautions that choices do not exist in a vacuum, they are always and necessarily circumscribed within specific contexts. For woman, her choices are more heavily restricted by patriarchy, and often come with considerable existential costs. April finds herself in a situation that offers few options. Accepting its horrendous risks, she chooses abortion as the only way to save not only her marriage, but in truth her sanity. If traditional marriage is the American tragedy for the couple as Kazin says, then this tragedy would have been experienced most profoundly by the woman who had little protection from unwanted pregnancies, in an era that neither recognised her sexual autonomy nor condoned abortion, and one that viewed the rejection of motherhood as a psychological disorder or a moral failure.

This is the tragic context of April's choice, one that would cost her dearly. It leaves her feeling alone and abandoned, with no one to turn to, least of all her husband Frank. We see an irate Frank telling April that he was sickened by the thought of aborting the foetus. Refusing to understand how April can 'make it sound like having children is a punishment', Frank angrily dismisses her decision as a selfish choice that 'a normal sane mother' would never make (Haythe 2008: 68–69). In demanding that April accept the pregnancy as he has, Frank chooses to remain in denial of April's oppression and autonomy, and rationalises that a woman cannot truly be a loving mother to her children if she decides to terminate a pregnancy. April responds by pressing her husband with the question, 'Do you really want another child?' This dialogue is compelling in that it brings out the essence of elective abortion in current political drama surrounding the subject. April chooses abortion not because they cannot afford another child. They can. She chooses abortion not because they have no room for another child. They do. April chooses to abort because she does not *want* a third child. Whereas Frank believes that a 'normal' woman is one who submits herself to her biological and social destiny, April takes the decisive step to control her own destiny, even if it costs her her life. The abortion scene in the film chillingly shows a calm and methodical April preparing to administer the procedure on herself, all the while knowing that she is putting her life in grave danger. But the determination on her face tells us that, for her, the alternative is worse than death. Mendes's camera skilfully follows April's last hour by showing small drops of bright red blood slowly dripping onto – and soiling – the plush beige carpet of April's clean and tidy house, a reminder of her castle and prison that are about to be destroyed. April's bold choice is the moment of courage that writes the tragic ending. Her struggle to live authentically is captured in her own ominous advice to Frank: 'Takes backbone to live the life you want' (Haythe 2008: 65).

Revolutionary Road is still compelling some fifty years later. If only the tension between responsibility and freedom in the Wheelers' marriage were not so gripping and familiar to us. A scene near the end of the film shows a grief-stricken Frank running down the street of their once serene neighbourhood, sobbing helplessly over his wife's violent death. *Revolutionary Road* ends on a realist note. In the final scene, the neighbourhood is restored to its normal tranquillity. Howard Givings (Richard Easton), the husband of the Wheelers' realtor, is seen sitting in his living room with his newspaper, where he passively silences his wife's idle chatter by turning off his hearing aid rather than confronting her. Complacency is indeed the attitude of choice for most people. With remarkable sensitivity, Yates and Mendes paint a gripping picture of the American tragedy. Rather than pass judgement on April's choice to abort, we come to appreciate her struggle and her determination to strive for freedom by reclaiming her body from another pregnancy. Similarly, we understand Frank's choice to bear down on his role as provider and to reject abortion as a solution, and ultimately, his resolve to raise his children on his own. It is rather discouraging that the situation surrounding April Wheeler's choice has not changed entirely today; women still encounter many of the same obstacles to reproductive freedom. Even though most people have access to methods of contraception, unplanned pregnancies still happen despite the best of intentions. And even with the decriminalisation of abortion in many countries, the stigma against elective abortion, especially for married women, still makes it an unspeakable choice, and social supports that could spread the burdens of childrearing beyond the nuclear family often do not exist. Perhaps that is why we can identify with the Wheelers' situation and see that Beauvoir's message on motherhood is still relevant today. She opens her chapter on that topic not with blissful tales of nursing mothers enthralled with their children, but with a harsh condemnation of anti-abortion laws. This has led to the Vatican's banning of *The Second Sex*, as it also explains why the feminism Beauvoir embraces years afterwards was focused on the fight to legalise abortion in France.[4]

Yates's realism shows us the Wheelers' failures when we wanted to see them succeed, so we could believe that we, too, can surpass our situations triumphantly. It is Beauvoir who offers us a glimmer of hope. While Beauvoir forcefully maintains that marriage and motherhood are institutionally designed to set people up for failure, she does not foreclose the possibilities of free love between women and men, nor does she refrain from fighting for radical, sweeping social change. Having experienced fulfilling relationships in her own life, primarily with Sartre but also with other men and women, Beauvoir provides us with a rough sketch of the authentic couple based on her own commitment to existential morality. In an authentic relationship, she says, the partners must strive to sustain 'a friendship that does not hamper their sexual freedom'; they must resist the temptation to close off their freedom from the world, or to seek in each other 'their exclusive reason for living' (520). However, Beauvoir also believes that authentic relationships will always risk the danger of collapsing into bad faith, so long as they are forged within the existing marriage institution 'that is perverted at its base' (520). Meaningful relationships must be nurtured in a social setting that promotes freedom without imposing conformity. Without sweeping social transformation, people will continue to face many of the struggles that marked the Wheelers' relationship. It is this conviction that prompted Beauvoir to end *The Second Sex* with the chapter, 'The Independent Woman'. There Beauvoir calls for the ultimate liberation that only a socialist world can provide. Liberal feminists opened the door to freedom by gaining certain important political rights for women, such as the right to vote, and demanded fuller participation for women in the labour force and public life. But such rights, as important as they are, do not address many other obstacles women encounter (721). We see that clearly in April Wheeler's case. In the end, Beauvoir believes that, in addition to reproductive and political freedoms, the road to revolution must be an economic one that offers women and men more than what is offered to men at present – namely, a society that ensures our full human subjectivity without regard to gender, race, sexual orientation or class. Only then will women and men be able to avoid the American Tragedy that marked the Wheelers' lives.

Notes

1. Beauvoir began working on *The Second Sex* in 1946, after finishing *America Day by Day*. In January of 1948, she wrote to Algren that she had finished her book about America 'and I came back to my essay about women. I told you, I never felt bad for being a woman, and sometimes I even enjoy it, as you know. Yet when I see other women around me, I think they have very peculiar problems and it would be interesting to look at what is peculiar in them' (Beauvoir 1998: 135).
2. Beauvoir grants that this is changing, even in the 1940s when she was writing. Her own life is an example of that change. However, Beauvoir insists that many women will still find themselves in that situation so long as they are economically dependent on men.
3. It should be noted that not all feminists share Beauvoir's view of homemaking as inherently oppressive. Iris Marion Young (2002), for example, adopts a Heideggerian perspective and attributes certain values to the home as a personal space that supports an individual's identity and subjectivity. These values include personal safety, the preservation of one's past, and privacy.
4. Beauvoir was deeply troubled by the illegality of abortion in France as evidenced by a letter she wrote in English to Algren: 'There are lot of abortion affairs just now in France,

and I feel quite indignant about them. They have no kind of birth control here: it is forbidden. They just arrested a doctor I knew very well and to whom I had sent a lot of worried girls; he helped the poor ones as well as wealthy ones. Another surgeon jumped by the window last week, because he had been taken in this kind of bad affair' (Beauvoir 1998: 263). (The editor of her letters to Algren, Sylvie le Bon de Beauvoir, chose not to correct Beauvoir's English.) Toril Moi reminds us that in 1943, Marie-Jeanne Latour, a known abortionist, was the last woman sent to the guillotine in France (Moi 2004: 60).

Bibliography

Ascher, C. 1981. *Simone de Beauvoir: A Life of Freedom.* Boston: Beacon Press.

Bailey, B. 2003. *A Tragic Honesty: The Life and Work of Richard Yates.* New York: Picador.

Beauvoir, S. de. [1947] 1976. *The Ethics of Ambiguity*, trans. B. Frechtman. New York: Citidel Press.

———. 1998. *Transatlantic Love Affair: Letters to Nelson Algren*, S. le Bon de Beauvoir (ed.). New York: The New Press.

———. [1954] 1999. *America Day by Day*, trans. C. Cosman. Berkeley: University of California Press.

———. [1949] 2009. *The Second Sex*, trans. C. Borde and S. Malovany-Chevallier. New York: Alfred A. Knopf.

Friedan, B. [1963] 2001. *The Feminine Mystique.* New York: W.W. Norton & Company.

Haythe, J. 2008. *Screenplay for Revolutionary Road.* Universal City: DreamWorks, LLC.

Le Doeuff, M. 2004. 'Towards a Friendly, Transatlantic Critique of *The Second Sex*', in E. Grosholz (ed.), *The Legacy of Simone de Beauvoir*. Oxford: Clarendon Press, pp. 22–36.

Moi, T. 2004. 'While we Wait: Notes on the English Translation of *The Second Sex*', in E. Grosholz (ed.), *The Legacy of Simone de Beauvoir*. Oxford: Clarendon Press, pp. 37–68.

Sartre, J.-P. [1938] 1969. *Nausea*, trans. A. Lloyd. New York: New Directions.

———. [1943] 1984. *Being and Nothingness*, trans. H. Barnes. New York: Washington Square Press.

Seymour-Jones, C. 2009. *A Dangerous Liaison.* New York: Overlook Press.

Yates, R. [1961] 2000. *Revolutionary Road.* New York: Vintage Books.

Young, I.M. 2002. 'House and Home: Feminist Variations on a Theme', in C. Mui and J. Murphy (eds), *Gender Struggles: Practical Approaches to Contemporary Feminism*. Lanham: Rowman & Littlefield Publishers, pp. 314–46.

Filmography

Mendes, S (dir.).1999. *American Beauty*. Dreamworks. Jinks/Cohen Company.

———. 2002. *Road to Perdition*. Dreamworks. Twentieth Century Fox Film Corporation. Zanuck Company.

———. 2005. *Jarhead*. Universal Pictures. Red Wagon Productions. Neal Street Productions.

———. 2008. *Revolutionary Road*. Dreamworks. BBC Films. Evamere Entertainment.

———. 2009. *Away We Go*. Focus Features. Edward Saxon Productions. Big Beach Films.

5

SIMONE DE BEAUVOIR, MELODRAMA AND THE ETHICS OF TRANSCENDENCE

Linnell Secomb

Todd Haynes's 2002 film, *Far From Heaven*, opens with a descending crane shot moving from a transcendent, god's-eye-view perspective to the level of the mundane and quotidian. Panning past the treetops outside Hartford train station the camera slides toward the street where it follows the main protagonist Cathy Whitaker (Julianne Moore) as she drives to collect her daughter from her ballet class before tracking her as she passes along suburban streets toward the family home. This opening sequence iterates Douglas Sirk's 1955 film, *All That Heaven Allows*, in which the opening credits roll over a similar scene of a clock tower overlooking suburban streets below. The camera sweeps across autumnal treetop foliage before cutting to a shot of Cary Scott's (Jane Wyman's) friend, Mona (Jacqueline de Wit), emerging from her car outside Cary's home. These opening arcing descents, from the firmaments to the everyday materiality beneath, metaphorically represent themes that each film implicitly elaborates: of movement from a transcendental morality to a human-created ethics. The movement from the omniscient view overseeing the whole of Hartford into the street and the family home parallels, I will argue, a movement from the sacred to the secular and human. This expresses, visually, a transition from a traditional morality (understood as a preordained, religion-based code of behaviour) to an ethics, developed by human societies in response to specific historical and cultural contexts, that these films elaborate.

A central function of melodrama is to explore new ethical frameworks in the context of the demise of conventional morality and this is evident in conflicts surrounding class, race and love depicted in these films. These themes will be examined in relation to Beauvoir's analysis of ethics in *The Ethics of Ambiguity* (1994) and her critique of the subordination of women in *The Second Sex* (2009). This enables a nuanced reading of the ethical frameworks and love relations they depict. Moreover, her vivid characterisation of bad faith and her examination of the constraints on women's freedom reveal the continuing subjugations and denials that remain intrinsic to the 'new' ethics they represent.

In *Far From Heaven* and *All That Heaven Allows* the transition from conventional morality to a newly emerging ethics is also associated with a refiguring of transcendence. Just as the camera descends from the god's-eye-view to the streets below so, too, a new human-created understanding of transcendence is evoked. Beauvoir's understanding of transcendence, as a freedom enabled by the multiple possibilities offered by the future, enables a complex and layered interpretation of the depiction of transcendence. This is a transcendence that may be achieved by participation in the creation of new worlds and open futures that these films portray.

Ethics in Melodrama

The American film director, Todd Haynes, is renowned for his postmodern film style involving non-linear narrative structures, mixing of genres, techniques of pastiche and imitation, representation of fluid identities, and depiction of transgressive themes. His first feature film, *Poison* (1991), for example, draws on Jean Genet's writings and combines several film genres – documentary, sci-fi and prisoner love story – to critique conventional perceptions of homosexuality. *Velvet Goldmine* (1998) explores the 1970s glam rock era, focusing on the fluid identities, styles and sexualities of the period and playfully reworking the myths and rumours surrounding figures such as David Bowie, Iggy Pop and Lou Reed. His 2007 film, *I'm Not There*, engages with the life and music of Bob Dylan using fictional characters who each represent an aspect of, or influence on, Dylan. The film challenges the biopic genre by refusing to create a simple life narrative and revealing instead the multiple trajectories, influences and musical personas evident in Dylan's music.[1]

Similarly, Haynes's 2002 film, *Far From Heaven*, uses the postmodern techniques of pastiche and imitation, recreating and also transforming Douglas Sirk's 1950s melodramas and especially his film *All That Heaven Allows*. In *Far From Heaven*, Cathy Whitaker is a young wife and mother who, with her husband Frank (Dennis Quaid), appears to live the perfect 1950s suburban middle-class life. Yet, her marriage is not all it seems: Frank's repressed homosexuality begins to find expression in secretive encounters with other men – in toilets, cinemas and bars; Cathy forms an attachment with her 'Negro' gardener Raymond Deagan (Dennis Haysbert). Reprisals follow: arrest by the police and psychiatric treatment for Frank and verbal warnings, physical attacks and ostracism in the case of Cathy, Raymond and their children.

Haynes's film is deeply indebted to Sirk's oeuvre and it imitates the cinematic style, rich colour palette and controversial themes elaborated by Sirk. In Sirk's *All That Heaven Allows* – one of the five films by Sirk generally taken to be emblematic of film melodrama – a repressive community opposes and restricts the desires of the heroine and ethical questions regarding love, responsibility and conformity are explored. The widowed Cary Scott falls in love with her younger and socially unconventional gardener, Ron Kirby (Rock Hudson), foreshadowing the illicit love relation between Cathy and Raymond in the later film. Her neighbours and children oppose this romance, forcing her, at least initially, to renounce her desire. They consider Cary too old for this younger man, while Ron is too unconventional and not sufficiently conformist and middle class.

The class and age issues in *All That Heaven Allows* are replaced by the race issue in *Far From Heaven*, and the unconventional bohemian lifestyle in the earlier film is reprised in the illicit homosexual love of the latter, drawing attention to the impossibility of depicting gay love in the first film and recalling the need for its lead actor, Rock Hudson, to remain closeted because of the endemic homophobia of the time. While the specific issue is transformed, the broader themes in each film remain the same: each represents the conflict between traditional mores and moralities and newly emerging attitudes and ethics. The main protagonists question pervasive beliefs about class, race and romantic relations and introduce a more progressive and empathetic perspective. The old conventions are in this process redefined as noxious and anachronistic and the new attitudes (though they do not necessarily prevail) are depicted as creating or heralding a more ethical, just and equal society.

These themes, conflicts and transitions are not, of course, unique to these two films. Indeed, while film melodrama was not until recently a valued genre it is now recognised for its portrayal of precisely these dilemmas. Within film theory, melodrama was, initially, largely overlooked and under-valued. Perceived as a 'woman's' genre, it was frequently construed as superficial, sentimental and unsophisticated. The work of feminist film theorists (Gledhill 1987; Klinger 1994; Williams 1998) challenged this disdain and disregard by revealing the political and social importance of melodrama. This re-evaluation was further enhanced by the application of Peter Brooks's influential theories of melodrama in theatre and literature to film melodrama.

In *The Melodramatic Imagination* (1995), Brooks reconsiders the origins, mode and function of melodrama, suggesting that it emerges as a form during periods of political and social turmoil when conventional beliefs and traditional moralities begin to be questioned. Brooks argues that melodrama (in literature and theatre) has its origins in the period during and after the French Revolution (Brooks 1995: 15). In this context, melodrama is a form that explores contentious and difficult personal relations that raise ethical dilemmas and elaborates an alternate ethics that emerges within particular historical and cultural situations (Brooks 1995: 15).

Brooks's analysis of melodrama has influenced the development of film theory. Linda Williams, for example, suggests that melodrama is not a limited and specific genre but is the mode that underlies American popular movies as a whole. She suggests that melodrama 'seeks dramatic revelation of moral and irrational truths through a dialectic of pathos and action' and, she continues, 'It is the foundation of the classical Hollywood movie' (Williams 1998: 42). Williams, like Brooks, argues that melodrama is concerned with creating new ethical values and delineating acceptable behaviours. Importantly, she points out that the conflict evident in melodrama derives from the struggle faced by the protagonists whose virtue is not recognised by the other film characters (who adhere to a more conventional moral code).

The film narrative within both *All That Heaven Allows* and *Far From Heaven* may be understood in relation to Brooks's and Williams's contention that melodrama represents the struggle to replace traditional morality with a human-created and culturally and historically specific ethics. In each film the 'new' ethics of anti-classism and anti-racism advocated by the main protagonists challenges traditional mores and prejudices. In response to widowhood and to divorce, Cary and Cathy hope to recreate fulfilling lives by following their romantic attraction to men from different class and race backgrounds. Yet, the conventional attitudes of their families and friends forbid such relationships. These films depict the conflict that arises between established beliefs and moralities and a newly emerging ethos and ethics. Importantly, this conflict between differing moral and ethical systems suggests that there is no universal preordained morality and that, instead, ethical beliefs and behaviours are constantly evolving and transforming in response to new situations and dilemmas.

While Brooks's theory of melodrama provides some insight into the underlying issues explored in these films, Simone de Beauvoir's analysis of the ambiguity of human-created ethical systems enables a more nuanced and richer understanding of the ethical conflicts and dilemmas portrayed. For Brooks, the characters of melodrama are either good or evil and the purpose of melodrama is to explore and recreate a new ethics in the context of the loss of a Christian-based morality. Good and evil are internalised within and expressed through the uni-dimensional characterisations of melodrama. This polarisation is evident in character construction – characters are reductive figures whose attributes are communicated through pronouncements about and depictions of their honesty, virtue and respectability or on the contrary their cruelty and tyranny. Beauvoir's reflections on the varying forms of bad faith or false consciousness may, however, enable a more nuanced reading of character in melodrama.

Beauvoir's *The Ethics of Ambiguity* foregrounds both the uncertainty that attends ethical decisions and choices and the vacillations and fallibility of human existence. Beauvoir sees human life as a never-completed process that involves disclosing meaning in and imposing meaning on the world. Importantly, neither the desire to uncover nor to create meaning is fully achievable. This failure may be concealed by the assertion of absolute truths and moralities. These, however, are evasions that refuse to acknowledge the limits of human capacities and knowledges and ignore the indeterminacy of the future. Human existence involves the ambiguous process of discovering and inventing meaning though many, too intimidated by the uncertainty this creates, seek assurance by clinging to predetermined beliefs and ideas. In addition, ethics is ambiguous insofar as choices and actions take place in complex and not fully knowable contexts and insofar as the disclosure and invention of meaning are necessarily incomplete and partial (Beauvoir 1994; see also Arp 2001).

In *The Ethics of Ambiguity*, Beauvoir identifies those who, intimidated by the complexities of the ethical world and by the difficulties associated with freedom, cling to old certainties and beliefs. She distinguishes these from those who seek their own freedom but in doing so undermine that of others. Finally, she describes those who pursue their own freedom while also facilitating the freedom of others. These different character types enable a deeper understanding of the melodramatic characters deemed simply 'good' or 'evil' by Brooks's analysis. Using Beauvoir's analysis of the ethics of ambiguity reveals instead a complex functioning of bad faith and false consciousness as well as more and less successful attempts to attain ethical freedom. For Beauvoir, ethics is founded on freedom: on the expression and recognition of one's own freedom in the context of acknowledging and enabling the freedom of others (Beauvoir 1994: 73). The 'sub-man' fails to recognise either the freedom of the self or of the other. He repudiates freedom and instead denies and flees this possibility. The sub-man refuses to seek meaning or to create meaning and takes the world to be a pre-determined fact. Having no projects, passions or interests, being an inert passivity, the sub-man is easily recruited to the ideologies and causes of others (Beauvoir 1994: 44).

Similarly, the 'serious man' denies freedom by unquestioningly accepting the childhood values of parents and teachers or by adopting similarly certain and absolute new values. Beauvoir argues that some are trapped in this character type through their circumstances: the slave, the woman in a sexist society, have little option but to accept the world as given. However, others deny the freedom available to them and adopt the attitudes of the serious. The serious man sacrifices himself and others to his ideology and is therefore dangerous; he is, for Beauvoir, a natural tyrant (Beauvoir 1994: 46–49). The 'nihilist' also has links with the sub-man and the serious man in his denial of freedom. The nihilist rejects all given authority and institutions and beliefs but in so doing confirms these values. Like the sub-man and the serious man he threatens existence, negating his own life and that of others (Beauvoir 1994: 53–55).

These three character types refuse to express their own freedom and willingly restrain or destroy that of others. In *Far From Heaven*, the man on the street who shouts at Raymond 'Hey boy. Hands off,' when Raymond touches Cathy's arm, personifies the sub-man. He accepts unquestioningly dominant racist ideologies, denigrating Raymond by calling him a 'boy' and forbidding intimacy across racial boundaries. In *All That Heaven Allows* Cary refuses the advances of a sleazy married acquaintance, and he, discovering her involvement with Ron, abuses her, accusing her of playing him 'for a prize sucker' and of 'going into that perfect lady routine'. His accusations reveal a dichotomous view of women as either 'perfect ladies' or as sexually available to all men. He denies Cary agency and choice in her romantic liaisons, negating her freedom while also conforming to and perpetuating rigid and misogynist ideologies through his tyrannical abuse of her.

These character types may be contrasted with others that Beauvoir identifies who pursue their own freedom while denying it to others. The 'adventurer' engages in war, love, conquest, politics and exploration with ardour. This ardour is capricious and free-floating; he has no investment in the ends but merely takes pleasure from the conquest. While the adventurer seeks his own freedom he has no regard for that of others (Beauvoir 1994: 58). The 'passionate man' creates an absolute rather than adopting a pre-given absolute (as do the sub-man and serious man). He insists on the autonomy of his passionate project but fails to appreciate the significance of subjective inter-connection. As a result of his obsession with his own projects and his failure to recognise that of others, he obstructs the freedom of others in his pursuit of his own freedom (Beauvoir 1994: 65).

These character types seek their own freedom while negating that of others: Cary's children, for example, insist that she remains entombed in her widow-hood while pursuing their own freedom through travel, education and love. Similarly, Cathy's husband Frank, who finally allows himself to express his repressed homosexuality while accusing Cathy of an inappropriate, scandalous friendship with Raymond, pursues his own freedom while condemning Cathy and restraining her desires. All these may be contrasted with those who seek their own freedom while also facilitating freedom for others.

For Beauvoir, it is only the final character type, the 'writer-artist', who is able to fully express and facilitate freedom for both self and other. Artists and writers represent existence in their work and in so doing they necessarily reveal the lack that is inherent in being. If they don't succumb to making of art, and of themselves, an idol then they can express their own freedom and enable that of others, opening, through their art, new meanings and possibilities (Beauvoir 1994: 69).

The hero figures in *Far From Heaven* and *All That Heaven Allows* may be interpreted as artist-writer figures insofar as they pursue their own freedom while encouraging others in their quests for freedom. Neither do this through art or writing. They are, however, each associated with creativity. Ron's bohemian social world includes the diverse marginalised creativity associated with exotic and foreign culture and cuisine, with artists and writers. Raymond's appreciation and knowledge of modern and religious art links him with creativity. Both ignore convention and prejudice, seeking for themselves and others a future beyond the confines of their restrictive societies.

While these various character types may be easily identified, more import-antly, Beauvoir's analysis reveals how the manifestation and effects of bad faith (or self-deception) operate within these characters and within the films. The characters surrounding the central couple in each melodrama manifest this bad faith to varying degrees and through diverse attitudes and actions. Most significantly, though, an oscillation between bad faith and recognition of self-responsibility is evident in the decisions and dilemmas faced by the main protagonists. Early in *Far From Heaven*, Cathy, indulging in bad faith, allows herself to conform to the expectations of a middle-class, stay-at-home, 1950s suburban wife and mother. Subsequently, throwing off this self-deception, she briefly reaches for freedom that she believes may be attained through her relationship with Raymond. This attempt, however, is snatched away by the violence that an inter-racial friendship and love provokes. Here, Beauvoir's recognition of the limits to freedom is confirmed – as a result of their constrained situations certain groups (women, minorities, slaves) may not have the capacity to attain or even to reach for freedom. Raymond's character, too, illustrates the ambiguities and complexities of an ethics of freedom. Willing to risk social censure, isolation and even violence he entertains the possibility of love across the colour line. He recognises that he is responsible for his own life choices and attempts to create his own destiny. But when the resulting violence threatens his daughter's future well-being, Raymond recognises the limits of his situation. He does not return to a state of bad faith but prioritises his daughter's safety and future freedom over his own present pursuit of freedom.

Beauvoir's ethics of ambiguity enables a more subtle reading of the forces of good and evil that Brooks identifies in melodrama. Melodrama explores new possibilities in contexts of transforming political and social relations but, as Beauvoir's analysis demonstrates, these new futures that melodrama gestures toward involve complex, ambiguous, heterogeneous formations and uncertain outcomes.

Transcendence

Melodrama is not only a vehicle for exploring new ethical frameworks, it also reinterprets transcendence, transforming it into a state attainable within human experience. Within the western philosophical tradition, transcendence or the transcendental refers to that which is beyond, prior to, or superior to human experience – the 'Good' in Plato or 'God' in the Christian tradition, for example. Beauvoir's phenomenological conception of transcendence differs, though it is not entirely unrelated. For her, transcendence involves reaching beyond the constraints of immanence, beyond entrapment within biology, social convention and repetitive domesticity, embracing freedom through active involvement in the public world. Contributing to a phenomenological philosophy, Beauvoir conceives transcendence as a purposive projection toward the future within, rather than beyond, the human realm (Beauvoir 2009: 737–68).

In *The Second Sex*, Beauvoir distinguishes between the transcendence that is possible for man and the limited possibilities available to woman due to social expectations and conventions. Beauvoir explains that:

> The man knows that he can reconstruct other institutions, another ethics, another code; grasping himself as transcendence, he also envisages history as a becoming; … as the woman does not participate in history she does not understand its necessity; she mistrusts the future and wants to stop time.

(Beauvoir 2009: 656)

For Beauvoir, transcendence is the freedom available to man – but less so to woman – to construct the world and to reach out toward the future and the new options, possibilities and actions that it enables.

Peter Brooks also discusses transcendence and in particular explains its function within melodrama. His use of the concept, however, reflects the more established, traditional use of the term. Though he proposes that melodrama emerges in a period characterised by a declining belief in the traditional sacred transcendental, he, nevertheless, identifies a reincarnation of this sacred transcendental in the battle between good and evil that structures melodrama. In Brooks's analysis, the lost sacred transcendental returns but is now immanent within human relations. This 're-sacralisation' of man parallels the theological formulation of 'God' who now appears not as transcendent to, but as immanent within, man.

By contrast, Beauvoir's transcendental is stripped of this quasi-religious signification. Rather than representing the descent of the *mysterium* from the heavens to man, Beauvoir's conception involves a conscious decision to pursue freedom for the self and for the other through an orientation toward the possibilities offered by the openness of the future: 'The individual who is a subject, who is himself, endeavours to extend his grasp on the world if he has the generous inclination for transcendence: he is ambitious, he acts' (Beauvoir 2009: 700). This alternate conception enables a different and, perhaps, more nuanced reading of melodrama to emerge.

Brooks's identification of a transposition of the *mysterium* from the heavens to man is represented in the descending crane shot described in my introduction. His interpretation suggests that in both *Far From Heaven* and *All That Heaven Allows* this lost transcendental, sacred realm is reincarnated in the everyday world and, in particular, in the male lead characters. As gardeners who engage with and enhance the beauty of the natural world, Raymond and Ron are each associated with nature and the mystery and sublime aspect of the universe. Raymond's speculations on modern abstract art as a form of sacred art reinforces this connection as does his quasi-religious poetic references to a 'shining place' 'beyond the fall of grace'. Though not as explicit in Ron's character, here, too, there is a charisma and calm about his personality that suggests a spiritual wisdom. Brooks's observation that melodrama involves a re-sacralisation enables a reading of Raymond and Ron not just as unconventional but also as the incarnation of the sacred transcendental that appeared to be lost with the decline in traditional western religious belief.

In these films, Cathy and Cary are the innocent and ethical characters who recognise the good, the reincarnated sacred, evident in Raymond and Ron, and who struggle against the evils of racism, convention and class prejudice represented by their family and friends. Cary's children oppose her romance with Ron, favouring an older middle-class suitor, while Cathy's friends abandon her when they understand that rumours about her association with her 'Negro' gardener are true. Evil is associated with restrictive, prejudiced, convention while good is expressed in 'true' love between the quasi-transcendental heroes and their innocent, empathetic, female leads.

This reincarnation of the transcendental within man is further elaborated in a crucial scene in *Far From Heaven* involving an encounter between Cathy and Raymond when he, responding to her pronouncement that their friendship 'isn't plausible', asks whether it might be possible to 'see beyond the surface, beyond the colour of things ...'. Seeing beyond the surface as Raymond explains it involves a vision of another world beyond the restrictions of everyday life. Expressed in quasi-theological terms, Raymond ruminates: 'Just beyond the fall of grace, behold that ever shining place ...'. Redemption and salvation from the present situation of disgrace or of dishonour and ignominy are evoked here as Raymond reveals his vision of a 'shining place' beyond.

Beauvoir's alternate formulation of transcendence enables a more directly political interpretation of this scene. Raymond's wish is not so much for the re-emergence of a state of theological grace but a desire for a new future of freedom from the prejudices and racism of the present. A Beauvoirian under-standing of transcendence as active engagement with the world and projection toward the future suggests that Raymond's vision expresses hope for a future beyond colour segregation when inter-racial friendship and love would be embraced rather than condemned.

While Beauvoir advocates reaching for transcendence, she recognises that this possibility is rendered more difficult by the situations of particular groups – for example, women's situation and her possibility for transcendence is limited by acculturation to a position of subservience within male-dominated culture (Beauvoir 2009: 651). Beauvoir suggests that:

> the universe as a whole is masculine; it is men who have shaped it, ruled it, and who today dominate it; as for her; ... it is understood she is inferior and dependent; ... the passive opposite to these human-faced gods who set goals and standards.
>
> (Beauvoir 2009: 654)

Beauvoir also recognises other groups who are deemed inferior and who, as a result, are restricted in their search for transcendence. The privilege associated with the male sex only applies to those in the appropriate class and race position. From the white perspective, for example, 'the native is not a man' and, like the woman who 'is shut up in the kitchen or a boudoir' so that 'her wings are cut' (Beauvoir 2009: 660), the racial other is also constrained in her search for freedom and public participation and action. In *America Day by Day*, Beauvoir comments on the unjustified white fear of the black other, speculating that it arises from within the white person who has 'the face of the oppressor' (Beauvoir 1999: 35). 'It's this face that frightens him' (Beauvoir 1999: 35), Beauvoir observes, but this fear of having to confront his own violence is projected onto the black other who is then repudiated and subjugated. This racism undermines the capacity of the cultural other to envisage and project toward a future of equal freedom, mutual dignity and respect.

This limitation on transcendence is evident in *Far From Heaven* when Cathy offers to visit Raymond in Baltimore where he is forced to move following the white and black assaults against him and his daughter. He refuses her implicit offer of a new life, declaring: 'I've learned my lesson about mixing in other worlds. I've seen sparks fly – all kinds.' It is Raymond who now recognises the impossibility of their relationship understanding that the 'shining place', the 'other worlds', 'beyond' are not yet within reach. Raymond's transcendence toward a new future collapses as the intransigence of racism destroys the possibility of a better world beyond the colour line.

While Brooks proposes that melodrama represents a redefinition of trans-cendence that transposes it from an omniscient God into a quality of virtue and divinity identifiable within man, Beauvoir's understanding of transcendence enables a more radical transformation to be acknowledged within the style and sensibility of melodrama. Beauvoir's interpretation of transcendence as the movement toward freedom offered by the open-ended possibilities of the future suggests that it is not so much the sacred and ethical qualities within each character that are significant but rather the decision to actively re-define and re-create the world in the pursuit of greater freedom for all. It is not just the characters who embody transcendence in this perspective but melodrama as a genre to the extent that it explores new possibilities and opens new worlds to its audiences.

Entombed Love

While melodrama may represent and facilitate transcendence by questioning conventional mores and proposing greater freedoms, it is, nevertheless, itself constrained by the moralities and customs of its time. In particular, film melodrama frequently depicts heterosexual love as the main mechanism for its female protagonists to gain freedom and to transcend the limits imposed by society. Beauvoir's analysis of love contests this pervasive portrayal of love suggesting instead that it may produce not liberation but a further entrapment for women. While film melodrama frequently valorises love, depicting it as the vehicle through which the female protagonist is able to escape her 'entombment' in a superficial and sterile world, Beauvoir's acerbic observations about love warn that this seeming escape may yet be another form of servility and subordination.

Beauvoir's chapter in *The Second Sex* on 'The Woman in Love' explores the centrality of love for the existence of the woman and elaborates the distortions of love by the repression of female transcendence. For Beauvoir, the second sex has been restricted to a life of immanence; she has been restricted to a limited life dominated by carnality and by the repetitions of reproduction and domesticity (Deutscher 2008). Transcendence beyond this realm – reaching toward futural freedom experienced in productive (rather than reproductive) projects and occupations – is possible for the woman but is rendered more difficult by her situation. Her upbringing and culture confine her to home, family and corporeality and this undermines her capacity to seek freedom beyond the limits of domesticity (Beauvoir 2009: 654–60). In addition, women are acculturated to love and serve, rather than to desire the other, and this forecloses her ability to perceive and prioritise her own needs and feelings. In this limited situation the woman turns to love as a means of fulfilment but this will inevitably fail to provide transcendence for, rather than achieving the freedom of involvement with the world, she remains dependent on her beloved to give her life meaning and to affirm her existence and identity.[2]

For Beauvoir, conventional heterosexual romance entraps women as love involves total devotion and unquestioning faith. Beauvoir argues that in the conventional love relation the woman gives herself totally while the man in love always holds something in reserve (Beauvoir 2009: 699). The man remains a 'sovereign subject'; the woman abdicates herself 'for the benefit of a master' (Beauvoir 2009: 699). The woman transforms her lover into a god who she worships and serves (Beauvoir 2009: 700).

While Beauvoir describes love as enslavement and self-abnegation, *Far From Heaven* and *All That Heaven Allows* represent love as the pathway to freedom and as an escape from the restrictions of widowhood and of conventional and repressive social mores. *All That Heaven Allows* depicts widowhood as an entombment. Cary's daughter explains to her mother that in ancient Egypt widows were entombed along with their husbands and expresses the view that this no longer occurs. Cary responds: 'Doesn't it? Well, perhaps not in Egypt'. Cary's entombment is visualised through the cinematography: she is repeatedly depicted looking out into the world through barred windows, or framed in reflected images (on her TV screen and the reflective surface of her piano), emphasising her containment within domestic space (Mercer and Shingler 2004: 60–68). Only Ron offers freedom: his bohemian lifestyle, his disdain for social convention, his love of beauty and nature, his passion, all indicate the possibility of a love that facilitates freedom. In *All That Heaven Allows* widowhood is represented as the loss of freedom, love as release from this imprisonment.

Yet *All That Heaven Allows* also, paradoxically, betrays its own intentions by revealing that it is Cary who must change to conform with Ron's life and that the reverse is unimaginable. Fighting over the negative reactions of family and friends, Cary suggests they take things more slowly, allowing others to get used to the idea of their relationship. Ron responds:

> You mean we'll be invited to the cocktail parties. And of course [Cary's friend] Sarah will see to it that I get into the Country Club. Dear Howard [Cary's failed seducer] and I will shake hands and forget. And you'll flatter [town gossip] Mona so she won't be malicious. And then [daughter] Kaye won't mind so much because we'll be living just as you always have, probably in your home.

Ron here expresses his rejection of her entire lifestyle, refusing to adapt or adopt any aspect of her existence. She responds:

> What's wrong with that? Suppose we did live in my house. It's only for a little while. And it would make things so much easier. It wouldn't change you, Ron. You couldn't change.

Refusing this compromise Ron insists he is only willing to pursue the relationship if she moulds herself to suit his way of life. *All That Heaven Allows* portrays this love as the means to her freedom at the same time as it also hints at the cost involved. From a Beauvoirian perspective, this scene reveals that this seeming freedom is only available on the condition that she moves from her current entombment in her dead husband's home to a similar imprisonment in his newly converted old mill-house. She must re-style herself in his image and become an appendage, an accessory, to his bohemian life.

In Brooks's reading of melodrama, Ron would be conceived as emblematic of the good, and as the incarnation of the sacred that has descended from on high to the earth below. Beauvoir's phenomenology of love and ethics suggests, not only that Ron as a 'human-faced god' may represent yet another entombment for Cary but, also, that his apparent laudable virtue and integrity are inflected by human failures. Ron may represent the good and the sacred for Brooks but a Beauvoirian analysis reveals a certain bad faith that shadows his intentions. Wishing for an unconventional, unconstrained life for himself he insists that Cary conform to his desires, and refashion herself to fit within his chosen lifestyle. Her desires, choices, projects and freedom are ignored as he determines the context and conditions of their shared future.

Far From Heaven, like *All That Heaven Allows*, depicts an opposition between the un-freedom of single life and the freedom to be found through love. With her marriage at an end, Frank having left her for his young male lover, Cathy faces a lonely life as a divorcee. Like Ron, Raymond offers an escape from loneliness and from the restrictions of social convention. While Raymond is treated as inferior by the racist 1950s society depicted in the film, nevertheless, the film portrays him as having god-like qualities. Raymond's speculations about modern art as a contemporary form of religious art associates him with divinity. He has the capacity to open a new world for Cathy 'on the other side of the colour line' and through his greater connection with both nature and the divine. While Cathy initially ends her connection with Raymond she, like Cary, is ultimately prepared to give up all, offering to follow Raymond when he is forced to leave town.

From a Beauvoirian perspective, however, these films partake of bad faith or false consciousness about love. Beauvoir represents the woman in love as worshipping her beloved as though he were a god. *Far From Heaven* and *All That Heaven Allows* perpetuate this idolisation of the male hero figure and the subordination of the worshipping female character, reinforcing the mythology of love as the ultimate attainment for the woman and the focus and meaning of her existence. While these films represent the possibility of transcendence, they also undermine this possibility, at least for the woman, by valorising and romanticising traditional, unequal relations. There is, then, an ambiguous and contradictory signification in these films. They simultaneously challenge while also perpetuating conventional mores: class and race prejudice are questioned and orthodox love relations critiqued but at the same time the subordinate role of the woman in love is overlooked and even validated.

For Brooks, the characterisations of Raymond and Ron would illustrate the humanised re-sacralisation that replaces the traditional religious transcendental. For Beauvoir, however, this construction of the male heroes as transcendent beings replicates an old and troubling feminine fantasy in which the enslaved and subordinated woman in love worships her god-like lover. For the melodramatic heroine, he is the means for her escape from imprisonment in convention, the transcendence she herself cannot achieve but can worship. While Brooks proposes that melodrama attempts to re-establish divinity in the wake of the death of God, Beauvoir reveals the deceits and dependency, the subjugation and servitude, which this romantic fabrication conjures and conveys.

In *Far From Heaven* and *All That Heaven Allows* the transcendental function has been reformulated constructing ethics not in relation to commandments and gospels but in relation to love. The transcendental deity has been transmogrified into an earthly hero and the woman's traditional role of religious worship and self-sacrifice is only changed insofar as she now subordinates herself to the male hero rather than to a conventional divinity.

While Brooks's analysis of melodrama reveals the incarnation of the sacred within the human in the context of the diminishing relevance of western religion, Beauvoir's reflections on heterosexual love make clear the cost of this relocation of the sacred. Haynes's and Sirk's films represent their male leads as saviours of the entrapped, lonely and isolated divorced and widowed feminine figures but Beauvoir, reading between the lines, may contest this depiction pointing to the invidious and impossible choices open to women in sexually divided and unequal societies. The woman alone may be trapped by social conventions but so too, she argues, is the woman in love.

Love as Transcendence

While Beauvoir focuses on the illusions and distortions associated with romantic love, she also acknowledges the possibility of a more positive authentic love that may facilitate freedom and transcendence. This authentic love brings together two freedoms neither of whom rescind their transcendence nor martyr themselves for the other. This love is an 'enrichment of the universe' and a revelation of 'values and ends in the world' (Beauvoir 2009: 723). Authentic love involves the freedom of each and 'discovers new heavens and new earths even in the landscape where we have always lived' (Gusdorf, quoted in Beauvoir 2009: 723). This form of love, however, is difficult to attain in the context of repressive societies within which woman is subordinated to, and dependent upon, man.

While, in general, *Far From Heaven* and *All That Heaven Allows* depict a traditional love relation in which the woman worships a transcendent male beloved, there are also moments that surpass this limited form of unequal love gesturing toward the authentic love that facilitates transcendence of which

Beauvoir speaks. This is especially evident in *Far From Heaven* in three encounters between Cathy and Raymond – three moments when touch, rather than dialogue, communicates the complexity of their mutual desire.

As Cathy's racial panic, early in the film, recedes, following her realisation that the stranger in her yard is the son of her previous gardener, she places her hand on Raymond's shoulder. Learning of his father's death, Cathy's touch is a gesture of sympathy for his loss, but it is also an indication of tolerance, and the beginning of desire. Standing above him on the porch this gesture expresses her assumption of superiority – she both keeps him at arm's length and almost anoints him with her touch. Her racial tolerance (which like all tolerance assumes the power to determine what is to be tolerated and makes abject that which is tolerated), her 'kindness to Negros', her superiority, are all announced in this moment but so too is her desire. The scene moves rapidly from fear to sympathy to toleration to desire and each emotion is conveyed in this placing of her hand on his shoulder.

This touch is reprised and reversed, in the scene discussed earlier, when Cathy explains to Raymond that their friendship is not possible. He, pleading for his vision of a 'shining place' beyond the colour line, touches her arm. Simultaneously the music crescendos and the man on the street warns, 'Hey boy. Hands off'. His contact with her, though expressing love, is intolerable and forbidden. The touch expresses love; the response to it is the 'implausibility' of love and the pervasive power of racism.

The final touch again recalls and reverses the first. As Raymond tells Cathy that he is leaving, and explains that he has learned not to venture into other worlds, he places his hand on her shoulder and she covers it with her own. He is elevated on the back steps of his house and she is turned away from him as he asks her to 'have a proud life, a splendid life'. The touch communicates the pathos of thwarted love but also his paradoxically empowered position. While she had previously instigated the end of the friendship he is now the one who determines that it is impossible. This touch is an expression of respect and regard: it forgives her earlier racial fear and awkward claims to racial tolerance; and expresses the deep sorrow and love that neither he nor she are able, are not permitted, to express. Previously, her touch had both anointed him and kept him at bay; now he wishes and hopes for her a fulfilled future life, a life of transcendent freedom perhaps, despite the restrictions that thwart their love.

The penultimate scene of the film, in which they part at Hartford station, echoes the era of silent film, there being no spoken communication. Instead gesture and facial expression convey intensely the meaning and affect of parting. The ultimate image is of his hand still waving from the departing train. The touch – the symbol of love, power, racial tension, sympathy and freedom – is broken, but the waving hand is a lingering reminder of this touching affect. The departing train, travelling toward a new life, and the enduring waving hand suggests not an ending, but a transition toward a future, a movement, that is, toward the freedom that the future makes possible. This last moment of lingering contact and forward movement evokes Beauvoir's concept of a futural transcendence made possible by their visionary and utopian love.

While Cathy and Raymond's love is forbidden by their society, these scenes gesture toward an authentic love that challenges each of them to embrace the opportunities offered by the future. Each gives to the other recognition of their equal value and dignity. Each offers the other respect, affection and desire. Within their relation neither is subordinated, power shifts and moves between them, and for each the other inspires in them visions of new worlds, new possibilities, beyond the restrictions of the present. If their mutual trans-cendence is ultimately thwarted, they, nevertheless, glimpse together what may be possible in the future beyond the limitations enforced by their present situation.

This transcendence of the present toward an open-ended future is further reinforced by the film's final scene. As Cathy leaves the station and returns to her car the camera pulls back and up, ascending once again into the treetops. Whereas Cathy and Raymond's romance started with the autumn and was thwarted in a bleak and cold winter, the film closes with a branch of blossom representing the return of spring and with it new life. While racism has separated the lovers, the film ends with renewal: the spring, the transgressive love relation, and the new ethics of freedom practised by the protagonists all portend new possibilities that will continue to challenge the old moralities and open up new trajectories and new futures.

Conclusion

Peter Brooks's study of ethics and transcendence in melodrama has been crucial to the renewed interest in melodrama as a genre that challenges conventional moralities and established social conventions. Simone de Beauvoir's analyses of ethics, transcendence and love, however, enable a richer and more nuanced interpretation of these issues, revealing the ambiguities and paradoxes that emerge as melodrama explores alternate ethical and social possibilities. A Beauvoirian reading suggests that ethics, love and transcendence are complex projects that involve an ongoing process of interpreting and creating new, dynamic and open relations with others and with the world. This perspective reveals how *Far From Heaven* represents transcendence as an escape from convention through the invention of new lives, loves and futures. By defying established moralities, exploring new ethical frameworks and more equal love relations, and by hinting at untold futures, *Far From Heaven* creates alternate visions and new interpretations of existence. In doing so, it does more than merely represent transcendence, authentic love and alternate ethical possibili-ties: it also opens new worlds, futures and perspectives to its audiences, encouraging us all to question convention and pursue and facilitate our own and others' freedoms.

Notes

1. For further discussion of Haynes's oeuvre see Morrison 2007.
2. For further analysis of Beauvoir on love see Bergoffen 1997; Secomb 2007; Vintges 1996.

Bibliography

Arp, K. 2001. *The Bonds of Freedom: Simone de Beauvoir's Existentialist Ethics*. Chicago: Open Court.

Beauvoir, S. de. [1947] 1994. *The Ethics of Ambiguity*, trans B. Frechtman. New York: Citadel Press.

———. [1949] 2009. *The Second Sex*, trans. C. Borde and S. Malovany-Chevallier. London: Jonathan Cape.

———. [1954] 1999. *America Day by Day*, trans C. Cosman. London: Phoenix.

Bergoffen, D. 1997. *The Philosophy of Simone de Beauvoir: Gendered Phenomenologies, Erotic Generosities*. Albany: State University of New York Press.

Brooks, P. 1995. *The Melodramatic Imagination: Balzac, Henry James, Melodrama, and the Mode of Excess*. New Haven and London: Yale University Press.

Deutscher, P. 2008. *The Philosophy of Simone de Beauvoir: Ambiguity, Conversion, Resistance*. Cambridge: Cambridge University Press.

Gledhill, C. (ed.). 1987. *Home is Where the Heart Is: Studies in Melodrama and the Woman's Film*. London: British Film Institute.

Klinger, B. 1994. *Melodrama and Meaning: History, Culture and the Films of Douglas Sirk*. Bloomington: Indiana University Press.

Mercer, J. and M. Shingler. 2004. *Melodrama: Genre, Style, Sensibility*. London: Wallflower.

Morrison, J. (ed.). 2007. *The Cinema of Todd Haynes: All That Heaven Allows*. London and New York: Wallflower Press.

Secomb, L. 2007. *Philosophy and Love: From Plato to Popular Culture*. Edinburgh: Edinburgh University Press.

Vintges, K. 1996. *Philosophy as Passion: The Thinking of Simone de Beauvoir*. Bloomington: Indiana University Press.

Williams, L. 2008. 'Melodrama Revised', in N. Brown (ed.), *Refiguring American Film Genres: History and Theory*. Berkeley: University of California Press.

Filmography

Haynes, T. (dir.) 1991. *Poison*. Bronze Eye Productions.

———. 1998. *Velvet Goldmine*. Channel Four Films.

———. 2002. *Far From Heaven*. Focus Features and Vulcan Productions.

———. 2007. *I'm Not There*. Killer Films.

Sirk, D. (dir.) 1955. *All That Heaven Allows*. Universal International Pictures.

6

LA PETITE JÉRUSALEM:
FREEDOM AND AMBIGUITY IN THE PARIS BANLIEUES

Claire Humphrey

In *The Ethics of Ambiguity*, Beauvoir argues that our existence is characterised by different forms of subjective and temporal ambiguity. They shape how the world is seen and experienced by each individual, and can cause a number of behaviours as responses to the tensions and uncertainties they bring. This chapter will consider how ambiguity is related to freedom in a discussion of a French film entitled *La Petite Jérusalem* (Albou 2005). Set in an Orthodox Jewish suburb of Paris, it follows the evolving self-deceptions of Laura (Fanny Valette), an adolescent girl trying to achieve an objective form of freedom by ignoring her environment and her relationships with others and living by strict, self-imposed rules. She discovers instead how the ambiguity she avoids is both part of our everyday existence and crucial to creating our future.

For Beauvoir, individuals are situated, meaning that they must recognise the contingency of their knowledge and experience, as well of as their relationships with others. Those who deny this and try to fully grasp the world live out a tragic situation, since each subject in fact 'knows and thinks' their anguish at the impossibility of this task (Beauvoir 1976: 9). The paradox of this anguish is that it is this failure, or lack, which joins us to others and grounds our collective experience, since it is felt by every individual. Our relationships with others are particularly paradoxical, since we are able to deny their existence, and yet we must turn to them for confirmation of our own being. Beauvoir argues that to ignore the ambiguity between individual and collective and instead rely on political, religious or aesthetic confirmation of the self can lead to a number of self-deceptions or 'attitudes', each of which leads us further away from realising our freedom (1976: 76). The circuitous relationship between ambiguity and freedom in Beauvoir's work is reflected in the failure of Laura's muddled attempts to live freely. The film charts her progression as she comes to recognise herself as dependent on others, and in doing so, to understand the ambiguous nature of freedom. This chapter will argue that the Beauvoirian reading of ambiguity and freedom in the film is reinforced by its distinctive cinematography and occasions of narrative ellipsis.

La Petite Jérusalem was the first feature film of Karin Albou, a female writer, director and actress of 'Arab-Jewish' heritage.[1] Although it did not receive a wide release the film won a screenwriting award at Cannes in 2005 and also received César nominations for Fanny Valette for 'most promising actress' and Albou for 'best first feature'.[2] The film situates its characters within a number of ideological oppositions as it follows the tensions lived by Laura (Fanny Valette) and her elder sister Mathilde (Elsa Zylberstein) between their lived experience and their religious and philosophical beliefs. They live together in an apartment situated in the *banlieues*, the impoverished outer regions of Paris, with their mother (Sonia Tahar), Mathilde's children and her husband Ariel (Bruno Todeschini), who is head of the household. Mathilde's adherence to Orthodox customs gives her a community role outside of the home but in her domestic life her marriage is threatened by a lack of sexual intimacy. Little sister Laura studies Kantian philosophy and is inspired by her lectures to regulate her life 'like clockwork', dedicating her existence to working, studying and going on daily walks. Her steadfast detachment from the world is at one stage entirely usurped by her sexuality when she has a relationship with Djamel, a Muslim co-worker (Hédi Tillette de Clermont Tonnerre). When the relationship ends Laura attempts suicide. At the end of the film, against a backdrop of increasing anti-Semitic attacks in the area, Mathilde and her husband decide to move to Israel with the mother. Laura stays behind, moving from Sarcelles, the *banlieue* where the family lived, into her own studio apartment in Paris.

From the opening credits of the film it is made clear that Laura's identity is in question, and that this is related to her body. The first shot begins in silence with close-up of thick wool net tights being put onto feet. As they are pulled up the camera moves up too and we see thighs being squeezed into the tights. The boundaries of the body are blurred due to the unfocused lens and the sound is amplified to the extent that we hear breath and the rustling of fabric. Partial shots of a neck and a back further elicit curiosity on the part of the viewer, who is being drawn into intimacy with Laura's body without seeing her face, which is shown last, in a dark profile which outlines her nose and lips. The focus on surface and texture frames Laura as an enigma, yet at the same time the camera emphasises her identity as linked to her body. As she finishes putting on her modest clothing we understand that she also lives within a religious context in which her body is fully covered. In the following scene she is at the ritual of Tashlikh, a New Year ceremony, which is taking place by the lake. People are stood in a line throwing stones in the water, and the women are making fanning gestures and shaking. Their chanting confirms their unity as a group as they cast sins away and shake out demons. The shot is taken from a high vantage point in a helicopter, placing the viewer at some distance from the action. Laura is filmed as a lone separate figure before the camera pans out over the geometric lines of the high-rise apartment blocks in Sarcelles and over the traffic flowing around the motorway. The shot links the idea of Paris with transcendence by ending on the horizon, where through sun spots the Eiffel Tower is visible.

Through the two successive opening scenes the film establishes a visual language of near and far perspectives, corporeal and social/religious spaces. They suggest a pervasive tension between the individual subject who is at the same time part of a community. In Beauvoir's discussion of individual and collective freedom in *The Ethics of Ambiguity* (1976), the self is ambiguous on two counts relating to separation and unification: with other people and with the world itself. The first, intersubjective ambiguity, is based on the paradox that each individual must recognise that they are both subject and object: 'In turn an object for others, he is nothing more than an individual in the collectivity on which he depends' (Beauvoir 1976: 7). The second, the relationship with the world, is characterised by another paradox, which is that they form part of the world and yet are unable to fully grasp it: 'He is still a part of this world of which he is a consciousness … and he also experiences himself as a thing crushed by the dark weight of other things' (Beauvoir 1976: 7). In *La Petite Jérusalem* Laura denies both ambiguities. As a reaction to the strict religious doctrines of her family and her community, she is inspired by her study of Kant to elevate her existence to what she sees as the objective 'world of ideas'. She asserts during a philosophy lecture that freedom is obtained through obeying laws, and so Laura does not engage with the world as if she were a part of it, instead refusing to make choices and in particular to engage with others, including her family.

Laura demonstrates her separateness by living her everyday life in a different rhythm to her family, a fact communicated by scenes where she studies all night, and through the tension at the dinner table as she walks out during the middle of their dinner in order to take her daily 7 pm walk. Her abrupt departure is left unexplained until halfway through the film where reference is made to Kant's famous walks in one of her philosophy lectures. Kant himself is described by the lecturer as a 'besieged city', his daily rituals constituting 'ramparts' which prevent his body and senses from overwhelming him. Laura has adopted what Beauvoir names 'the aesthetic attitude' in *The Ethics of Ambiguity*: 'a position of withdrawal, a way of fleeing the world'. This refers to a way of looking at the world from a contemplative standpoint in order to deny the subject's situatedness in the present (Beauvoir 1976: 76). She resists her family's attempts to involve her in their life and instead spends hours either studying or on her walks.

Laura's motivation for removing herself to 'the world of ideas' is explained in terms of her motivation to succeed in her studies and leave Sarcelles for a studio apartment in Paris. That she will give into her emotions seems inevitable, since even her lecturer describes her in bodily terms, writing 'You do not think, you tremble' in her report. Her resistance to engaging with others removes her from the potential violence of the relationship, and after her love affair turns sour and she attempts suicide we see just how vulnerable she is. Although Laura represents two extremes of this relationship, Beauvoir held that the view of the self as 'split' between object and subject is a natural state as well as being the basis for conflict and violence. Following Hegel, she suggests that each consciousness feels 'a fundamental hostility to any other consciousness' (Beauvoir 2009: 7). This is based on the desire to be the 'essential' subject rather than the 'inessential' object (Beauvoir 2009: 7). Laura attempts to deny this tension by sidestepping it, instead seeing herself as uniquely autonomous.

Beauvoir argues that this reaction is characteristic of 'the tragedy of the unhappy consciousness; each consciousness seeks to posit itself alone as a sovereign subject' (Beauvoir 2009: 163). A scene at the start of the film shows how Laura withdraws from others. Her body language with Eric (Michaël Cohen), who is set up as an ideal boyfriend (a handsome medical student), communicates her discomfort throughout their meetings. During their first chat early on at a metro station it is also the first time we hear her name, as he calls her back to talk to him. Eric leans in to kiss goodbye and Laura is shot from a high angle, mirroring his point of view. Since he is much taller, her comparatively diminutive stature is emphasised. When he kisses the other cheek her face is completely obscured by his at the same time as the alarm of the closing doors sounds. Laura runs into the carriage, her face visibly perturbed by the exchange. Later on she refuses her mother's entreaties to start a relationship with him as she states it would entail giving in to 'primitive emotions'.

Laura's resistance to recognising herself as 'object for others' is further developed by introducing gendered and cultural aspects in scenes where she walks around the high-rise estate of Sarcelles during the evening. Within the spaces of Sarcelles, characterised by high rise buildings and desolate-looking areas of wasteland, Laura clearly finds a sense of relief. This is emphasised as soon as she leaves the building, with the wind blowing through her hair as she opens the doors. The piano chords and muted blue tones of the buildings and sky at dusk add to the impression of freedom and space, in contrast to the claustrophobic nature of family life in the small apartment. Yet the transgressive nature of Laura's movement is hinted at by the camera, which follows a few paces behind her, as if she is being threatened or stalked. During the course of her first walk she makes eye contact with a man who is watching her, seated alone on the floor. We can see from his clothes that he does not practise Orthodox Judaism, unlike many of the other men she passes. The next shot, unsteady and partially obscured, is of her entering her apartment block and suggests she is still being watched, which is confirmed as the camera turns round to reveal the same man. From inside her kitchen, we see Laura peer through the net curtains and then draw back quickly. The potential violence hinted at here is compounded when she is later forbidden to go out by her brother-in-law after anti-Semitic attacks in the area.

Laura's efforts to detach herself from the world must also be seen in the context of her life as a young woman in Sarcelles. In *The Second Sex* Beauvoir elaborates how subject–object ambiguity is inflected with gender bias, since women who are brought up in a patriarchal world are positioned as feminine objects. For women, the subject–object ambiguity involves a struggle at an individual level, and at the level of 'situation', or culture: 'Woman's drama lies in this conflict between the fundamental claims of every subject which always posits itself as essential, and the demands of a situation that constitutes her as inessential' (Beauvoir 2009: 17). Moi argues that the way in which these two interactions mirror each other is a metaphor upon which *The Second Sex* is based; 'the social oppression of women, [Beauvoir] implies, mirrors or repeats the ontological ambiguity of existence' (Moi 1992: 98). Laura's struggle not to be denied her subjectivity by others is therefore both an ontological conflict found in each subject and a struggle which involves her being situated within a specific gendered and cultural context.

The film argues for the embodied nature of subjectivity and freedom for Laura, while at the same time situating the characters and spaces within the context of the Jewish population which left Tunisia and other North African countries in the post-war period. Of those who came to France, many settled in Sarcelles, the 'Little Jerusalem' of the title. It is a district on the outskirts of Paris which houses a Jewish population of around 20,000, the largest concentration in France (Chrisafis 2006). The film's attempt to emphasise the bodies of the two sisters as expressions of opposing ideologies mirrors Beauvoir's commitment to link individual consciousness to wider social and political tensions. Yet it has been seen by some critics as portraying migrant and Orthodox communities as oppressive. Carrie Tarr argues that 'the film's vision of the minority community as inward-looking, rigid and constrained works to justify dominant negative perceptions of communitarianism' (Tarr 2009: 79).[3] Hiller writes on a Jewish culture blog that 'the film, which means well in its attempt to touch on Kantian philosophy, racial divides, sex and orthodoxy, and secularism versus religion, manages to insult each one of these heavy subjects' (Hiller 2006). Albou does not shy from portraying the Orthodox community in the film in ways which highlight current debates on immigrant assimilation and national identity in France. However, these tensions are explored not from a political perspective but rather in terms of how ideologies, whether secular or religious, cannot be seen as separate from lived experience.

The film shows us through its narrative how the personal is always imbricated with the social, and it further underlines this point through a cinematic style which uses many lingering close-ups of the blurred edges of the body. This continually reminds us that the body is the focal point of her ideological struggles, as is the case in the opening scenes outlined above. This is particularly true of the two sisters, and the film's focus on adolescence reflects Beauvoir's emphasis on this period as crucial to women's embodied subjectivity. Whereas in childhood boys and girls experience their world 'as a transcendence', able to live out their desires freely, during adolescence cultural distinctions between genders start to take effect: 'the future not only moves closer, it settles into her body' (Beauvoir 2009: 353). Laura must negotiate gendered cultural and religious ideologies as she moves through the world, and yet in her body and her movements she is already a product of this world. As she learns, freedom is not to be found in the objective transcendence of the material world, but instead in accepting that her body and her perception of the world are bound together.

At the start, the camera's perspective appears to contradict Laura's view of herself. The camera pays close attention to Laura and her immediate surrounds in a manner which continually suggests a reciprocal relationship between her body and her surroundings. The film's distinct cinematography can be described using Marks's definition of the 'haptic', part of the phenomenological turn in film studies which sees the experience of watching film as involving sensory processes beyond vision. Marks describes haptic viewing as 'a form of visuality that yields to the thing seen, a vision that is not merely cognitive but acknowledges its location in the body, seems to escape the attribution of mastery' (Marks 2000: 132). The frequent scenes involving skin and touch, as in the first scene, are filmed through a haptic perspective which invites the viewer into a close tactile relationship, using the eyes as organs of touch and contact. Scenes focusing on the minutiae of Laura's body and gestures act as a parenthesis in the story and recall 'haptic visuality' as they force the viewer 'to contemplate the image itself instead of being pulled into the narrative' (Marks 2000: 162). Albou's use of the haptic joins image and narrative, since although it provides a contemplative space for the viewer, it also provides a comment on Laura's struggle, encouraging the viewer to identify her as an embodied sub-jectivity despite her own desire to transcend her body. In contrast to the haptic, Marks deems 'optical' shots to depend on 'a separation between the viewing subject and the object' (Marks 2000: 162). In the scene by the lake this sense of distance reflects the transcendent aims of those at the ceremony. Laura's struggle is therefore made into a visual language which is shared by the viewer.

These moments highlight that re-considering our experience of time is vital to recognising subjective ambiguity, and to achieving the sense of creative freedom Beauvoir describes in *The Ethics of Ambiguity* (1976: 27). It is significant that Laura's distancing endeavours are centred on her disjointed experience of time, as she keeps to a different timetable to her family and then loses herself in certain moments. Beauvoir sees temporality as grounding the experience of ambiguity on an intersubjective basis as well as in terms of individual freedom, a point on which Beauvoir and Sartre differ. Langer argues that while Sartre sees consciousness as a temporally constant experience of 'lack', for Beauvoir we are 'the positive existence of a lack' (Langer 2003: 93). The permanent experience of lack means we are forced to justify our existence and through this process can develop a 'creative freedom' (Beauvoir 1976: 28). This is an ongoing process for every individual, who must always return to their actions and justify them 'in the unity of the project'. Their goals must be continually surpassed so that they avoid 'congealing into unjustified facticity' (Beauvoir 1976: 28). It is this link between temporality and freedom which Langer emphasises as distinguishing Beauvoir's philosophy of ambiguity as positive. For Langer, the way Beauvoir sees temporality is that it allows us 'to develop our will, choose a goal, decide on a course of action, implement our decisions, confirm our freedom, and justify our existence' (Langer 2003: 96). This is reflected in the film through Laura's experience of time, which evolves as she moves towards freedom. She does so by experiencing intersubjectivity as temporal ambiguity in scenes where she takes the metro to and from university.

During these scenes the dynamic between haptic interior and exterior optical scenes is frequently blurred. External spaces, in which we are repeatedly shown the touching of hands or bare skin, are filmed using 'haptic' techniques in order to emphasise the intersubjective relationship between individuals. These moments prove crucial to Laura's ability to find an in-between space away from the constraints which structure her everyday life. In the five scenes of Laura in the metro, she gradually moves from shyness and hostility to taking pleasure in being among a crowd. The camera emphasises the different lives of those around her, all headed to and from Paris for a variety of purposes. During her first journey she stares out the window with the camera directly behind her. The train is in darkness in a tunnel and external lights reveal the scratches on the window. As the train surfaces overground the darkness changes to a bright white light outside. The next shot appears to be two arms at an angle, followed by two hands grasping the pole, both shots filling the screen. The camera lingers on the passengers in close-up, each absorbed in their own activity or inner worlds. Laura is not centred on screen, and we can pick her out among them, seated next to the window, simply one of the crowd. She smiles at the small child next to her. Her temporary loss of self in these scenes is an important step in letting go of her commitment to live 'like clockwork' and her attempts to distance herself from the world.

This scene is repeated later on, with the train busy and Laura standing up. She closes her eyes and seems relaxed. There is a power cut, and a hand reaches out to hers. It is Djamel. In a close-up shot lasting nearly twenty seconds, their fingertips meet and caress around the pole. The unsteady camera lingering on the surface of the hands emulates the sensation of touch. Touching hands is a metaphor Merleau-Ponty used to describe the point of interchange between subject and object: 'a reversibility of the seeing and the visible, of the touching and the touched' (Merleau-Ponty 1968: 147). Coincidence between the two can never be achieved as it is impossible to be subject and object simultaneously. In *The Second Sex* Beauvoir takes this 'lack' to be the basis for a positive ethics, when she describes the ideal relationship of 'reciprocity' between subjects: 'The conflict can be overcome by the free recognition of each individual in the other, each one positing both itself and the other as object and as subject in a reciprocal movement' (Beauvoir 2009: 163). This is not easily accomplished, and, as in the case above, often requires an erotic context to achieve 'the keenest consciousness of the other and the self' (Beauvoir 2009: 426). Beauvoir links this intersubjectivity to freedom, since it is only with the presence of the other that my freedom can be confirmed. The other person must be 'present to himself: that is, true alterity is a consciousness separated from my own and identical to it' (Beauvoir 2009: 163). It is here that temporality takes on an important role, since the relationship of reciprocity and generosity requires a constant effort to 'renounce possession', which is 'a struggle endlessly begun, endlessly abolished' (Beauvoir 2009: 163).

This underlines the importance of movement to the narrative and to the cinematographic style. Laura moves between subject positions just as she travels between Sarcelles and Paris. Marks argues that the haptic situates the viewer within 'an elastic, dynamic movement, not the rigid, all-or-nothing switch between an illusion of self-sufficiency and a realisation of absolute lack' (Marks 2000: 163). Through the haptic, the viewer experiences a similar shift in subjectivity which parallels Laura's movement from detachment to recognising her situatedness. At the start the film fails to provide a contrasting temporal ambiguity. The narrative is set largely in the present tense, without reference to past or future events, and Albou repeats certain shots and spaces in order to emphasise the contained and ritualised nature of Laura's existence. However, as the film progresses certain objects or events interrupt the present-tense narrative and the viewer is forced to re-contextualise their knowledge.

When Laura is on her walks around Sarcelles the same framing of shots is used each time, and only the light changes – a technique which Albou compares in the director's commentary to Monet's repetition of subject and form. The presence of the Orthodox Jewish population in Sarcelles juxtaposes high modernism with ancient modes of dress and behaviour. In spite of this contrast the family's presence in Sarcelles is not explained. Early on there is a scene in which the mother and Mathilde speak about Ariel in Arabic. He asks Laura for a translation, but she only knows a few Arabic words. This complex dynamic between French, Hebrew and Arabic at the dinner table is not explained to the viewer, and so this personal history is erased within the narrative. We never learn the mother's name, and despite her poignant attachment to old photographs, her history is largely untold. Instead of these personal histories the daily rituals of the family and Laura of dinner, prayer, *mikveh*, walks and metro are a collective present tense which mask the past.

The objects which intrude upon this temporality are all again linked to the body. The blond hair found by Mathilde on her husband Ariel's trousers confirms suspicions which are never articulated; instead we are shown repeated scenes of their platonic bedtime routine. The pearl necklace received by Laura in a letter suggests that her relationship with Djamel is at a far further stage than we have witnessed, seeing them so far only as strangers who make eye contact. They situate the body within a specific moment and yet leave a trace which brings together past and future. The hair is brazenly open in comparison to Mathilde's hair-covering, the necklace breaks as Laura writhes with it on her bed, and the wedding ring given from the mother to Laura was hidden from corrupt authorities in her bra and produced at dinner one night. These objects force the viewer to recreate the past but also for the characters they act as catalysts for the future as Mathilde seeks help, Laura initiates her sexual relationship with Djamel, and the mother gives Laura the ring to finance her dream of a studio in Paris.

In the final scene Laura breaks out of her routine and moves towards the future. She is shown standing still on a walkway which takes passengers through a long tunnel in the Paris metro. She is not walking, but is nonetheless being carried along towards her direction. Her family have left Sarcelles for Israel after a number of anti-Semitic attacks on the community, and Laura is about to realise her dream of living independently in a studio apartment in Paris. This dual migration out of Sarcelles parallels the mother's own emigration from Tunisia in the 1960s, and Laura's new independence will be financed by her mother's wedding ring. The ambiguity of Laura in the present is made into a metaphor by the automated walkway. Can we detect a willed movement or is she simply being carried along in the moment? The question reflects the ambiguity between subjectivity and temporality through which freedom and meaning are created. Even if her freedom is temporarily achieved, Beauvoir stresses that for the subject to be indeed free such a goal 'must appear to me as a point of departure toward a new act of surpassing' (Beauvoir 1976: 27). Laura's journey cannot be seen as an end, and for this to take place a sense of temporal ambiguity between present and future must continually be re-asserted, just as the reciprocal relationship between self and other is also a permanent struggle.

Although this may seem disheartening, since freedom is a value forever postponed, it is counterbalanced by the way in which Beauvoir conceives of failure. As Langer points out, in Beauvoir's writings the notion of failure is ambiguous. Whereas for Sartre it is characteristic of the 'inevitable failure' to attempt to synthesise our subject and object positions, Beauvoir emphasises that failure involves making ethical choices and justifications (Langer 2003: 91). This is shown to be the case in a number of situations within the narrative. For example, Laura's walks, which are initially a method of suppressing her embodied nature, lead her to Djamel. Likewise, her lectures on Kant means that she leaves Sarcelles regularly, unlike her family who are not pictured outside of domestic and religious contexts. Her studies equip her to give philosophy lessons and meet Eric, a potential suitor. Lastly, after her relationship with Djamel ends, Laura attempts suicide and her family recognise her will to live independently. Albou therefore sets up a number of paradoxes where Laura's attempts at detached contemplation fail, yet through making decisions and taking action, they nonetheless bring about new relationships with others and with the world.

The film seems to assert its own ideology in the presentation of Laura moving away from her own constraints and towards freedom, which for Albou also implies a necessary separation between Laura and her family. Laura is the only character to stay behind in France, and as Tarr suggests, the film 'perhaps unwittingly, offers the prospect of integration only to the individual who chooses to abandon both family and community' (Tarr 2009: 84). Despite troubling the ideological boundaries of one character, the film arguably equally seems to take a political position in its presentation of a minority community in relation to Paris. Yet at the same time, a Beauvoirian reading of the 'haptic' cinematography and of the relationship between Sarcelles and Paris as they are presented in the film recognises the parallel relationship between individual and collective self–other relations, and so acts as a counterpoint to accusations of heavy-handedness or political dichotomies.

Indeed the film itself evokes a wide range of ideological oppositions: Mathilde is caught between religion and sexuality, whereas Laura is torn by her commitment to Kantian philosophy and her lived experience. The sisters themselves form a contrasting pair of traditional and modern lives, and both are struggling to negotiate their sexual desires with their idea of themselves. Djamel is a political refugee yet must accept the conservatism of his Muslim family and reject Laura, and Ariel is a pious man who makes the decisions for the family, yet who has betrayed his wife's trust. Although the emphasis on oppositions reinforces the idea of the film's narrative dualisms as 'natural' this wealth of tensions also arguably helps to give a more nuanced picture of the *banlieues* than is often the case. Each position is an attempt to negotiate between body and world, and yet in each case a particular ideology, whether Orthodox Jewish, Muslim or secular, intervenes in the relationship. However, each character must reconsider their own relationship to their body before engaging with the ideologies which constrain them, a process which recognises the situated nature of subjectivity, and which is reinforced through the 'haptic' cinematography which invites the viewer to do the same.

The idea of an embodied viewing position has been particularly relevant to French cinema's attempt to represent lives at the margins of society without fetishizing difference. As Beugnet writes, 'where cinema becomes a cinema of sensation, the questioning about identity and otherness is evoked not merely in narrative and representational terms, but through the very texture of the films' (Beugnet 2007: 125). Laura's journey between Sarcelles and her university involves a continual movement between the marginalised space of the *banlieues* and Paris. Beugnet summarises the distinctions between *banlieue* and Paris in representation through the crossing of the *périphérique*, the motorway which divides historic Paris from the wider Île-de-France region. This 'signals the passage from "normal" life to social, economic and mental alienation, from the land of the living to a kind of purgatory' (Beugnet 2004: 290). The *banlieues* and their inhabitants are contextualised through oppositional discourses in relation to Paris and both sites have transcended their material situations to become ideological constructs in relation to one another. As Beauvoir identified, this tendency is part of a specific historical context and yet also relates to a universal self–other distinction whose pattern originates in consciousness: 'The category of *Other* is original as consciousness itself ... alterity is the fundamental category of human thought' (Beauvoir 2009: 6). What distinguishes Albou's film from the genre of *banlieue* cinema, a body of films inaugurated by Kassovitz's *La Haine* (1995) concentrating on the marginalisation of those living in France's poorer districts, is that the Orthodox Jewish community depicted in Sarcelles are shown to desire their own separateness by observing strict religious and social practices. The fact of asserting this difference has political consequences when situated in relation to the ideology of French Republicanism, which opposes such distinctions in favour of assimilation and unity.

La Petite Jérusalem portrays ideologies in a dualistic manner in its consideration of the impact of religious and secular beliefs on the everyday life of Laura and Mathilde. Yet this is problematised by the ways in which the narrative, cinematography and spatial relations in the film all overcome tensions between self and other and between social spaces through an emphasis on the body as a situated, contingent perspective on the world. Albou uses haptic cinematography to expose the ambiguous relationship between self and other in moments which are both a parenthesis in the narrative and a catalyst for Laura's reconsidered idea of herself. That such scenes take place on repeated journeys between the *banlieues* and Paris brings together these two spaces which are frequently set up as symbolising opposing political ideas. A Beauvoirian reading of the film recognises that the ideological and social boundaries it presents are a reflection of its situatedness in a specific historical and cultural context.

La Petite Jérusalem offers a convincing portrayal of the ambiguous relationship between perception and situation and enacts this through the cinematography, which invites the viewer to adopt a situated viewing position. The film uses the individual struggle of Laura as a metaphor for how ideology must be seen in terms of its lived experience, and this demonstrated through its portrayal of Laura's repeated movements between *banlieues* and Paris. Albou therefore effectively communicates the relationship between ambiguity and freedom through narrative and cinematography and suggests, following Beauvoir's philosophy of ambiguity, that it is impossible to separate freedom from intersubjective ambiguity.

Notes

1. Albou states in a 2009 interview with Esther: 'I am French or Arab-Jew or whatever (I don't know exactly what I am!)'.
2. The César awards are the French national film awards, chosen by an academy of film professionals.
3. A term referring to communities within France whose identity is apparently based on ethnicity or culture, in contrast to French Republician values of universalism and secularism.

Bibliography

Beauvoir, S. de. [1948] 1976. *The Ethics of Ambiguity*, trans. B. Frechtman. New York: Citadel Press.
———. [1949] 2009. *The Second Sex*, trans. C. Borde and S. Malovany-Chevallier. London: Jonathan Cape.
Beugnet, M. 2004. 'French Cinema at the Margins', in E. Ezra (ed.), *European Cinema*. Oxford: Oxford University Press, pp. 282–99.
———. 2007. *Cinema and Sensation: French Film and the Art of Transgression*. Edinburgh: Edinburgh University Press.
Chrisafis, A. 2006. 'Jewish Attacks Hint at Deep Malaise'. *The Guardian*, 21 March. Retrieved 29 May 2010 from http://www.guardian.co.uk/world/2006/mar/21/france.angeliquechrisafis1

Esther, J. 2009. 'Exclusive Interview: Karin Albou.' Retrieved 3 January 2011 from http://jestherent.blogspot.com/2009/11/exclusive-interview-karin-albou.html

Hiller, J. 2006. 'Movies That Bang: La Petite Jérusalem.' Retrieved 29 May 2010 from http://bangitout.com/reviews119.html

Langer, M. 2003. 'Beauvoir and Merleau-Ponty on Ambiguity', in C. Card (ed.), *The Cambridge Companion to Simone de Beauvoir*. Cambridge: Cambridge University Press, pp. 87–106.

Marks, L. 2000. *The Skin of the Film: Intercultural Cinema, Embodiment, and the Senses*. Durham: Duke University Press.

Merleau-Ponty, M. [1964] 1968. *The Visible and the Invisible*, trans. A. Lingis. Illinois: Northwestern University Press.

Moi, T. 1992. 'Ambiguity and Alienation in *The Second Sex*', *Boundary 2*, 19(2): 96–112.

Tarr, C. 2009. 'Community, Identity and the Dynamics of Borders in Yasmina Yahiaoui's *Rue des Figuiers* (2005) and Karin Albou's *La Petite Jérusalem* (2006)', *International Journal of Francophone Studies* 12(1): 77–90.

Filmography

Albou, K. (dir.). 2005. *La Petite Jérusalem*. Gloria Films. Film par Film.

7

'How Am I Not Myself?'
Engaging Ambiguity in David O. Russell's
I ♥ Huckabees

Bradley Stephens

I ♥ Huckabees (2004),[1] directed and co-written by David O. Russell, wants to engage its audience with the dilemmas of contingent being that Beauvoir herself explored over half a century earlier in her essay *The Ethics of Ambiguity* (1947). The film's reflections on the isolating and bewildering effects of modern living mirror Beauvoir's own insights into how we are alone in the world and exist without guarantees. A comparative reading of Russell's film and Beauvoir's essay reminds us of the ongoing relevance of Beauvoir's ethical thinking towards how we relate to ourselves and to our world, especially following the 'big September thing' as one character in *Huckabees* puts it with reference to September 11. Both the film and Beauvoir embrace ambiguity so as to disassemble supposedly unchanging and self-evident ways of being in favour of a more dynamic existence. For Beauvoir, such an embrace is an inherent aspect of human consciousness. As self-aware entities, our existence is incapable of being fixed into a determined state. 'The original scheme of man is ambiguous' (1976: 23): he yearns to disclose the meaning of his world and at the same time seeks to give that space his own meaning. At once embodied and self-conscious, he is both object and subject of his world without being able to unite those two modes of being into a self-enclosed and unmistakable whole. Embracing the ambiguity of such an indeterminate existence becomes imperative to the ethics of individual responsibility that Beauvoir constructs out of her existentialist thinking. This ambiguity enables her to access a logic of responsibility and reciprocity rather than one of a single all-determining power.

> The fact is that no behaviour is ever authorised to begin with, and one of the concrete consequences of existentialist ethics is the rejection of all the previous justifications which might be drawn from civilisation, the age, and the culture: it is the rejection of every principle of authority.
>
> (Beauvoir 1976: 142)

Huckabees demonstrates an obvious sympathy for this kind of spirited rejection of absolutes so as to respect our fundamental freedom as individuals. The film obliges both its characters and its audience to assemble meaning without any sense of closure and to understand experience 'all along the road', to borrow Beauvoir's metaphor (1976: 153), rather than rely on fixed ideas of how we should behave as individuals.

Equally, as what Russell describes as his 'existential comedy',[2] the film returns us to a tricky dilemma at the heart of Beauvoir's ethics. In resisting what Beauvoir calls the spirit of seriousness that perceives the world in definitive and therefore reductive terms, how do we avoid lapsing into the opposite spirit of the absurd when searching for answers to how we should live? Beauvoir's response is to reject absurdity outright: 'To declare that existence is absurd is to deny that it can ever be given a meaning; to say that it is ambiguous is to assert that its meaning is never fixed, that it must be constantly won. Absurdity challenges every ethics' (1976: 129). But *Huckabees* is something of a farcical film that does not entirely do away with the absurd when thinking about how and why we act. The film makes undeniable use of narrative irony and dramatic silliness. In so doing, it raises intriguing questions as regards the refusal of absurdity that an ethics of ambiguity demands.

In the film, a young poet-activist called Albert Markovski (Jason Schwartzman) seeks the help of a detective agency unlike any other. After becoming concerned that a series of chance encounters involving a Sudanese doorman hold some secret to the meaning of his life, the dainty Albert hires Bernard and Vivian Jaffe (Dustin Hoffman and Lily Tomlin): a pair of married metaphysicians known as the 'Existential Detectives', who intrusively investigate every element of their clients' lives in order to 'dismantle' their reality. They urge their clients to collapse their self-centred lives and recognise an infinite connection between all existence. In Albert's case, they pair him with another of their confused clients who they see as his 'Other', a disillusioned burly fire-fighter named Tommy Corn (Mark Wahlberg), and trace much of his anxiety back to his escalating conflict with Brad Stand (Jude Law). Brad is a flashy executive climbing the corporate ladder at Huckabees, the 'everything store' that is seeking to acquire local woodland for a new retail site. This move initially outrages the environmental coalition that Albert chairs, but Brad uses his charm to win over many members. He also tries to outdo the easily excited Albert further by hiring the Jaffes for himself, only for them to dig deeper into his ambition and explode the picture-perfect existence that he shares with the 'face of Huckabees', the model Dawn Campbell (Naomi Watts). Meanwhile, the Jaffes' former student Caterine Vauban (Isabelle Huppert) arrives to discredit her tutors' positive search for 'interconnectivity' by seducing Albert and Tommy with a nihilistic view of their hardships. But as their desire for meaning gives way to the despair of meaninglessness, the fallout yields unexpected results. Albert and Tommy begin to see that these two impulses towards fullness and emptiness ironically demand as much as deter one another, discovering that the answers are neither fully reassuring nor entirely dispiriting.

Albert ends where he began, in the woodland he is trying to save from the Huckabees corporation, with the frame dissolving back into the unfocused wash of colours that opened the film. The implied cycle does not close, however, and the return to a blurred screen offers a visual suggestion of what Albert has come to realise: nothing remains in clear focus forever, and our existence is indeterminate. As he tells Tommy, he will not be 'getting off the ride', since our efforts at giving meaning to our world are as ongoing as his environmental campaign.

Huckabees marketed itself as 'a film about what it's all about', and the verbal punning of this tagline indicates the kind of intelligent mischievousness at work throughout. The film is motivated by an unremitting spirit of playfulness that only ever offers multiple answers rather than any definitive and singular response. The film's very title smacks of perplexity rather than clarification even before any viewing has commenced, confirming its referential ambiguity. The icon of the heart in the film's title mirrors the famous slogan printed across countless T-shirts available to tourists in New York City, implying a thematic concern with potentially contrary feelings of escape and belonging; similarly, the name 'Huckabees' alludes to a political bent by calling to mind Mike Huckabee, who was the Republican governor of Arkansas at the time of the film's release. Nevertheless, the title is never referred to in the film itself, leaving us to gauge its potential meanings for ourselves. Beyond this curious title, we are drawn further into uncertainty by the formative opening scenes. Setting an inquisitive tone, Albert asks himself 'what am I doing?', only to reply 'I don't know what I'm doing'. Albert's self-questioning marks our point of entry, thereby shaping our relationship to the film. His monologue about his own purpose comes from off-screen, as the blank frame comes to focus on the woodland he is defending. His voice is disembodied, giving it a narrative character that the audience themselves process as a personal stream of thought. From there, the camera follows Albert in his journey through a maze of corridors in a commercial building as he searches for the Jaffes' offices. This uninterrupted tracking shot, combined with Albert's puzzled yet determined expressions and the introduction of the title credits, establishes the impression of a labyrinthine journey of discovery that will typify the film to come. Moreover, the fact that he is looking for a pair of detectives is markedly ironic. His own detective work, following directions on a slip of paper, has brought him to yet another stage of detection, leaving us with the inkling that Albert's quest will be neither quick nor self-sufficient. Subsequent point-of-view shots during Albert's dream sequences whilst in therapy with Bernard Jaffe, themselves accompanied by his off-screen voice, confirm that this character and his investigation are integral to our encounter with the film, not least since the camera never aligns itself with another character's point of view.

If Albert's expletive-ridden outbursts at the start subtly revise the classic philosophical question 'who am I?', it is perhaps Brad Stand's own moment of self-reflection that best channels the film's restlessly investigative nature. During a defiant encounter with the Jaffes, he asks: 'How am I not myself?' His dismissive tone reveals that this is initially nothing more than a rhetorical question in his view. To the golden boy of Huckabees, with his hair as blond as his skin is tanned and his eyes as blue as the sharp suits he sports, the idea that he may not entirely identify with his prosperous existence is ridiculous. Yet the almost choral repetition of this supposedly simple question by the Jaffes soon erodes Brad's self-certainty, provoking an emotional breakdown that costs him his professional reputation. The audience is subtly persuaded to recognise the validity of this self-negation by the well-known English actor Jude Law's portrayal of the American high-flyer, since such casting suggests that Brad is himself a performed identity rather than an authentic person. The negation inherent in Brad's question is no accident, sharpening the critical edge of the questions Albert poses at the start. In effect, his question accentuates the self-alienation that characterises both the Jaffes' and Vauban's methods as a some-what paradoxical means towards a more authentic sense of self. Like Albert and Tommy, Brad comes to understand that the ways in which we may not be who we think we are opens up fresh possibilities for our future.

These philosophical ideas about identity, otherness and human interaction have prompted numerous references to French existentialist thinking in critics' reviews. Although other elements of modern French culture are evident and reveal a broader Gallic influence on Russell's thinking,[3] it is Jean-Paul Sartre who in general is most often cited as the main philosophical reference point, given the existentialist overtones of the film (Garrett 2005; Queenan 2004). An emphasis on self-negation as a key to self-affirmation, not to mention a critical attitude towards the cultural conformism and environmentally destructive consumerism of western society, yields clear connections with the 'pope' of existentialism. Yet the connections between *Huckabees* and Beauvoir seem equally fruitful, if to date overlooked. The looks of Vivian Jaffe and Caterine Vauban both evoke a 1950s continental style often associated with Beauvoir, not to mention the fact that Vauban is a Parisian philosopher played by a French actress who is renowned for the intelligence of her performances.[4] Moreover, the amorous relationship between the Jaffes and Vauban, which Albert suspects may lie in their shared history, resembles the notoriously unconventional private lives of Beauvoir and Sartre at the core of their so-called 'family' of lovers in post-war Paris.

These cultural markers aside, the most interesting connections between Beauvoir and *Huckabees* run at the deeper level of sharing the same conceit. The ideas that the film raises undeniably chime with Beauvoir's existentialist conviction that the individual is the agent of his or her own self-conscious being, and must take responsibility for that existence through an engaged attitude towards both his or her own agency and that of other subjects. In particular, Beauvoir believes that the lack of determinism in human existence enriches rather than impoverishes the meanings we give to life, and her ideas enhance the dynamic approach towards existence that *Huckabees* enacts. The question 'how am I not myself?' reveals itself as a key philosophical strategy that is reminiscent of the ways in which Beauvoir frees up and engages multiple modes of being as the only authentic ethical response to a contingent universe. Her conception of existence in *The Ethics of Ambiguity*, like that of *Huckabees*, relies on the undetermined, rather than the unambiguous, in order to understand the human condition as one of perpetual *becoming* as opposed to definitive *being*. 'To exist is to *make oneself* a lack of being; it is to *cast* oneself into the world' (1976: 42). Beauvoir refigures the notion of being in existential rather than essential terms so as to identify an ethical response to a Godless world in which existence precedes essence. The human individual is an embodied consciousness, aware of its own physical presence as a body and yet not fully identical with that physicality precisely because of being self-aware. This consciousness is caught in traction between the material mode of being-in-itself and the mindful mode of being-for-itself. It always strives (but necessarily fails) to fuse these two modes of being together into an absolute state of self-coincidence. Human consciousness acknowledges its own lack of essential being and desires a concrete nature for itself, but is forever prised loose from such fixity by its own self-awareness. It is this tension which liberates us from any fixed nature and grants us our freedom as self-determining entities: 'Man's being is lack of being, but this lack has a way of being which is precisely existence' (1976: 13).

Strictly speaking, insists Beauvoir, we therefore cannot *be* anything in a world that lacks pre-determination. On the contrary, the human individual is 'that being whose being is not to be' (1976: 10), seemingly anticipating Brad's self-questioning; 'in construction, as in rejection, it is a matter of reconquering freedom on the contingent facticity of existence' (1976: 156), resembling the eventual interaction between the Jaffes' essentialism and Vauban's nihilism. For Beauvoir, such absolutes of idealism and nihilism are suspect in their refusal of indeterminacy. 'That is why it is incumbent upon ethics not to follow the line of least resistance', compelling existentialist philosophy to renounce such straightforward directions in the search for answers as to how we should live (1976: 154). Categorical notions of identity must be problematised or 'othered' in order to prevent the human being from attaining what is ultimately a misleading sense of stasis and plenitude. In turn, we develop a personal attachment not only to our own existence but also to that of others. We find solidarity in our mutual alienation from essential being: we realise that neither of these sentiments of connection or isolation can ever win out (1976: 158), hence the need to engage with existence in a mobile and unrestricted manner.

What is at work here is what Christina Howells, when reading Sartre, has usefully identified as a 'transformative logic' (1988: 201). Such logic is integral when Beauvoir refuses any synthesis of, or exit from, the tensions between conscious and pure being.

> Rather than being a Hegelian act of surpassing, it is a matter of conversion. For in Hegel the surpassed terms are preserved only as abstract moments, whereas we consider that existence still remains a negativity in the positive affirmation of itself. To attain his truth, man must not attempt to dispel the ambiguity of his being but, on the contrary, accept the task of realising it.
>
> (Beauvoir 1976: 13)

Both Cartesian dualism and modernist absurdity, themselves reflective of the Jaffes and Vauban respectively, are rejected in favour of a more interactive and less categorical relationship between the subjective and objective modes. Neither consciousness nor physicality can be privileged over one another, any more than they can be neatly joined together. For Beauvoir, the closest we can come to transcending such difference is by entering into it whilst always seeking an impossible exit. In turn, she evaluates any struggle to reconcile subject and object (and, by extension, self and other) as worthwhile, noting however that 'a conquest of this kind is never finished' (1976: 157). Beauvoir reiterates that the individual need not choose somehow between 'the contingent absurdity of the discontinuous and the rationalistic necessity of the continuous' (1976: 122). The point, rather, is to multiply the possibilities open to the self whilst at the same time recognising these ensembles as part of the desire for an idealised certainty of being. Such an outlook on human experience anticipates Albert's own realisation that the restless negotiation of our experiences, and not some complacent resolution of them, is the only authentic way to exist. As Russell argues in his commentary on the film: 'It's about which side you're on: the nihilist side, the Isabelle Huppert side, the chaos side; or are you on the more affirmative, connected side? And of course, ultimately, they are part of one position, because you can't really reside in either one and still remain human'. This respect for the complexity which makes us human is why Beauvoir believes the notion of ambiguity must be rescued from its relegated place in traditional philosophy as an illogical flaw.

Just as Beauvoir urges us to 'assume our fundamental ambiguity' (1976: 9), so do Albert and Tommy therefore come to believe that human subjectivity and material objectivity cannot ignore one another. Where the Jaffes teach them to refigure their perspectives on the world in an endless kaleidoscope of imagined connections, clearly exercising their being-for-itself, Vauban pulls them back from such self-reflexive approaches into an immanent physical mode of being-in-itself. To prove that the indifference of material existence is inevitable, she callously engineers an arson attack on Brad's house, so as to free Albert from any moral illusions as to the nature of 'pure' being. But this moment, itself coinciding with Brad's breakdown, is revelatory. Albert sees himself in Brad's crying face, believing that there is a connection between them after all through their shared self-alienation. Vauban intended the fire to liberate Albert from Brad, but instead it touchingly bonds the two in what Albert calls the 'insanity of pain'. Albert joyously affirms that his warring mentors espouse 'two overlapping, fractured philosophies'. When isolated, these philosophies are either 'too dark' or 'not dark enough', but when brought to bear upon one another they prove more vigorous as a way of living with both self-respect and respect for the other.

Albert's and Brad's final confrontation in a hotel lift at that afternoon's Huckabees fundraiser reiterates how this interaction of difference leads to more fruitfully interactive human relationships. The scene begins with a medium close-up accentuating the characters' differences. The small, dark and unkempt Albert, wearing a cheap grey suit, contrasts against the tall, fair and well-groomed Brad in his tailored sky-blue shirt. But the subsequent fisticuffs momentarily force these opposites together as they pull one another to the floor. The two men mimic one another's enraged gestures as they fight, eventually slumping against the wall at the same height and in the same pose on screen. Calling a truce, Albert gives Brad Vauban's card and advises he temporarily leave the Jaffes. Albert knows from experience that Brad must pass through Vauban's lessons as well if he is to make sense of his heartache. Symbolically, Brad has also now shifted from his usually central, sometimes divisive, location in the middle of the frame to a less sovereign, more unfastened position towards the edges of the screen. The film subsequently closes with Albert and Tommy discussing how the Jaffes' constructivist method and Vauban's nihilist approach only work best when they engage one another in our efforts at self-knowledge. Tellingly completing one another's sentences, Albert and Tommy agree: 'The interconnection thing is definitely for real. It's so fantastic! But it's also nothing special, because it grows from the manure of human trouble. The detectives just wanted to gloss right over that; but in fact, no manure, no magic.' As the dissolving visuals and narrative thrust suggest, this is not however an endpoint, but a fresh beginning.

Just as Brad asks how he is not himself, so too does the film throw itself into question. It pluralises its own meanings up until and beyond this finish, thereby confirming that its underlying philosophy is one of contrast, not uniformity. To the soundtrack of composer Jon Brion's whimsical score flitting between quirky overtures and wistful signatures throughout, the audience must continue to negotiate an indeterminate relationship between the Jaffes' 'cool' notion that essential truth connects us all and Vauban's opposite resolve that we must 'deconstruct our mind to the blackness'. We are required to remain engaged with the film as with our own existence, and such engagement remains at once resistant to fixity and yet reactive to the demand for meaning. To this end, *Huckabees* repeatedly questions the boundary between what we see and what is real. The film exhibits an anxiety towards what Russell believes to be the 'please don't ask questions' culture of conservative western society, which he argues encourages certainties based purely on pre-determined concepts of knowledge, especially fantasies or fears of security. Such fantasies smack of existentialist bad faith: the ways in which we deceive ourselves by pretending that our existence is entirely fixed in what Beauvoir calls an 'infantile' manner (1976: 37). Key to this spirit of scrutiny is the film's visual aesthetic, encouraging us to look closely at what occurs. Cinematographer Peter Denning's use of light and production designer K.K. Barrett's use of space creates a bright, open world where nothing is hidden from our gaze and where evasion seems impossible. All the interior locations, from the Jaffes' office to Brad's house, possess large windows that allow light to flood in to their clean and spacious rooms, whereas the use of tall glass panels acting as partitions between the Huckabees offices opens up the space of the frame more evidently still through their transparency. This consistent exposure leaves the viewer with the sense that there is nowhere to hide from the film's searching gaze, especially since the cover of night is never allowed to materialise. Exterior location shots either take place bathed in flat daylight, or under a softer light suggestive of the transitional moments of dawn or dusk, which are themselves symbolic of the changes in perception that the film asks of us.

The character of the blonde model Dawn offers an excellent illustration of how the film encourages us to scrutinise what we assume is real, indicating its antagonism towards a culture of self-righteousness and patriarchal authority (embodied by several peripheral characters, including Albert's parents). When we first see Dawn, she is an image in one of Albert's Jaffe-induced daydreams who demands that he (and, by implication of the point-of-view shot, we) stop looking at her. Yet in several early scenes, Dawn is always catching our eye in the seemingly endless publicity commercials and posters which bear her image around the Huckabees offices. She is a represented object rather than an actual presence: her appearances in this commercialised form signal a culture whose reality lacks authenticity, and in which image is everything.[5] Dawn is in fact the object of the film's first close-up shot during an advertisement video. Whereas this technique is more usually deployed to suggest psychological realism, here Dawn is rendered yet more artificial by her theatrical nature. Her forced wide eyes and abundant smiling match her exaggerated manoeuvres as she recycles elements of the American national anthem for Huckabees' publicity slogans. Bedecked in top hat and tails coloured in red, white and blue, her appearance and manner are more befitting of a circus act or magician's assistant than Uncle Sam, and create a telling visual association of American identity with perform-ance and illusion. The replication of her image into three symmetrical clones on screen stresses her objectification through the ease of its reproducibility, whilst the empty white background of the video enhances this effect through its capacity for projection. Given that this sequence includes the film's first close-up, the audience is encouraged to recognise the emptiness of the image and the absence of a more immediate and embodied way of being. Even in such close proximity, Dawn remains an object to behold, and only when she is removed from the commercial image by the Jaffes is she able to develop a more personal identity. The cameo appearance of the singer Shania Twain during Albert's and Brad's lift confrontation stresses this questioning of image and reality yet again. Herself only seen as a Huckabees publicity image or talked about in one of Brad's self-promoting stories up until this point, the singer here appears in the flesh to berate Brad for his scheming. Not by coincidence, she seizes the central position within the frame that had been Brad's standard domain, emphasising the importance that the film lends to a more material, rather than solely visual or imagined, way of being.

Notwithstanding the feminist overtones of these two examples and how they might echo Beauvoir's call for femininity to be rescued from the objectified role of 'other', their comedic nature could be seen to diverge away from an ethics of ambiguity towards one of absurdity. This threat pervades the whole film, in that *Huckabees* incites us to ridicule the characters as much as sympathise with them. Albert's opening poem in his first scene is woefully kitsch in its simplistic language as he pays homage to a large rock in an effort to save the woodland around it: 'Nobody sits like this rock sits. You rock, rock!' When we learn that Albert's family name is in fact Silver and not Markovski, suggesting that he has changed his surname to pay homage to the famous Bulgarian poet, he appears to us as someone with an ambition to be something he is not, making his cause yet more embarrassing. Tommy equally has difficulty in coming to terms with himself and getting his message through to others. As he pleads with his wife Molly not to leave him, his thoughts come across as unnecessarily heavy-handed and the film denies him any audience admiration. Quoting dense phrases from Vauban's book, scaring his young daughter with tales of third-world sweatshops, and punching a colleague who tries to keep the peace, Tommy is overbearing. The muscular frame of actor Mark Wahlberg lends him a threatening air that is made all the more apparent by the fireman's boots that he always wears, as if dressed for combat. A confrontational dinner with the adoptive father of the Sudanese doorman and his religiously zealous nuclear family may evoke admiration for the non-conformist pair, especially as they boldly challenge the sickeningly smug family's beliefs. Flared tempers and amusingly offbeat one-liners ('You're the Hitler!') ensure, however, that these discussions seem more outrageous than serious. Afterwards, their exercise of smacking one another with a large inflatable red ball, as part of Vauban's lesson in abandoning emotion for 'pure' being, does little to restore solemnity. No character is immune from this sense of farce. Turning to the Jaffes, Dawn abandons her bikinis and make-up in favour of dungarees and Amish bonnets, filming a series of comically abstract advertisements about increased self-awareness. Similarly, the Jaffes' eccentricity makes it difficult for the audience to take them seriously. Vivian throws herself into the back of a car, leaps across lawn sprinklers, and dives into a wheelie bin as she carries out her investigations; Bernard seals his clients in giant body blankets for therapy sessions. The couple also revel in the 'Mancala Hour' that they organise for their depressive clients to drink cocktails and play board games. Their former student Vauban likewise suffers from moments of incredulity, not least when repeatedly plunging Albert's face into a mud pool before enjoying a bizarre outdoor sex romp.

Huckabees thereby destabilises the split between farce and earnestness as consciously as it blurs the divide between the Jaffes' and Vauban's philosophies, and such instability throws even further into question any final analyses we may seek to make. The danger here, from a Beauvoirian perspective, would be that the film is lost to the absurd through such farcical elements. Even after a second viewing, the respected film critic Roger Ebert (2004) offered 'a shiny new dime to anyone who can figure out what the joke is', whilst David Denby (2004) agreed that 'this authentic disaster' was too crowded and dense a film to be truly funny or smart. *Huckabees* is certainly problematic on both a narrative and dramatic level, with ideas that are more quick-firing than slow-burning and a characterisation that is sometimes thin. But within the interpretive context of Beauvoir's ethics, and despite the film's structural shortcomings,

Huckabees never confuses its own comedic moments with pure nonsense. To say that the film *is* ridiculous or even *is* serious is, in part, to work against its own posing of the question 'how am I not myself?', hence what Peter Travers (2004) identifies in his review as 'a philosopher's eye for absurdist humour' in the film. Both Ebert and Denby seem compelled to offer definitive readings which ignore the film's teasingly open-ended nature. In Russell's own opinion, if the ambiguity of our attempts to fit in to this world was to retain its power as a deeper meaning to human experience, then any spirit of seriousness needed to be kept well in check, marking a break with the sombre video documentaries of his early career. *Huckabees* invites us not to take it or ourselves too seriously, lest its own philosophical position would lose its dexterity and energy. 'You keep getting undermined in this movie,' Russell observes. 'If you're not laughing, you're not getting it', suggesting that the answers the film provides to the questions it poses are necessarily as comical as they are credible. Their meaning can only be determined in a subjective sense and lacks objective validation.

The film consequently forces the notion of existential ambiguity into a more intimate and even uncomfortable relationship with the absurd than might at first be apparent in Beauvoir's essay. Importantly, however, this relationship is not inconsistent with Beauvoir's ideas, even if her own writing lacks the blatant comedy of a film like *Huckabees*. Whilst a spirit of seriousness may be invited in the search for meaning, Beauvoir is clear in pointing out that it must not be allowed to take full hold, lest the 'subjective tension of freedom' is lost: 'The serious man puts nothing into question', as she notes, and 'keeps himself from existing because he is not capable of existing without a guarantee' (1976: 48–50). When the 'serious' individual opens their eyes to our indeterminate reality, such earnest worldviews fail, since 'the serious is one of those ways of trying to realise the impossible synthesis of the in-itself and the for-itself' (1976: 52). The threat of falling into nihilism emerges, of course, but itself only as yet another attempt at objectifying reality. 'The nihilist is close to the spirit of seriousness: he conceives his annihilation in a substantial way. He wants to *be* nothing' (1976: 52). The dynamism of ambiguity therefore needs to be considered on its own ever-shifting terms rather than within the fixed confines of an objective standpoint, so that the subject is sure 'to have given freedom a content without disavowing it' (1976: 55). This dynamism may be otherwise understood as 'an "ambiguity" of ambiguity in Beauvoir's ethics' (Card 2003: 4), through which ambivalence is not an object in itself, but a condition of existence.

If engaging in a mobile mode of being between the idealistic and the nihilistic means rejecting seriousness as much as affirming positive choice, then it follows that absurdity cannot be entirely removed from this existential dynamic of being. Any legitimacy of meaning must contend with the reality of meaninglessness in an endless but empowering dialogue which, according to Toril Moi, was an at once 'comforting and utterly daunting' aspect of Beauvoir's work in its refusal of clear-cut solutions to how we should live (Moi 1994: 257). This ambiguous relationship – less a balance than an interaction of opposing modes – has to maintain its volatility rather than be frozen into the kind of definitive analysis that Debra B. Bergoffen proposes, for example, when reading Beauvoir. For Bergoffen, pleasure, more than Sartrean angst, describes our feelings when confronted with our freedom. 'We are not condemned to be free; we take delight in our freedom. Further, my freedom marks a primordial relationship between myself and the other. Hell is not necessarily other people' (1995: 185). The danger lies in the binary opposition that Bergoffen relies on between anxiety and delight. Beauvoir engages a repeated cycle passing through the two states that will not cancel one opposite out, nor totalise the two into an ordered whole. We must not confuse the condition of being free for some objective or thing-like state: 'Freedom wills itself genuinely only by willing itself as an indefinite movement (…); as soon as it withdraws into itself, it denies itself on behalf of some object which it prefers to itself' (Beauvoir 1976: 90). To claim that Beauvoir focuses on delight rather than despair subsequently risks objectifying what is, in fact, a subjective experience of freedom, thereby limiting its capacity for self-determination.

Nowhere is this vibrant challenge to the 'seriousness' of objectivity more accessible for Beauvoir than in art, hence her attraction to writing (and, arguably, Russell's own interest as well). Where the philosophical essay could sketch out the dynamic ambiguity of being, the work of art could animate those same complexities and bring them to life. 'Art reveals the transitory as an absolute', Beauvoir argues: it qualifies itself and the world it depicts as a 'constructive activity' through its emphasis on creation and interpretation (1976: 80–81), ensuring that her own thinking would always remain open to transformation and never ossify in her successful literary career (Fallaize 1988: 7). As Beauvoir insists in her essay, 'existentialism does not offer to the reader the consolations of an abstract evasion [from indeterminism]: existentialism proposes no evasion'. The calmness she experiences when reading Hegel becomes merely 'the consolations of death' the moment she leaves the library: 'and again I wanted to live in the midst of living men' (1976: 158–59). If existentialism is a philosophy of ambiguity for Beauvoir, then the dramatic creativity of art indeed offered the necessarily supple framework in which to throw life's contrasts into sharper and more agile relief, enabling what might be called 'a developmental understanding of subjectivity' (Busch 2005: 178). Understanding philosophy in this responsive way has become increasingly important to film studies, where Daniel Shaw has argued for a more nuanced approach to the question of philosophy than that he sees in other film theorists such as Stephen Mulhall (2002). He notes that 'a film need not unequivocally answer the philosophical questions that it raises in order to be properly considered as [philosophical]' (Shaw 2008: 109): in other words, as 'something beyond mere argument and rather more of the nature of the discovery of the deepest and most difficult truths of human experience' (Carroll and Choi 2006: 384).[6]

It is on these terms, in a refusal of generic identity and consistent posture, that *Huckabees* reveals itself in fact to echo rather than quieten the kind of discourse on existential ambiguity that Beauvoir develops. Ultimately, the absurd remains under check rather than unconditional in the film. When using *The Ethics of Ambiguity* as a reference point, it becomes clear that a cinematic lightness of touch does not evacuate meaning from the film, and that its eccentricity should not be confused with silliness. Genre need not be overly deterministic: *Huckabees* should no more be categorised in absolute terms as being absurd than Beauvoir's bestselling *The Mandarins* (1954) be approached simply as a historical novel. *Huckabees* undercuts any positions it seemingly underpins, in order to reaffirm the dynamic premise which engages the ambiguity of its own philosophical view of life. The film obliges its audience to understand the process of being as a repeated and unavoidable engagement with indeterminism. As with the other so-called 'American Eccentrics' of filmmaking, such as Spike Jonze and Wes Anderson, Russell's feature films have used offbeat humour to probe a sense of estrangement in mavericks like Albert who try to make sense of the world.[7] The heavy repetition throughout the dialogue of questions such as 'what are you talking about?' and, more emphatically still, 'what the Hell does that mean?' enhances the film's obstinate will towards ongoing investigation rather than instant understanding. Likewise, this underlying will recalls Beauvoir's observation that any authentic answer to how we should exist 'does not furnish recipes' (1976: 134). The similarity to Beauvoir's thinking in turn lends *Huckabees* considerably more insight into human behaviour than reviewers like Ebert and Denby give credit for.[8] At the same time, I would suggest that the film prises open a productive role for humour that is not usually identified amidst the avowals and apprehensions of being in Beauvoir's work, but which can help propel our engagement with ambiguity all the same. This point could readily be downplayed in readings of Beauvoir's philosophy and literary writing, since neither sees Beauvoir engage with the absurd in as overt a manner as *Huckabees*. Nonetheless, the encounter between her essay and this film identifies a mutual resistance of both self-importance and meaninglessness, ethically rendering both different to themselves.

Notes

1. Herewith referred to as *Huckabees*.
2. All quotations are taken from Russell's audio commentary accompanying the 2005 DVD release.
3. Bernard Jaffe's descriptions of how to look at reality differently replicate a cubist aesthetic akin to Georges Braque's: they are accompanied by visual dissolves of the frame into a variety of floating particles that move above, and realign onto, the original image. The surrealist movement that succeeded cubism in Paris is also present in the bowler hat and melons seen in Jaffe's office, recalling Magritte's famous painting 'L'Homme au chapeau melon' ('The Man in the Bowler Hat').
4. For more on the kinds of rich screen roles that Huppert is associated with, see Ursula Tidd's discussion in this volume of the maternal bond in her recent films (chapter two).
5. Here, *Huckabees* could well be referencing Guy Debord's thinking on the prominence of the image as the principal determinant of reality (1994).

6. For more on the theoretical uses of ambiguity in filmmaking, see Murray Smith (2006).
7. Such dark humour is displayed in Russell's 1990s successes, such as the incestuous farce *Spanking the Monkey* (1994) and his war satire *Three Kings* (1999). His most recent film *The Fighter* (2010), however, turned towards mainstream drama, suggesting a new direction.
8. The Internet Movie Database (http://www.imdb.com/title/tt0356721/ratings) records that the film received a seven out of ten rating or higher by some 70 per cent of nearly 40,000 online reviewers, with younger audiences responding especially well.

Bibliography

Beauvoir, S. de. [1947] 1976. *The Ethics of Ambiguity*, trans. B. Frechtmann. New York: Citadel.

Bergoffen, D.B. 1995. 'Out from Under: Beauvoir's Philosophy of the Erotic', in M.A. Simons (ed.), *Feminist Interpretations of Simone de Beauvoir*. University Park: Pennsylvania State University Press, pp. 179–92.

Busch, T.W. 2005. 'Simone de Beauvoir on Achieving Subjectivity', in S.J. Scholz and S.M. Mussett (eds), *The Contradictions of Freedom: Philosophical Essays on Simone de Beauvoir's 'Les Mandarins'*. Albany: State University of New York Press, pp. 177–88.

Card, C. 2003. 'Introduction', in C. Card (ed.), *The Cambridge Companion to Simone de Beauvoir*. Cambridge: Cambridge University Press, pp. 1–23.

Carroll, N. and J. Choi. 2006. *Philosophy of Film and Motion Pictures: an Anthology*. Oxford: Blackwell.

Debord, G. [1967] 1994. *The Society of the Spectacle*, trans. D. Nicholson-Smith. New York: Zone.

Denby, D. 2004. 'Review of *I* ❤ *Huckabees*'. *New Yorker*, 11 October. Retrieved 20 March 2011 from http://www.newyorker.com/arts/reviews/film/i_heart_huckabees_russell

Ebert, R. 2004. 'Review of *I* ❤ *Huckabees*'. *Chicago Sun Times*, 8 October. Retrieved 20 March 2011 from http://rogerebert.suntimes.com/apps/pbcs.dll/article?AID=/20041007/REVIEWS/40920003/1023

Fallaize, E. 1988. *The Novels of Simone de Beauvoir*. London: Routledge.

Garrett, D. 2005. 'David Owen Russell's *I* ❤ *Huckabees*', *Offscreen* 9(1). Retrieved 20 March 2011 from http://www.offscreen.com

Howells, C. 1988. *Sartre: the Necessity of Freedom*. Cambridge: Cambridge University Press.

Moi, T. 1994. *Simone de Beauvoir: The Making of an Intellectual Woman*. Oxford: Blackwell.

Mulhall, S. 2002. *On Film: Thinking in Action*. London; New York: Routledge.

Queenan, J. 2004. 'Review of *I* ❤ *Huckabees*'. *The Guardian*, 27 November. Retrieved 20 March 2011 from http://www.guardian.co.uk/film/2004/nov/27/culture.features1

Shaw, D. 2008. *Film and Philosophy: Taking Films Seriously*. London; New York: Wallflower Press.

Smith, M. 2006. 'Film Art, Argument and Ambiguity', in M. Smith and T. Wartenberg (eds), 'Thinking Through Cinema: Film as Philosophy', *Journal of Aesthetics and Art Criticism* 64(1): 33–42.

Travers, P. 2004. 'Review of *I* ❤ *Huckabees*'. *Rolling Stone Magazine*. 30 September. Retrieved 20 March 2011 from http://www.rollingstone.com/movies/reviews/i-heart-huckabees-20041001

Filmography

Russell, D.O. (dir.). 1994. *Spanking the Monkey*. Fine Line Features.

———. 1999. *Three Kings*. Warner Brothers.

———. 2004. *I ♥ Huckabees*. Fox Searchlight Pictures.

———. 2010. *The Fighter*. Paramount Pictures.

8

ENCOUNTERS WITH THE 'THIRD AGE': BENGUIGUI'S *INCH'ALLAH DIMANCHE* AND BEAUVOIR'S *OLD AGE*

Michelle Royer

> In order to understand the meaning and the reality of old age we are therefore obliged to look into the place that has been allotted to the elderly and the image that has been formed of them, in different times and different places.
> (Beauvoir 1972: 37)

> One also begins to exist when one sees images of oneself.
> (Yamina Benguigui, interview with Yasmina Medani)

The topic of old age receives considerable attention from Simone de Beauvoir in her theoretical texts and in her autobiographies. She devotes a chapter of *The Second Sex* to maturity and old age, and an entire book, *Old Age* (*La Vieillesse*) to the question. Described as 'a fascinating work for readers familiar with *The Second Sex*' (Deutscher 2003: 289) *Old Age* revisits many of Beauvoir's themes from her earlier study and is similarly structured. Part I analyses old age from 'without' by focusing on biological, ethnological, historical and social perspectives. Part II is devoted to 'The being-in-the-world' and deals with the lived experience of old age. Beauvoir's interest in ageing arose from her recognition that the topic is taboo in a society that 'looks upon old age as a kind of shameful secret that it is unseemly to mention' (Beauvoir 1972: 1). Her book aims at breaking the 'conspiracy of silence' (Beauvoir 1972: 2) and at exposing the myths and clichés about ageing. Like *The Second Sex*, *Old Age* was prompted by personal experience: 'I was on the threshold of old age, and I wished to know the bounds and the nature of the aged state' (Beauvoir 1972: 147). Her study shows that old age is not a universal category and that to understand its meaning it is essential to consider how the individual's experience of ageing is always situated in a cultural, social, geographical and historical context. Women and men for example experience ageing differently because of their differing roles in patriarchal societies. Beauvoir also highlights the fact that class struggle informs the experience of ageing.

In *The Second Sex* her analysis of gender led her to conclude that woman is a cultural construct; similarly *Old Age* demonstrates that ageing 'is not solely a biological state but it is a cultural fact' (Beauvoir 1972: 13). Beauvoir argues that in western culture the aged are the Other of those who are economically active and there is a generational power relationship between the dominant group (young active men) and the oppressed (the aged): 'by the way in which a society behaves towards its old people it uncovers the naked, and often carefully hidden truth about its real principles and aims' (Beauvoir 1972: 87).

Beauvoir argues that 'old age is more apparent to others than to the subject himself' (Beauvoir 1972: 284), and that 'within me it is the Other – that is to say the person I am for the outsider – who is old: and that Other is myself' (Beauvoir 1972: 284). In other words, the old person has no choice but to eventually accept the Other's view of her as an old person. One of the more interesting aspects of Beauvoir's study is the challenge old age presents for existentialist philosophy: considering the lack of a future associated with ageing and its social and physical constraints, how is one to transcend limitations and engage in authentic projects? Is it a moral fault or in existentialist terms 'bad faith' to understand ageing as a loss of vitality, desire and physical abilities and as a result to restrict one's possibilities in the world or reduce one's life to repetitive tasks (Deutscher 2003: 290)? Deutscher (2003: 300) suggests that Beauvoir's study of old age is an important contribution to her philosophy because it has 'prompted her to rethink the adequacy of an account to which practical freedom may be limited, but ontological freedom is not'.

Films are valuable not only because they entertain us but 'because they cause us to reflect on issues that bear on the meaning of life' (Pamerleau 2009: 1). As mentioned earlier, Beauvoir has demonstrated the importance of focusing on lived experience to analyse old age. Yamina Benguigui's historical melodrama *Inch'Allah dimanche* (*Inch'Allah Sunday*, 2001) provides an excellent tool to investigate and discuss Beauvoir's theory of ageing, as it realistically portrays the experience of women in 1970s France in the migrant and host cultures, and how they dealt with intergenerational conflict. Through a contrasting examination of the relationship between the old and young generations, this chapter will use Beauvoirian theories of old age to provide a critical analysis of the filmmaker's cinematic representation of ageing women. Before we turn to the cinematic analysis, it will be useful to briefly situate the film within the context of Benguigui's body of works and contemporary cinema.

Yamina Benguigui is an important French film director from an Algerian background. She was born in Northern France and raised in an Islamic family in the 1960s. She received acclaim for her documentaries on immigration *Femmes d'Islam* (1994), and for *Mémoires d'immigrés, l'héritage maghrébin* (*Immigrant Memories: The North African Inheritance*, 1997), a 160-minute documentary, the result of 350 interviews conducted across France with North African immigrants, policy makers and industrialists. *Mémoires d'immigrés*, which was the first filmic transgenerational reconstruction of over thirty years of labour migration, was broadcast on television and received the 'Sept d'or'

(French television award) for best documentary as well as several other film awards. The film was hailed as *the* testimony on immigration.

Inch'Allah dimanche is Benguigui's first fiction film; it has been very well received inside and outside of France and has won a variety of awards at international film festivals, including the top prize at the Marrakech International Film Festival, the FIPRESCI Award at the Toronto Film Festival and the Audience Prize and Golden Wave Winner at the Bordeaux International Festival for Women in Cinema. The film has touched migrant communities in France, and has attracted considerable attention from film scholars in Europe, Britain and the United States.

Benguigui's films have been associated with *cinéma beur* or *cinéma de banlieue*, terms which describe 'a set of independently released films by and about the *beurs*, that is, second-generation immigrants of Maghrebi descent' (Tarr 2005: 2). Beur filmmaking, which began in the mid-1980s, turned French cinema into 'a site of struggle for constructions of French national identity based on the realities of France as a multicultural, multi-ethnic society' (Tarr 2005: 86). Originally, gender difference had very little place in this site of struggle. However, this was challenged in the 1990s by women filmmakers of Maghrebi descent who began making films that focused on women's lives. Although some scholars and filmmakers have challenged the merits of the category of *cinéma beur*, Benguigui is seen as part of this film trend. Her films, in particular *Mémoires d'immigrés* and *Inch'Allah dimanche*, have enriched and renewed scholarly debate about the construction of migrant collective memory (Freedman and Tarr 2000) and notions of identity and hybridity (Fauvel 2004; Tarr 2005).

Inch'Allah dimanche is a portrait of immigration and its impact on women, a memoir of the story of Algerian immigrants at the time of family reunion authorised by the French government in 1974. The film recounts the story of an Algerian woman Zouina (Fejria Deliba) who arrives in France to join her husband Ahmed (Zinedine Soualem) established in Northern France as an industrial worker for the past ten years. She is accompanied by her three young children and Aïcha, her mother-in-law (Rabia Mokeddem, a non-professional actress). The film, constructed from Zouina's point of view, chronicles the first month of the protagonist's transition to living in France during the emerging feminist movement of the 1970s. Abused by her husband, oppressed by her mother-in-law, and harassed by her old racist neighbour Mme Donze (France Darry), Zouina is also influenced by her young feminist neighbour Nicole and helped by Mme Manant (Marie-France Pisier), the widow of a French officer killed in Algeria during the independence struggle. *Inch'Allah dimanche* explores intergenerational relations in the migration context and Zouina's emotional struggle for mobility and sovereignty as she attempts to make sense of her surroundings and come to terms with new relationships and with people beyond her close family. The story ends with a scene showing Zouina's dramatic and assertive claim for greater freedom and the downfall of her mother-in-law's traditional authority.

The era depicted in the film coincides with the peak of Beauvoir's influence on a generation of young women. In *Inch'Allah dimanche*, the changes in sexual mores and women's condition which were sweeping across French society are represented through the friendly character of Nicole Briat, a young neighbour who wants to help Zouina emancipate herself by lending her books, giving her make-up and inviting her to participate in her women's discussion group. Not without humour, the propagation of the 'popularised' version of Beauvoir's ideas is alluded to when Nicole makes a vague allusion to *The Second Sex*: 'I have to bring you the book of that woman. What is it called? The word sex is in the title. This woman says we have to manage our sexuality. Your body belongs to you'. She has set up a women's group for divorced women so that they can 'hang out, go out and dance'. Although it is only a short sequence, it captures the climate in which young French women were living and the changes in French society taking place at the time of Zouina's arrival. It also invites spectators to read Zouina's story of adaptation to modern French society as a narrative of emancipation from the oppressive agents of Algerian cultural traditions and patriarchal ideology represented by marriage and the older generation.

In her introduction to *The Second Sex* Beauvoir explains her perspective on freedom and more specifically on women's freedom. She writes that the perspective she has adopted is 'one of existentialist morality' (17) and explains that freedom can only be accomplished through projects and that there is no other justification for existence than 'its expansion towards an indefinitely open future' (Beauvoir 2009: 17). Freedom implies transcendence that is the surpassing of limitations, and responsibility. To fail to engage in projects and to consent to that degrades one's existence: 'Every time transcendence lapses into immanence, there is degradation of existence into "in-itself", of freedom into facticity; this fall is a moral fault if the subject consents to it: if this fall is inflicted on the subject, it takes the form of frustration and oppression: in both cases it is an absolute evil' (Beauvoir 2009: 17). In patriarchal societies, women are deprived of their transcendence and are condemned to live in immanence, without personal projects although every subject has a fundamental need for transcendence. For Beauvoir, 'Woman's drama lies in this conflict between the fundamental claim of every subject, which always posits itself as essential, and the demands of a situation that constitutes her as inessential' (Beauvoir 2009: 17). In *Inch'Allah dimanche*, the female protagonists, the old woman Aïcha and the young wife Zouina, are confronted with this very conflict: on one hand they live in a patriarchal family structure which severely limits their freedom and their mobility; on the other, in the society they have migrated to, women are demanding more freedom. In Benguigui's film the tension created by the constraints imposed on women's mobility is represented through the construction of a spatial dichotomy between inside and outside.

The representation of space in *Inch'Allah dimanche* reflects the opposition between the confined space of Algerian women and the physically unconstrained world of men and of French society. From the first scene of the film, dichotomic spatial representations underlie the meaning of the film. Zouina's emotional separation from her mother, framed behind heavy bars, is paralleled with the physical journey of migration. Through a series of shot/reverse-shots, wide shots and tight framing, Zouina's departure, although painful for her and her family, is portrayed as pertaining to an open space evoking freedom unlike her mother's prison-like space.

Algerian women who decided to join their husbands in France had to break close ties with their mothers, sisters and a traditional extended family that served as a support system: 'Much of Zouina's trauma on arrival in France is portrayed as resulting from the grief over the loss of this maternal bond' (Fenner 2007: 104), which is also the bond to her Algerian roots. A background song adds emotional depth to the departure scene. Throughout the film extradiegetic Algerian melodies like in the opening scene will serve to evoke Zouina's nostalgia for her family and her country while 1970s French songs will permeate the space to invoke the process of adaptation of the protagonist. The older generation of women, represented at the beginning of the film by the mother and later by the mother-in-law, will function as an obstacle to Zouina's desire for mobility and integration into French society. To achieve integration, Zouina will need to transgress the physical and psychological boundaries of spatial confinement set by the Algerian family structure.

Algerian women are not allowed to go outside of their home on their own and while Aïcha complies with this interdiction, Zouina rebels against it. Cinematic techniques translate the sense of imprisonment of the female protagonists in their home by an abundance of shots of closed spaces, of the inside of the house and the enclosed garden. Barred windows shot from the inside and locked front doors delineate a claustrophobic space similar to that of a prison. The female protagonists are tightly framed with medium, close shots and close-ups which create a sense of restriction and isolation from the outside world. Aïcha and Zouina are portrayed as doomed to live in immanence, confined to a repetitive existence and deprived of transcendent personal projects. Although a power relation is at play between them, both women are similarly imprisoned. However, Zouina is often seen standing in doorframes as if wanting to move beyond spatial limitations, as if willing to overcome restrictions on her physical freedom. While Aïcha never ventures outside on her own, Zouina will. The old woman has integrated the patriarchal interdiction and cannot even envisage breaking it – to her it would be a sin; however, for Beauvoir, as we have previously seen, to give consent to the deprivation of one's freedom would be a 'moral fault'. Conversely, the young Zouina experiences the outside world as a space where she can exercise her freedom, as a transcendent space. A low angle shot of Zouina walking and smiling in an open field when she secretly leaves her house illustrates very powerfully the sense of satisfaction that emanates from her being able to engage in the world.

Beauvoir devotes the second part of *Old Age* to the 'Being-in-the world' of old people and deals with their lived experience from their own point of view, an approach which she followed in *The Second Sex*. In cinema, the ageing subject is seldom the focus of the narrative, because dominant cinema celebrates first and foremost youth and beauty. As explained by Beauvoir 'old age arouses a biological repugnance: from a kind of self-defence one thrusts it from oneself' (Beauvoir 1972: 217). Benguigui's film is no exception and apart from a few scenes where the point of view is that of Mme Donze or Aïcha, old women are portrayed from a young woman's viewpoint: Zouina's. As we will see, her perspective on ageing women (Aïcha, Mme Donze and Mme Manant) supports and challenges Beauvoir's description of the aged as the Other.

Beauvoir argues that in the demand for reciprocal relationships, the old person 'is defined by an *exis*, not a *praxis*: a being not a doing' (Beauvoir 1972: 217) because time is carrying the aged towards death, which is unavoidable and not part of a personal project. Thus, the aged are not perceived as transcendent subjects. In *Inch'Allah dimanche*, however, it is Aïcha, the old woman, who turns the young Zouina into the 'Other', she is domineering and abusive, she spies on her, belittles her and even threatens to have her son's second wife emigrate to France, because Zouina is not serving her well enough. As the mother-in-law and an old woman she has the responsibility for perpetuating Algerian traditions: she prays and often invokes god, she makes couscous, sits on a sheepskin on the ground and tells her grandchildren stories that terrify them. As soon as she enters the house on their arrival in France, she claims the role of 'master' of the house by taking control over the food cupboard. She dominates her son who, in return, respects her, but she also makes sure that Zouina obeys him and submits to patriarchal rules.

For Aïcha, adapting to her new country is not an option, it is unthinkable, and she treats every French person she comes in contact with as the Other. In relation to Nicole and to Zouina, Aïcha adopts a masculine role as she takes the place and role of her son when he is away: she posits herself as the 'absolute subject'. She stands straight, looks very self-assured and is always shot from a low angle, which magnifies her and diminishes Zouina and Nicole. When she sits on the floor she prudishly rearranges Nicole's clothing and seems to be towering over other characters. Although Aïcha is old, she, at first glance, does not appear to be deprived of projects; on the contrary, her life aims at the protection of the patriarchal family and the transmission of Algerian culture and customs. Beauvoir argues that there is no universal experience of ageing: 'A man's ageing and his decline always takes place inside some given society: it is intimately related to the character of that society and to the place the individual in question occupies within it'[1] (1972: 37). *Inch'Allah dimanche* is a good illustration of Beauvoir's argument on the cultural specificity of ageing as the film explores the specificity of the lived experience of an aged immigrant Algerian woman. The mother-in-law has a powerful role in the Algerian family that western women do not have. She has acquired power because of her age and because she is the mother of a son, and exercises it by oppressing her daughter-in-law and scaring her grandchildren.

The relation between Aïcha and Zouina is a power struggle in which Aïcha objectifies Zouina and attempts to turn her into a slave. While Zouina is never seen openly rebelling against her husband's sovereignty, she challenges Aïcha's authority. In one sequence, she violently throws the carrots into a pan as a sign of protest against Aïcha's bullying. Zouina refuses a submissive existence and eventually disobeys her mother-in-law and her husband by going out secretly with her children to find Malika, an Algerian woman with whom she wants to celebrate *Eid*, a traditional Muslim festival. However, Zouina transforms *Eid* into a place of revolt to assert her existence as a free being. Conversely, Aïcha does not use her freedom to invent or engage in new projects; she maintains and reproduces traditions but does not create new meanings around them. She only mimics patriarchal power and her role does not grant her autonomy. In Beauvoirian terms, her life is inauthentic. According to Beauvoir, work 'becomes meaningful and dignified only if it is integrated into existences that go beyond themselves, towards the society in production or action' (Beauvoir 2009: 497). Far from enriching or enfranchising Aïcha's life, her traditional role makes her dependent on her son, her daughter-in-law and her grandchildren. She justifies her existence through them and is only a mediator, living her life as her son's proxy, so that the patriarchal family structure is maintained without being altered by or contaminated through contact with French culture.

One may wonder however if Aïcha, as an old woman, should be expected to rebel against her condition. Can she really choose to exercise her freedom? Benguigui's point of view on the mother-in-law is clearly negative, as she is mostly portrayed as a harsh and even cruel woman who is an obstacle to Zouina's freedom. But is it fair to portray old Algerian women in such a way? Aïcha's behaviour is due to a combination of factors: physical, social, historical and economic (Barakat 1993: 97). Time is also an essential factor. Beauvoir argues that 'Age changes our relationship with time: as the years go by our future shortens, while our past grows heavier' (Beauvoir 1972: 361). Because of the years that have passed, Aïcha is fixed in traditions and unable to project herself into the future, which would involve embracing different traditions and new ways of living. In *Old Age* Beauvoir offers a somewhat pessimistic analysis about the freedom that is possible in old age in western society. This departs from *The Second Sex* where she strongly criticised women who accepted prejudices about women's limitations. In *Old Age* she shifts the focus from moral responsibility to the factors that contribute to old people's marginalisation. As suggested by Deutscher, 'for Beauvoir, since physical facts do not exist in abstraction from social, historical, subjective, and economic factors, it is the combination of all these elements that produced the state she analysed somewhat pessimistically' (Deutscher 2003: 297). Benguigui, while hinting at Aïcha's hard life, does not provide a sympathetic account of the role of the old Algerian woman in the situation of migration, but blames her for respecting and perpetuating patriarchal ideology. This perspective is more in keeping with *The Second Sex* than with *Old Age*, and one might be tempted to criticise *Inch Allah dimanche* for displaying an ageist approach to the topic of migration and by not providing details of the factors that contribute to old women's role and behaviour.

In *The Second Sex*, Beauvoir explains that: 'Travelling, a local is shocked to realise that in neighbouring countries locals view him as a foreigner which removes the absolute meaning from the idea of the other and brings out relativity: whether one likes it or not, individuals and groups have no choice but to recognise the reciprocity of their relation' (Beauvoir 2009: 7). This could apply indeed to any migrant settling in a new country. Benguigui has represented this shift in self-consciousness in the scenes situated in the Algerian family's backyard.

Inch'Allah dimanche is constructed not only from a female viewpoint but also from a Maghrebi perspective, and at first establishes the Algerian family as the point of reference, the essential one, and their new environment as foreign. The protagonists apprehend France as a hostile, lonely, cold and grey place. Aïcha perceives the French as foreigners and the young Nicole Briat as a threat to her moral values. She resents the fact that Zouina 'is always yakking with the French woman', and when Zouina shows signs of integrating into French society Aïcha disdainfully says to her: 'you forgot Arabic, you speak French now'. She perceives anyone not belonging to Algerian culture as a suspicious 'Other'. However, as soon as Zouina, Aïcha and the children arrive in their 'new home', the film positions them all as outsiders: the sparsely furnished house feels like a transitory place, and the suitcases in full view are a sure sign of their immigrant status; they are the foreigners. The backyard is the site of the first interaction between Algerian and French neighbours and where the struggle for recognition begins. The backyard is an enclosed liminal space that allows for interaction with the neighbours and for the exchange of gaze between the two families, Mme Donze's and Zouina's. Mme Donze, the old racist neighbour, is often seen at the window spying on the newly arrived migrants. She calls Aïcha and the children 'that old Indian and those brats', 'murderers, slaughterers' and likens Aïcha to a witch. In one regard the two old women, Mme Donze and Aïcha, are similar: they both consider their own culture as the essential one and will not attempt negotiation for reciprocity.

Beauvoir emphasised the necessity of reciprocity in the Self–Other relations which involve relating to others and to oneself as both subject and object. Benguigui's film provides an excellent illustration of the Self–Other relationships through the exchange of gaze. It is in the backyard scenes that Benguigui stages the Self–Other negotiation in the encounter between two cultures and two generations. As soon as Zouina, Aïcha and the children arrive in their new house, Mme Donze is seen looking at them from her window. Through a series of shot/reverse-shots, point-of-view shots of Zouina's and Mme Donze's backyards, and high camera angle shots, the relation between Self and Other is constructed: Mme Donze is presented as Subject of the look, as the active onlooker, and Zouina as Object of the look and the dominated Other. A low angle shot from Zouina's backyard portrays Mme Donze as dominant; she is even feared by Zouina. Interestingly, Aïcha and Mme Donze are often shot very similarly from the backyard in low angle shots. Mme Donze actively attempts to limit Zouina's freedom by interfering when she wants to make coffee in her garden (an Algerian custom), or by destroying the children's soccer ball when it inadvertently falls into her manicured garden. However, unexpectedly, Zouina resists her objectivised status and a struggle for sovereignty follows in which Zouina, in a rather comical sequence, has literally the upper hand as she knocks her to the ground, sits on her and tries to strangle her. Throughout the scene, Mme Donze is represented as an unpleasant character, obsessed by her garden and often ridiculous in her behaviour. Perceived as an enemy by Zouina and her children, Mme Donze deserves her fate. She is a rather stereotypical image of the old woman: intolerant, set in her ways and obsessed by useless personal projects, an image that Beauvoir has shown to be the result of societal pressures but to which Benguigui does not provide any challenge. After the fight between the two women, the policeman attempts to settle the dispute by asking the two parties to shake hands. In Beauvoirian terms, he is underlining the fact that while they have opposing claims for sovereignty they have no choice but to recognise the reciprocity of their relation if they are to live peacefully next to one another. While neither of them has chosen the situation they are in as neighbours coming from different cultures, each one must recognise the other as a free subject.

At the core of migration, there is always a struggle for reciprocal recognition but young and ageing women are placed in different situations. While the young people portrayed in the film readily accept reciprocity when dealing with others, the old women are shown to be inflexible. The young feminist neighbour and the young bus driver enter the Self–Other relation with Zouina as a reciprocal mode of being. Similarly Zouina will embrace French culture and will negotiate a new identity by establishing a link between traditional Algerian culture and modern French culture. On the other hand, Mme Donze and Aïcha will resist any attempt to achieve reciprocity. The relations between Zouina on the one hand and Mme Donze and Aïcha on the other will always be a struggle as Zouina refuses to be turned into an object and Mme Donze and Aïcha persist in denying Zouina the status of subject.

In *Old Age*, as already mentioned, Beauvoir argues that for the old, it is 'the Other' who is old and not the person they experience themselves as being. Eventually the old person will accept the image that others have of them but not without difficulties, a period that Beauvoir defines as an identification crisis. In her chapter 'Time, Activity and History' she claims that ageing transforms our relationship to time. If old people love to talk about the past, it is because in fact 'they refuse time' (Beauvoir 1972: 361) and do not want to see decline in themselves. They prefer to keep a fixed, unchanged image of themselves as a protection against the deteriorations of age. The world they live in is not the world they were used to; old people have not only seen the people of their generation die but a completely different world has also taken the place of their own (Beauvoir 1972: 436). The nostalgia expressed by Mme Manant for her past life in Algeria and her endless grief for her husband, although he has been dead for ten years, can be understood as the symptoms of this difficulty in coming to terms with ageing and its consequences.

Zouina meets Mme Manant during her escapade to find Malika, the Algerian woman with whom she wants to celebrate the *Eid* festival. They meet in the war cemetery where Algerians and French military personnel are buried. Impeccably dressed, Mme Manant represents the generation of wealthy colonists (*pieds noirs*), a middle class that now harbours feelings of guilt towards Algerians. The sequence allows Benguigui to provide spectators with a historical context about the Algerian war and to contrast the lives and the attitudes of the two communities and generations towards the past. When Mme Manant sees Zouina crying, she thinks she is shedding tears of nostalgia for Algeria, whereas Zouina is upset because she is lost and is facing setbacks in her project to find the Algerian family. Cut off from her past, Mme Manant is obsessed by it and tells Zouina about her husband's death during the war: 'It's been 11 years that I have lost my dear Henry, he is somewhere over there in Algeria, in Kabylie'. She is held captive by her nostalgia and has set up an image of herself as essentially a being living her life in the past. This is reinforced in another sequence when, through Zouina's eyes, a pan reveals the walls of Mme Manant's house covered with memorabilia of her life in Algeria and with portraits of her late husband. Unable to project herself into the future, Mme Manant wards off the decline of old age by attempting to relive the past. As explained by Beauvoir, old people 'set up a fixed, unchanging essence of themselves against the deterioration of old age, and tirelessly they tell stories of this being that they were, this being that lives on inside them' (Beauvoir 1972: 362).

However when Mme Manant meets Zouina, the future seems to open up again although everything comes between the two women: their social class, their history, their age and the death of Mme Manant's dog caused by Zouina's children. Yet, she is able to transcend prejudices when she visits her and invites her to her home and helps Zouina find Malika's family, an Algerian family who lives in the neighbourhood. But Zouina will assert her independence and her freedom to choose when she refuses to allow Mme Manant to drive her back home, thus relegating her to uselessness and depriving her from engaging in the present. Instead, Zouina rides home by bus with her children, and she is seen standing next to the young bus driver travelling in the open streets, metaphorically towards an open future, leaving Mme Manant behind. As shown by Beauvoir, in western societies, even when they attempt to engage in the world, old people are relegated to the status of object by the young. In Benguigui's film the quest for freedom and the divide between past and future is shown to be inseparable from the intergenerational relationship.

The end of the film provides us with a conclusion to our study as the issues of freedom and of the role and status of the aged in a migrant context come to a resolution. During the last scene Zouina arrives home as everybody is waiting anxiously for her: her mother-in law, Mme Donze, Mme Manant and her husband. The generational conflict takes on a new turn, as Zouina proclaims herself as a free being by looking at her husband and telling him she will take the children to school from now on. For the first time, he also looks at her. She is positing herself as a subject in her own right and is demanding that her husband recognises her as such. As Aïcha screams at Zouina, 'You idiot, we've been waiting for four hours', Ahmed tells the old woman to 'shut up' and to go inside, provoking in spectators a sense of satisfaction that justice is finally being carried out. Aïcha, the oppressive mother-in-law, has been disempowered by the patriarchal order for being unable to look forward to the future and hence to adapt to her new situation.

At the beginning of the film we had seen Zouina painfully tearing herself from her extended Algerian family. At the end, she stands alone in front of the older generation, demanding to have her new hybrid identity recognised, however, this has to be done at the expense of old people who represent traditional values. Hence the film maintains patriarchy's divide-and-rule over women of different generations as it ends on the victory of integration over the rigid maintenance of Algerian patriarchal traditions. It is also the victory of the future over the past and of the young over the old. The film shows that the old generation has to occupy the place of the Other for the new generation to act freely and the alienated life of the older woman serves as a catalyst for the younger woman not to follow in her footsteps. Through contact with French society the migrant extended family structure has been transformed: the old woman has lost her role as the guardian of cultural traditions and the young wife's place in the family is evolving and being westernised. The extended family model where the older woman has a powerful role in maintaining the structure of the family is modernised by the migration process to become a western nuclear family model where the old generation has no place. If such changes are represented by Benguigui as being positive and desirable because of the emancipation of young women, Lacoste-Dujardin's study points out that 'the parents find themselves faced with a new relationship, reduced to unforeseen duality which is difficult to manage in the absence of any ideology of the couple and of the nuclear family project' (Lacoste-Dujardin 2000: 58). Benguigui does not provide a critical point of view on this whereas in *The Second Sex* Beauvoir writes that solidarity between women is even less likely in the nuclear family context because women 'live dispersed among men, tied by homes, work, economic interest and social conditions to men – fathers or husbands – more closely than to other women' (8).

Benguigui's film provides both support for and a critique of Beauvoir's perspective on old age. The examination of the role of old women in the film reveals that the experience of old age is not universal. Family structure, patriarchal ideology and personal context define the experience. The old women in the film come from very different contexts, yet they exhibit a common trait in their inability to embrace change brought about by time and migration. Benguigui portrays them as obstacles to young people's freedom: old women represent the traditional values that have to be overcome in order for the young to negotiate a new hybrid identity or to access new freedoms. While young people are shown to be able to weave reciprocal relations, except for Malika who will become another Aïcha, the old women are isolated. Throughout the film, Benguigui offers a negative perspective on ageing, Mme Donze with her racism and her obsessions with gardening is ridiculous, and her fascination for flowers verges on the grotesque. Mme Manant and Aïcha have been marginalised by Zouina's actions towards greater freedom. By presenting the aged women from the point of view of the young, the film alienates old age, making it 'an exis rather than a praxis' (Beauvoir 1972: 217). The film constructs a narrative in which the alienation of old women and their Otherness are inevitable and necessary, and provides no real challenge or critical viewpoint to this ageist image. As such it corroborates the dominant discourse on old age in western societies, which Beauvoir denounced in *Old Age*.

Note

1. Beauvoir does not always distinguish women's experience as different from men's and often uses the term man to include man and woman, as is the case in this quotation.

Bibliography

Barakat, H. 1993. *The Arab World: Society, Culture and State*. Berkeley, Los Angeles, London: University of California.

Beauvoir, S. de. [1970] 1972. *Old Age*, trans. P. O'Brian. London: André Deutsch and Weidenfeld and Nicolson.

———. [1949] 2009. *The Second Sex*, trans. C. Borde and S. Malovany-Chevallier. London: Jonathan Cape.

Benguigui, Y. 2001. 'Culture Opens the Speech', interview with Yasmina Medani. Retrieved 17 January 2011 from http://www.euromedcafe.org/interview. asp?lang=ing&documentID=15

Deutscher, P. 2003. 'Beauvoir's *Old Age*', in C. Card (ed.), *The Cambridge Companion to Simone de Beauvoir*. Cambridge: Cambridge University Press, pp. 286–304.

Fauvel, M. 2004. 'Yamina Benguigui's *Inch'Allah dimanche*: unveiling hybrid identities', *Studies in French Cinema* 4(2): 147–57.

Fenner, A. 2007. 'Aural Topographies of Migration in Yamina Benguigui's *Inch'Allah dimanche*', *Camera Obscura* 66, 22(3): 93–128.

Freedman, J. and C. Tarr (eds). 2000. *Women, Immigration and Identities in France*. Oxford: Berg.

Lacoste-Dujardin, C. 2000. 'Maghrebi Families in France', in J. Freedman and C. Tarr (eds), *Women, Immigration and Identities in France*. Oxford: Berg, pp. 57–68.

Pamerleau, W.C. 2009. *Existentialist Cinema*. New York: Palgrave Macmillan.

Tarr, C. 2005. *Reframing Difference: Beur and banlieue Filmmaking in France*. Manchester: Manchester University Press.

Filmography

Benguigui, Y. (dir.). 1997. *Mémoires d'immigrés: l'héritage maghrébin* (*(Immigrant Memories: The North African Inheritance*). Paris: Canal+ Editions.

———. 2001. *Inch'Allah dimanche* (*Inch'Allah Sunday*). DVD. Film Movement.

9

EASTWOOD READING BEAUVOIR READING EASTWOOD: AGEING AND COMBATIVE SELF-ASSERTION IN *GRAN TORINO* AND *OLD AGE*

Oliver Davis

'Extraordinary events culminate in what may seem to be an anticlimax.'[1] Sat on his front porch with his decrepit dog Daisy by his side, on a lonely birthday shortly after the death of his wife, Korea veteran and retired car-worker Walt Kowalski (Clint Eastwood) reads aloud his horoscope. But he could just as well be reading Beauvoir's despairingly anticlimactic account of the ageing subject in her unjustly neglected essay, *Old Age*, or listening attentively in her autobiography to the curious backwash of depressive anxiety from the extraordinary events of her intellectual and semi-private life.

The discussion which follows is adamantly not a unidirectional 'application' of Beauvoir's thought to Eastwood's film. In refusing to 'apply' Beauvoir's thought to the film it endeavours to avoid repeating a subordinating move now so commonly decried, even if still so often repeated, as Alain Badiou complains (Badiou 2004), in the history of the relationship between art and thought in philosophical aesthetics. Before the obvious be stated elsewhere, let it be said here that Kowalski is of course *not* reading Beauvoir in the diegesis. Yet the risk in sticking with such compliant earnestness so closely to the dour evidence, as this anticipated objection does, is that an analysis of this film or any other in notionally Beauvoirian terms will betray one vital quality of her life and work. This quality, still too seldom recognised by detractors and enthusiasts alike, is the capacity for unabashed outlandishness (*All Men Are Mortal*), for preposterously plangent intensity ('j'ai été flouée', 'I was gypped', Beauvoir [1963] 1965: 658), her embrace not of the *kitsch* exactly but of what I want to call the *farfelu*, which I take to be another queer mode of excess, not just in her pioneering and necessarily improper experimentation with alternative family and kinship structures but also in those eccentric touches which deftly capture a moment and fragments of a collective self-concept: '[w]e spent our evenings together in my studio, dining on a slice of ham, talking and listening to records' (Beauvoir 1965: 576), a phrase reminiscent of one of Iris Murdoch's heroines too busily engaged in intellectual parlay to notice that a can of spinach was hardly dinner, except for Popeye. What if to be true to Beauvoir also meant – as well as the obligation to treat her intellectual, political and artistic work with the requisite seriousness, a duty which was recognised far too late by the critical establishment, if not by her ordinary readership, and is still only very imperfectly respected, especially in France – what if to be true to Beauvoir also meant to be able to strike that same cracked tone of *farfelu* excess as Brigitte Fontaine in her captivatingly intoxicated song-essay 'La Chanson de Simone'?[2] What if to be faithful to Beauvoir also meant sometimes, in addition, attending to that side of her work which is productively *farfelu*?

In reading combative Eastwoodian self-assertion in Beauvoir at the same time as it uses Beauvoir's work to illuminate Eastwood's account of old age in *Gran Torino*, this chapter is offered as a faithfully unfaithful Beauvoirian experiment in the productive power of the methodologically *farfelu*; productive in that it begins in the virtual mode *as if* Kowalski, or Eastwood, were reading Beauvoir and reciprocally, and in that it calls forth its argument from the virtuality of this (non-)encounter; *farfelu*, too, in the obvious political sense that the reassertion of violent, heroic, American masculinity and conservative sexual politics with which Eastwood's name is justly synonymous makes him as keen an antagonist to Beauvoir's legacy as could readily be imagined. For as well as the film's titular car, Walt bequeaths to his young adoptive son Thao (Bee Vang) a particular model of traditional masculinity in a series of pedagogical encounters which Walt himself describes as the 'manning up' of 'pussy boy' Thao. The film's presentation of hegemonic masculinity as a learned performance which, while no longer exactly compulsory, is still strategically advantageous for a man to learn is a strikingly cynical reterritorialisation of some of the ground won by constructivist second-wave feminism of which Beauvoir's *The Second Sex* was, in the US as in France, even if sometimes more by repute, *the* key text. The juxtaposition between Beauvoir and Eastwood I am essaying here is not ignorant of their evident political disagreement, even as I try to work an eccentric course around it. The argumentative yield of this critical approach will be to demonstrate that, for all that they differ in their gender politics, in their accounts of ageing Beauvoir and Eastwood share a strikingly similar commitment to vigorously combative self-assertion. My wager is that this *farfelu* tack will steer a safe course clear around the philosophical squalls which a superficially more modest 'application' of Beauvoir's thought to this film would unfailingly encounter.

'Extraordinary events culminate in what may seem to be an anticlimax.' Walt's horoscope is a neat summary of the film's storyline: *Gran Torino* sees inveterate racist Walt form an implausibly sudden and intimate bond with his new Hmong neighbours, respond with what, for an old man, is extraordinary violence to a gang intent on forcibly initiating his surrogate son Thao into a life of criminality and ends, atypically for Eastwood, in the anticlimax of the hero's own on-screen demise.[3]

Old Age as Alienating Anticlimax

The anticlimax foretold in his horoscope can also be understood as a succinct summary of the life-course of ordinary American men of Walt's class and generation; called on in their youth to perform acts of unspeakable violence in the service of their country, welcomed home as national heroes and the embodiment of a certain kind of hard, or 'hegemonic', masculinity, they then had to adapt, in the 1950s and 1960s, as Brian Baker has observed, to a suburban life of 'feminizing' reproductive domesticity invariably doubled by repetitive work in the semi-skilled lower echelons of American industrial manufacturing, in Walt's case on the very archetype of the production line, at a Ford car plant (Baker 2006: 1). The film shows us Walt kicking against this anticlimax, responding with astonishingly violent acts of self-assertion to the intrinsic disappointment of growing old; 'What a load of shit!' is Walt's response to his horoscope and his refusal of the anticlimactic 'load of shit' that is ordinary ageing is just as forthright. In the tormented violence of this refusal, if not the vulgar form of its linguistic expression here, Walt is with Beauvoir, not least when she complained, at the end of the Epilogue to *Force of Circumstance*, of feeling that she had been cheated by life. Some readers have gone to quite extraordinary lengths to explain away this infamous last line, as though to acknowledge that Beauvoir had experienced the unbearable were itself an unbearable admission.[4] I have argued elsewhere that, on this occasion, we should trust the surface of the text; the line's raging despair is entirely consistent with the philosophical core of *Old Age*, an essay in which Beauvoir's well-meaning 'gerontological' intention to explain away ageing in terms of contingent socio-economic and historical factors repeatedly founders on her 'ontological' conviction that ageing is inherently alienating (Davis 2006: 33–61, 145–55). It is to the bleak philosophical core of that essay that I now briefly return in order to show how it and *Gran Torino* share a common understanding of the ontology of the ageing subject and a common commitment to the value of violent self-assertion, or 'age rage' as I have called it, in response to that alienating predicament (Davis 2006).

'Within me it is the Other – that is to say the person I am for other people – who is old: and that Other is myself' (Beauvoir 1972: 284, translation adapted). According to Beauvoir, we are inevitably so thoroughly convinced of our enduring youthful self-sameness that we only become aware of our ageing in repeated traumatic encounters with other people, the mirror of whose gaze reflects back a distorted image of what we cannot accept we have become, or with the mirror in a literal sense. Beauvoir and Eastwood share a paradigm of ageing which, following Kathleen Woodward (1991), can be understood as a reversal, or undoing, of the process of self-formation theorised by psychoanalyst Jacques Lacan in his celebrated account of what he called the 'mirror stage' (Lacan 1977). Lacan's concept of the 'mirror stage' theorises the moment at around eighteen months when, from a collection of dispersed drives, the infant's identity emerges in an intrinsically alienating identification with the ego, the image reflected back in the mirror. Prior to the mirror stage the infant, for Lacan, has no sense of coherent identity or self; it is simply a collection of disorganised drives. In the mirror stage the infant recognises and also misrecognises itself in the image reflected back at it; this is both the foundation of a certain kind of selfhood and a moment of alienation, for the self or ego with which the infant identifies is relatively thin, or two-dimensional, and straightforward by contrast with the rich and turbulent agonistic conflict of drives of its fuller subjectivity. We twice see Kowalski in the film in front of a mirror, on both occasions coughing up blood in a traumatised encounter with the new reality of bodily infirmity which undercuts his sense of enduring self-sameness. Kowalski has fled to the bathroom on both occasions and stands with head bowed before the mirror, retching into the sink, reeling with the shock of defeat. In Beauvoir's model ageing is anything but a smooth process of change: to age is to have one's sense of self-sameness violently undermined in such repeated traumatic encounters with the mirror, or the mirror of another's gaze. For Beauvoir, in *Old Age*, getting older means to experience schizoid alternation between our conviction of our inner self-sameness and the revelation, which typically comes through the reactions of others, of our decrepitude. Ageing, as Beauvoir understands it, involves 'an insoluble contradiction [*une contradiction indépassable*] between the obvious clarity of the inward feeling [*entre l'évidence intime*] that guarantees our unchanging quality and the objective certainty of our transformation. All we can do is waver from the one to the other' (Beauvoir 1972: 290). There is a narrowable but ultimately unbridgeable gap between our enduring inner conviction of our own self-sameness and the external knowledge which comes from other people that we have become other (Beauvoir 1972: 290). I have argued that it is important not to lose sight of the fact that in Beauvoir's account there is a substantial remainder of something inherently inassimilable and alienatingly traumatic about ageing which cannot be overcome, not by socio-economic improvements, nor by changes to the way the elderly are represented, and certainly not by blithe faith in the power of positive thinking (Davis 2006: 39).

Contrary to Woodward's implication I would not wish to suggest that the Lacanian paradigm somehow has superior explanatory potential to the understandings of ageing already present in these two works by Eastwood and Beauvoir. In fact the encounter with the mirror, or the 'mirror' of another's gaze, which is shared by Eastwood and Beauvoir, is a common, even a commonplace, experience of ageing in our culture, as its frequent recurrence in other ostensibly unconnected contexts suggests. What is important about what Woodward calls 'the inverted mirror stage of ageing' is not the homology with a Lacanian structure of alienating (mis)recognition but rather the combative self-assertion which, for Eastwood as for Beauvoir, is proposed as the only viable response to this predicament (Woodward 1991: 180). Woodward's Lacanian parallel does, however, usefully emphasise two important common factors to Beauvoir's and Eastwood's age rage: first, in psychoanalytic terms, it is a drama of the ego. I shall return to this point later. Second, Woodward's

Lacanian parallel alerts us to the fact that there is an inherently visual, indeed spectacular, dimension to the experience of ageing for Eastwood and Beauvoir alike. The encounter with the image of a self which both is and is not recognised as one's self, with a withered shell which belies the sense of inner self-sameness, takes place in the field of the visual, is a repeated spectacular experience of trauma. Neither Woodward nor Proust, to whom her account is greatly indebted, have much to say about 'age rage' itself, a shared response to the alienation of old age about which both Beauvoir and Eastwood are similarly eloquent in ways I shall now explore.

Combative Self-Assertion as the Only Viable Response

Beauvoir's ontology of ageing is premised on the inevitability of violence and violation and posits an insular, self-contained and self-similar subject who is forcibly 'othered', alienated in its encounters with other people, or with its image in the mirror. In turn, and in keeping with the conflictual Hegelian model of intersubjective relations which strongly influenced both Beauvoir and Sartre, particularly but not exclusively in the earlier years of their philosophical formation, the subject who encounters this othering gaze can respond with resignation by accepting the judgment, which Beauvoir sees as an admission of defeat that can only hasten that subject's decline, or with violent refusal, with 'age rage'. 'For those who do not choose to go under, being old means fighting against age' (Beauvoir 1972: 304). Beauvoir's can be described as a militarised account in the sense that the encounter with the other is anticipated as the occasion of inevitable psychic injury; the other will inflict a wound which the subject can only survive intact by responding with violent agonistic struggle.

Gran Torino is full of such Beauvoirian age rage. In the scene immediately following Walt's reading of the horoscope, Kowalski's son Mitch (Brian Haley) and daughter-in-law Karen (Geraldine Hughes) come to visit and present him with two entirely inappropriate domestic aids for the elderly, for his birthday, a 'gopher' to help him reach things and a large-key telephone 'to make life easier', before trying gauchely and with unseemly haste to talk him into 'one of these great places', a retirement complex. These feckless mouthpieces for their culture's expectations of a normal old age are quite unable to think beyond its euphemistic clichés. They are sent packing by a stony-faced Walt, with a growl. This growl is itself a hallmark of steely Eastwoodian masculinity, familiar notably from the war film *Heartbreak Ridge* (Eastwood 1986). From the Sergio Leone Westerns of the mid-1960s on, Eastwood's characters are invariably as reticent with language (Neale 1993: 12; Smith 1993: 153) as they are economical in movement and gesture (Bingham 1994: 171); such is their phallic potency they need neither elaborately to articulate nor extravagantly to perform their desires in order for them to take effect. As Bingham has noted, the typical Eastwood hero 'is so immobile that motionlessness becomes equated with strength, making others in a scene into Others, making them look weak'

(Bingham 1994: 223). In the shot of Walt's growling refusal he is lit from back right and front left so as to cast shadow over half his face and both his eyes, rendering his gaze inscrutable and recalling the heavily backlit shots of early Eastwoodian masculinity (Smith 1993: 158).

Walt's growling refusal of the 'gopher', the telephone and the retirement complex is an emphatic gesture of self-assertion which reaches back to and draws strength from Eastwood's star persona before his oft-trumpeted 'revisionist' turn, as director, away from violence towards an exploration of its traumatic and destructive consequences, a turn which many academic and most non-academic critics concur was initiated in *Unforgiven* (1992) and perpetuated in his subsequent work, in particular *Mystic River* (2003) and the World War Two diptych from 2006, *Flags of Our Fathers* and *Letters from Iwo Jima* (Bingham 1994: 2–3; Cornell 2009: 185; Smith 1993: 264), an interpretive line Eastwood himself has been only too pleased to adopt but about which, for reasons I shall explain, I remain somewhat sceptical.

In *Gran Torino* Walt chooses sudden death in a violent final act of self-assertion, in full possession of his house, car and mind rather than accepting any of the demeaning compromises ageing tends to bring in our consumerist culture. In its representational choices the film endorses his violent rejection of ageing by presenting him as an exceptional figure for his age, 'standing strong', as a line in the title song says; although we glimpse him cough up blood these signs of infirmity do nothing to detract from the extraordinary hardness of his heroic body, serving rather to spur him on to his final act of heroically violent self-assertion. Rather than slowly slide into old age and infirmity, he chooses to die fully a man in his culture's own terms.

In the violence of Walt's refusal of the anticlimactic pattern of ordinary ageing lies his troubling affinity with Beauvoir, troubling no doubt for many Eastwoodians and some Beauvoirians alike. For although Beauvoir's essay, *Old Age*, calls repeatedly for the social and economic situation of the elderly to be improved and assiduously analyses the pernicious effects of socially circulated negative stereotypes of them, it ultimately rejects a redemptive vision of ageing as in any sense a positive experience; indeed it is relentlessly critical of such upbeat visions of the process, often attributing them to the false imperatives of American consumer capitalism. Beauvoir's is an unrelentingly and irredeemably despondent account of ageing and, in the final analysis, this is not for contingent and changeable, or indeed for personal, reasons, even though Beauvoir is also adamant that the way the elderly are treated could greatly be improved and even though she was both fascinated and depressed by her own decline. Penelope Deutscher has insisted of Beauvoir's work on ageing that '[o]ne must be critical of her most negative depictions' (Deutscher 2006: 301), yet it is my contention that it is only where Beauvoir is at her most extreme, her most 'negative', namely in the ontological account presented in chapter five of *Old Age* and outlined above, that she has something distinctive and enduring to say on the subject. Rather than being the regrettable qualification of a mainly redemptive account, in its unflinching self-awareness and its recognition of the necessity of combative self-assertion lie her distinctive contributions to knowledge of human ageing. Walt's growling refusal of his culture's demeaningly anticlimactic vision of ageing is an extreme case of Beauvoirian age rage and one which exaggerates and illuminates, albeit perhaps in rather a garish light, the latent 'Eastwoodian' violence of self-assertion in Beauvoir's ontology of ageing.

But What Eastwoodian Violence?

It may be objected that *Gran Torino* ends with an act of self-sacrifice rather than combative self-assertion and that rather than espousing violent self-assertion the film shows the destructive effects of it. In simple narrative terms it is of course tempting to see *Gran Torino* as a continuation of Eastwood's supposed revisionist turn away from the celebration of violent masculinity to the exploration of the traumatic effects of violence and the psychic wounds it inflicts on those who choose to be, or are forced in wartime to become, men of violence. The film was released two years after Eastwood's anti-war diptych, *Flags of Our Fathers* and *Letters from Iwo Jima*, which sought, as Drucilla Cornell has noted, to expose 'the psychic illness caused by the trauma of war' (Cornell 2009: 146). Moreover, by arousing and frustrating the spectator's Western-schooled desire for bloody revenge from the Eastwood hero, *Gran Torino* may seem to perpetuate the humanizing lesson Cornell discerns in *Mystic River*, where revenge is presented as 'a defensible urge and, simultaneously, as a terrifying danger' (Cornell 2009: 125). Certainly *Gran Torino* is also concerned with questions of guilt, forgiveness and expiation: Walt did 'unspeakable things' in Korea and the love of his wife Dorothy was clearly not sufficient of itself to erase the memory of those acts, just as in *Unforgiven* the love of a good woman may temporarily have calmed, but could not lastingly change, the killer William Munny (Eastwood).

I want to resist this comforting view of *Gran Torino* as a continuation of Eastwood's revisionist turn away from violence. Notwithstanding the rhetoric of self-sacrifice which accompanies it, Walt's choice of a violent death is a late renewal with, and reassertion of the need for, the hard and violent masculinity of the 'classic' Eastwood persona developed in the films of the 1960s, 1970s and 1980s, a persona trenchantly and comprehensively analysed by Bingham (1994), Jeffords (1994) and Baker (2006).[5] Not only does *Gran Torino* refuse to represent the steady decline of Walt's ageing and infirm body but it offers a new and insidious plea for the value of violent masculinity in the lives of ordinary working-class American men: for a man of Walt's class and generation, lost in the menacing and increasingly ethnically diverse suburban jungle, abandoned by his own unloving, ignorant, 'spoiled rotten', family, forgotten by an ungrateful nation and menaced by the onset of physical infirmity, violently self-asserting masculinity is offered up as the only credible response to the humiliating and anticlimactic compromises of old age. Moreover, the film suggests that this resolute masculinity is something which the ageing man has a duty to bequeath to his vulnerable male progeny.

In the film's gendered symbolic economy, as in American culture generally, the phallic instrument par excellence is the gun. Defending the perimeter of the home is the supreme test of masculinity and one which demands not only an inner preparedness to use, but the articulated threat of, violence. In the United States the right to use violence in defence of one's property, which is provided for in many state jurisdictions, is thoroughly entangled in symbolic terms with classic Eastwoodian masculinity. In those states which have enacted one, a 'Castle Law', so called in a reference to the adage about an Englishman's home, allows for the use of violence by the homeowner when faced by a trespasser. A 'Castle Law' (or 'Castle Doctrine' or 'Defense of Habitation Law') is more commonly known as a 'Make My Day Law', in a reference to the famous line uttered by maverick police inspector 'Dirty' Harry Callahan (Eastwood) in *Sudden Impact* (1983). *Gran Torino* is set in Michigan, which enacted its own 'Make My Day Law' in 2006, and this quintessentially Eastwoodian legal provision proves to be of some significance at critical junctures in the film, including and especially its violent denouement, even though that significance is not made explicit in the film.

When Walt first 'saves' Thao from the Hmong gang he does so not because he cares remotely for the boy but rather because the fight has trespassed over the invisible line dividing his front lawn from that of his neighbours. When he growls 'Get off my lawn', the threat of violence in this particular state, Michigan, is very real. The film cannot not reference – albeit probably as unwittingly as Walt saves Thao – this legal provision thoroughly entangled in symbolic terms with combative Eastwoodian masculinity. Given all the upbeat narrative consequences, entirely unintended on Walt's part, which follow from his defence of his own habitation – by unwittingly saving Thao he is drawn out of his isolation to recognise himself as part of a new and ethnically diverse community – the film suggests, perniciously in my view, that the readiness to use mortal violence to defend the boundaries of one's domestic space is not only compatible with, but an essential prerequisite for, people to live harmonious and fulfilling lives together in a community.

Similarly, in the final shootout it is crucial that when Walt calls to the gang members he is standing on the sidewalk rather than on their garden path or front lawn. Where he was standing is clear from where he falls, backwards away from the house towards the road. While the very obvious visual point about this shot is that his arms are outstretched as though he had been crucified, it is more significant, in my view, that the shot confirms that this unarmed man was *not* trespassing on private property when he was gunned down. As Walt taunts the gang before they gun him down he draws concertedly on violent Eastwoodian masculinity: 'You go ahead [...] now go ahead, pull those pistols, like miniature cowboys, go ahead'. The three 'go aheads' echo that same line from *Sudden Impact*, the here unspoken second half of which, 'make my day', lends its name to the abovementioned legal provision Walt and the film must, if perhaps unconsciously, circumvent if this final act is to produce its intended narrative effect, the conviction of the Hmong gang, concisely and without protracted courtroom argument. Even though Walt dies in a shootout, which is the first time an Eastwood character does, this simple fact is overwhelmingly offset by the saturation of this sequence with references to Eastwoodian violence, not just in the dialogue but also in the restrained minimalism of his hand gestures and in the scene's complex spatial negotiation of this Eastwoodian law on legitimate violence. Undermining the obvious visual allusion to Christ-like self-sacrifice this scene insidiously articulates the film's subtle plea: violent self-assertion is the dignified response to the contemporary social realities both of old age and of life in a complex multi-ethnic suburban community. In the representational choice not to show us Walt's gradual decline but rather his heroic end in a scene saturated with visual and verbal references to classic Eastwoodian masculinity, the film subtly revises Eastwood's alleged revisionism.

Beauvoir on the Warpath in the Land of Old Age

There are plenty of combatively self-assertive moments in Beauvoir's essay *Old Age*; not only is age rage put forward in the ontological abstract as the subject's only viable response to the alienating indignities of old age but this essay is itself enraged, speaking as it does of forcibly breaking the conspiracy of silence on the subject. Since my discussion here is situated within a volume of essays in film studies, my analysis of Beauvoir's 'Eastwoodian' self-assertion will now refer to another film, a rather obscure one which deserves to be better known, *A Walk Through the Land of Old Age / Promenade au pays de la vieillesse* (1974), a documentary about the plight of the elderly in France in the early 1970s directed by Swedish filmmaker and writer Marianne Ahrne.[6] For not only does Beauvoir herself feature prominently in that film, as its 'red thread', to use Ahrne's term, and not only did she collaborate extensively with Ahrne and her team in the conceptualization of the project and the script-writing, but there is every indication that the film was conceived by Ahrne and Beauvoir as a filmic transposition of the essay *Old Age* (Davis 2006: 201). Outlandish, *farfelu* in the extreme, though it may seem to want to make a film out of a lengthy philosophical, literary, medical, sociological and political treatise, the notion of such a transposition has an illustrious precedent in Eisenstein's project to film Marx's *Capital*. Ahrne's seventy-minute documentary was made for Swedish television and also shown in cinemas in Paris in 1978 after winning the critics' prize at the 1975 Hyères film festival. The film features many of the key locations familiar from *Old Age*, in particular the infamous state-run hospices for the elderly poor which bear more than a passing resemblance both to the Victorian workhouse and the madhouses of Charcot's day. I have shown elsewhere how this documentary transposes and dramatises Beauvoir's essay (Davis 2006: 164–69) and Ahrne herself has commented at length on the making of the film, both in my interview with her (Davis 2006: 197–204) and in a special issue of *Les Temps Modernes* devoted to Beauvoir's legacy (Ahrne 2008). Rather than rerun those discussions here I want to draw attention to the way in which Beauvoir's screen presence in one particular scene, in which she interviews a young nurse or care-worker from one of the hospices, embodies the imperative to combative self-assertion in the face of old age which I have been arguing is common to Eastwood and Beauvoir.

In this scene Beauvoir is supposed to be interviewing a nurse from one of the state-run hospices. The interviewee complains about her work and the insults she is forced to endure from her elderly charges. As the 'interview' progresses Beauvoir becomes increasingly irate, interrupting the nurse and eventually lecturing her on her responsibilities. The scene is comic in its way, not just because Beauvoir is clearly unable to respect the conventions of the interview form but more significantly in that the nurse is faced on screen with a differential repetition of her daily encounters with mouthy old folk; the difference being here that while Beauvoir's combative self-assertion in this scene is visibly affect-laden, she expresses herself not in a barrage of insults but with hyperarticulate rational argument; as the scene unfolds Beauvoir gradually reduces her young 'interviewee' to a state of largely gestural, mute, self-expression, not unlike the elderly inhabitants of the hospice who are 'silenced' by its institutional apparatus. In this scene we find Beauvoir embodying on screen the quintessence of 'Eastwoodian' combative self-assertion, resisting in exemplary fashion the alienating logic of her culture's treatment of the elderly.

Yet it is also *Promenade* which shows Beauvoir's response to ageing to be somehow different from, and in some sense superior to, Eastwood's. In *Gran Torino* Kowalski is violently self-asserting to the last and even beyond, for after his death on the sidewalk his fighting spirit returns, shooting from the hip in a pugnacious will which mischievously disinherits his affronted 'real' family by leaving his house to the Catholic Church and the film's titular car to Thao. Not even death brings an end to Walt's combative self-assertion. Beauvoir, by contrast, is more malleable, by allowing herself to be 'used' elsewhere in this film in ways which draw attention, in a spirit of autocritique, or 'collaborative altercritique', so to speak, to the privileges of her own position as a relatively affluent and intelligent elderly woman. Thus the film sets up, according to Ahrne with Beauvoir's encouragement, contrasts between her own relatively privileged experience of old age and that of the elderly and undereducated poor; we see her in her flat crammed with souvenirs of a life lived to the full and this scene is intercut with footage from the bedside of a woman who is too ill to get down the stairs and who died before filming was completed (Davis 2006: 204).

The scene with the nurse shows Beauvoir on the warpath, at her most combatively self-asserting, embodying the age rage which both she and Eastwood see as the only viable response to the alienating ontological predicament of old age. Yet in her consenting to the intercutting which serves as a critique of her own position of class privilege we find a Beauvoir more composed than Eastwood in the face of the alienation she personally faces in old age. She allows herself to be othered, to be *used* by others, on screen; when she saw the finished work Beauvoir's first comment to Ahrne was 'you have used me well' (Ahrne 2008: 374; Davis 2006: 204). Beauvoir's willingness to be 'used' for worthwhile purposes was not confined to her involvement in this film. Remarks by Geneviève Fraisse on Beauvoir's involvement in feminist intellectual and political struggles during the 1970s suggest that this was an example of her more general tendency willingly to consent to being used as a mirror, a surface onto which others could project their anxieties and the contradictions of their situation (Fraisse 2008: 190). In other words, despite the combative self-assertion which she shares with Eastwood in her response to ageing in *Old Age* [1970], as the 1970s advanced it seems Beauvoir was sometimes also capable of letting go, allowing her egoic self-preserving rage to subside and others to 'use' her, and in using her to *other* her. It would be misleading to characterise that decade as one of serene acceptance of old age for Beauvoir yet it would be fair to say that as the decade advances she seems no longer to be constantly in the midst of an egoic crisis of age rage.

Conclusion: The Egoic Character of Age Rage

In psychoanalytic terms the 'age rage' which Eastwood and, for a time, Beauvoir share must be thought of as an 'egoic' phenomenon, or in other words a drama of the ego; the self asserted against the alienating chaos of senescence is the ego. We witness Walt 'standing strong' just as we see Beauvoir standing up to the young care-worker; in the face of the alienating threat of old age both mobilise quasi-militarised egoic defences and throw their rage back at a world which would consign them to docile inconsequence, to 'one of those great places', a retirement home. The fact that age rage is the last stand of the ego helps explain why it is both fraught and futile. It also helps to explain why, at a time when the chattering classes in France were in the grip of a form of psychoanalytic thinking which sidelined the ego (Lacan's), Beauvoir's account of old age often seems remarkably out of keeping with the dominant intellectual obsessions of the day. Not only does *Gran Torino* echo Beauvoir's ontology of the ageing process in *Old Age* but in his last act of self-assertion, albeit through annihilation, it shares her conviction in that essay that combative egoic rage thrown back on the world is the only viable and humane response. Only a very superficial reading of the film could see it as a continuation of Eastwood's 'revisionist' turn away from non-violence; rather, the film is an insidious reassertion of the continued need, in difficult personal and social circumstances, for heroic Eastwoodian self-assertion and its associated violence. Amid the social disintegration of contemporary American suburbia and faced with the individual challenges of ageing, it is as though violent self-assertion had rediscovered its value and its innocence. Even though *Gran Torino* exhibits its immaculate titular car with what at times is almost comic witlessness, it also allows, even if it does not exactly encourage, a glimpse beyond or beneath that alluring trophy-object of post-war working-class American manhood to the particular anticlimactic shittiness of the life-course for someone like Walt. In the necessity of violent egoic rage as a response, Eastwood and the Beauvoir of *Old Age* stand strong together in unlikely agreement.

Notes

1. I am grateful to Douglas Morrey for his incisive comments on an earlier draft and also to the editors of this volume. Dates of publication given in square brackets are of the first edition in any language.
2. Brigitte Fontaine, 'La Chanson de Simone', from her album *Rue Saint Louis en L'Île*(2004); text adapted from Beauvoir's love letters to Nelson Algren by Fabrice Rozie.
3. As Hughes notes, Eastwood had died twice on screen before, in *The Beguiled* (Siegel 1971) and *Honkytonk Man* (Eastwood 1982), but this is the first time he dies in a shootout (Hughes 2009: 211).
4. Toril Moi has argued that Beauvoir's view of ageing can be explained by her depression (Moi 1994: 243–52). I argued against this reductive view, which Beauvoir herself anticipated and countered (Davis 2006: 148); coincidentally Deutscher (2006: 289) broadly agrees.
5. There is some danger here of oversimplifying a diverse body of criticism of a large number of films. Let me be clear then that most, but not all, Eastwood critics concur that his work of this early period projects violent hegemonic masculinity. However, Knee (1993) argues that there is some evidence of 'male hysteria' in a film as early as *Play Misty for Me* (Eastwood act. and dir., 1971). Similarly, Smith argues that while the films of the 1970s were decidedly unsubtle responses to the impact of feminism on American culture, they nevertheless concerned themselves with 'the difficult task of representing masculinity at the hysterical moment of its potential deprivileging' (Smith 1993: 171). With these two significant exceptions most Eastwood critics subscribe to the notion, quickly taken up from reviews by Eastwood himself in interviews, of *Unforgiven* (1992) as a Damascus moment in its turning away from this form of violent masculinity.
6. See the forthcoming transcription: '"A Walk Through the Land of Old Age": A Documentary Film by Marianne Ahrne, Simone de Beauvoir, Pépo Angel and Bertrand Hurault. Directed by Marianne Ahrne. Transcription by Justine Sarrot and Oliver Davis, Translation by Alexander Hertich' (Beauvoir, forthcoming).

Bibliography

Ahrne, M. 2008. 'Filmer la vieillesse', *Les Temps Modernes*, 647–48: 368–74.
Badiou, A. 2004. *Handbook of Inaesthetics*. Stanford: Stanford University Press.
Baker, B. 2006. *Masculinity in Fiction and Film: Representing Men in Popular Genres*. London: Continuum.
Beauvoir, S. de. [1949] 2009. *The Second Sex*. London: Jonathan Cape.
———. [1963] 1965. *Force of Circumstance*. London: Deutsch and Weidenfeld and Nicholson.
———. [1970] 1972. *Old Age*. London: Weidenfeld and Nicolson.
———. Forthcoming. '"A Walk Through the Land of Old Age": A Documentary Film by Marianne Ahrne, Simone de Beauvoir, Pépo Angel and Bertrand Hurault. Directed by Marianne Ahrne. Transcription by Justine Sarrot and Oliver Davis,

Translation by Alexander Hertich', in S. de Beauvoir, *Political Writings*, M.A. Simons and M. Timmermann (eds). Urbana: University of Illinois Press.

Bingham, D. 1994. *Acting Male: Masculinities in the Films of James Stewart, Jack Nicholson, and Clint Eastwood*. New Brunswick: Rutgers University Press.

Cohan, S. and I. Hark. 1993. *Screening the Male: Exploring Masculinities in Hollywood Cinema*. London and New York: Routledge.

Cornell, D. 2009. *Clint Eastwood and Issues of American Masculinity*. New York: Fordham University Press.

Davis, O. 2006. *Age Rage and Going Gently: Stories of the Senescent Subject in Twentieth-Century French Writing*. Amsterdam and New York: Rodopi.

Deutscher, P. 2006. 'Beauvoir's *Old Age*', in C. Card (ed.), *The Cambridge Companion to Simone de Beauvoir*. Cambridge: Cambridge University Press.

Fraisse, G. 2008. 'Le rire de l'historienne', *Les Temps Modernes*, 647–48: 186–91.

Hughes, H. 2009. *Aim for the Heart: The Films of Clint Eastwood*. London and New York: I.B. Tauris & Co.

Jeffords, S. 1994. *Hard Bodies: Hollywood Masculinity in the Reagan Era*. New Brunswick: Rutgers University Press.

Knee, A. 1993. 'The Dialectic of Female Power and Male Hysteria in *Play Misty for Me*', in S. Cohan and I. Hark (eds), *Screening the Male: Exploring Masculinities in Hollywood Cinema*. London and New York: Routledge, pp. 87–102.

Lacan, J. 1977. 'The Mirror Stage as Formative of the *I* Function, as Revealed in Psychoanalytic Experience', in Écrits: *A Selection*. London: Tavistock, pp. 3–9.

Moi, T. 1994. *Simone de Beauvoir: The Making of an Intellectual Woman*. Oxford: Blackwell.

Neale, S. [1983] 1993. 'Masculinity as Spectacle: Reflections on Men and Mainstream Cinema', in S. Cohan and I. Hark (eds), *Screening the Male: Exploring Masculinities in Hollywood Cinema*. London and New York: Routledge, pp. 9–20.

Smith, P. 1993. *Clint Eastwood: A Cultural Production*. London: UCL Press.

Woodward, K. 1991. *Aging and its Discontents: Freud and other Fictions*. Bloomington: Indiana University Press.

Filmography

Ahrne, M (dir.). 1974. *Promenade au pays de la vieillesse* (*A Walk Through the Land of Old Age*). Sveriges Television.

Eastwood, C. (act. and dir.). 1982. *Honkytonk Man*. Malpaso.

———. 1983. *Sudden Impact*. Warner Bros. and Malpaso.

———. 1986. *Heartbreak Ridge*. Jay Weston and Malpaso.

———. 1992. *Unforgiven*. Malpaso.

Eastwood, C. (dir.). 2003. *Mystic River*. Malpaso.

———. 2006. *Flags of Our Fathers*. DreamWorks, Warner Bros., Amblin Entertainment and Malpaso.

———. 2006. *Letters from Iwo Jima*. Amblin Entertainment and Malpaso.

Eastwood, C. (act. and dir.). 2008. *Gran Torino*. Malpaso and others. Released on DVD with the very special features 'Manning the Wheel' and 'Gran Torino: More Than a Car'.

Siegel, D. 1971. *The Beguiled*. Malpaso.

10

LES BELLES IMAGES? MID-LIFE CRISIS AND OLD AGE IN TAMARA JENKINS' *THE SAVAGES*

Susan Bainbrigge

The subjects of mid-life crisis and old age abound in the fictional and non-fictional writings of Simone de Beauvoir: these include the personal accounts of the deaths of her mother and Sartre in *A Very Easy Death* and *Adieux: A Farewell to Sartre*, her essay on ageing entitled *Old Age*, the fictional heroines in crisis in the three stories that make up *The Woman Destroyed*, as well as the generational 'crises' presented in *Les Belles Images*. With these, and the existentialist perspectives of *The Second Sex* in mind, Beauvoir's various insights and analyses offer potentially fruitful frameworks for analysis of contemporary films dealing with questions of crisis, ageing and old age. This chapter proposes to analyse the recent film, *The Savages*, in this light.

Written and directed by Tamara Jenkins (b. 1962), *The Savages* featured at the Sundance, Toronto and London Film Festivals of 2007, and won an Oscar nomination for Best Original Screenplay. This success builds on the director's earlier films, the semi-autobiographical *The Slums of Beverly Hills* (1998), in which she presents an impoverished family who struggle to survive there in the 1970s, and *Family Remains* (1994).[1] To date reception of her films has been scant. *The Savages* considers in humorous, thought-provoking and challenging ways questions about love, family, ageing and death, and offers scope for analysis in the context of Beauvoirian critical frameworks and insights. In particular, Beauvoir's analysis of ageing offers a means to bring existentialist frameworks into dialogue with gerontology and film studies.

The film tells the story of a middle-aged brother and sister, Jon and Wendy Savage (played by Philip Seymour Hoffman and Laura Linney), who, upon the death of the partner of their father, Lenny (played by Philip Bosco), are suddenly forced to care for him themselves. They have to make difficult decisions about how they will do this and where he will live. We learn that they have been estranged from him, that during their childhood he was a difficult and violent man who beat them when they were young, that their mother is dead, and that he now suffers from dementia. Although a somewhat bleak scenario, Jenkins succeeds in blending black humour with close observation to examine the contemporary mores and malaise amongst the educated middle-classes of the United States. As Jenkins comments in an interview that accompanies the DVD of the film, her own experiences of dealing with relatives with dementia drew her to an 'observational humour', which enabled her to articulate the universality of the experiences of ageing and death. Her film is rare in its attempt to avoid treating the subject matter with, as she puts it, 'schmaltz and sentimentality', and in finding humour in things that are not necessarily obviously funny. Like Beauvoir in *A Very Easy Death* and *Adieux: A Farewell to Sartre*, she confronts the subject of ageing in a very direct, concrete manner, and refuses to shy away from the realities of embodied, degenerating selves (Marks 1986).[2] Thus seemingly taboo subjects are broached in an unflinching way.

The film focuses on the way the elderly are cared for in old age (or what Jenkins calls 'the outsourcing of the elderly in our society'), in particular those with dementia, by means of a narrative that concentrates on the relationships between the three characters. Throughout the film the relationships between Jon, Wendy and this difficult man whose behaviour can be distressing and unsettling, are portrayed; in the process, the complex entanglements between brother, sister and father are revealed. Whilst Jon and Wendy find themselves suddenly confronted by the dilemma of how to care for an elderly person suffering from dementia, in turn their own mid-life crises are depicted alongside the degeneration and, finally, death of the father in a nursing home. By use of striking narrative and visual effects, various existential crises (how to live, how to love, how to die …) come under the spotlight.

This essay proposes to explore the ways in which a number of specifically Beauvoirian concerns are played out. Most obviously, there is the central question of how society manages those in the 'Third age'. In *Old Age*, Beauvoir wrote that 'Society looks upon old age as a kind of shameful secret that it is unseemly to mention' (Beauvoir 1972: 7). She argues that it is the society in which you live that shapes the way you are treated in your old age, and the status that is imposed on you (Beauvoir 1972: 15). Old age is therefore viewed not merely as a biological fact but a cultural one too, and of course, as noted earlier, Beauvoir would recount in vivid detail her first-hand experiences of these encounters. The publication of her monumental essay in 1970 would also, as Ursula Tidd notes, serve as 'a devastating exposé of the plight of old people by a figure at the height of her intellectual celebrity' (Tidd 2009: 145).

Embodied Selves: Degeneration and Death

The opening scenes of the film offer an obvious starting point for analysis of Jenkins' treatment of ageing, embodied selves. The camera rests on a house in a residential area, and then takes the spectator on a journey through that area, which, it transpires, is a retirement community, Sun City, in Arizona. Shots of groups of seniors engaging in various sporting activities (for example, tap dancing, golf, swimming, playing bowls and cycling) follow in succession, whilst in the background the song 'I Don't Want to Play in Your Yard' can be heard.[3] The sky is a cerulean blue, the streets are pristine, the hedges and shrubs immaculately kept, the streets quiet and calm. If life looks supremely comfortable for this particular community, there is an air of unreality about the scene: it looks artificially clean and unrealistically safe. Indeed, we could add to this the remark that in order to enjoy this type of retirement one would need to have the means to afford it. It is as if the reality of old people becoming infirm, suffering dementia, generally declining, or struggling in poverty (a point Beauvoir was keen to highlight in *Old Age*), has been elided.[4] When the camera then returns to the house featured in the opening shot, slowly approaches it, and goes inside, a very different reality is presented. Unlike the active seniors outside, the character Lenny is seated on the sofa slumped over a bowl of cereal whilst a home help tries to negotiate the basics of getting the old man to flush the toilet after himself, his wife pictured sitting on the edge of the bed staring vacantly into space. After being badgered to return to the bathroom to flush, we then see Lenny smearing his own faeces on the wall, clearly confused and angry. The stark facts of embodied existence which Beauvoir highlighted throughout her oeuvre come to the fore here. The loss of dignity in such situations is especially apparent. Like Beauvoir, and her much-criticised refusal to shirk away from exposing the realities of the ageing self when, for example, detailing Sartre's incontinence in his later days in *Adieux*, or her mother's fragile, vulnerable body in *A Very Easy Death* (Beauvoir 1969a: 18),[5] Jenkins is at pains here to document the reality of life for a dementia sufferer and his or her family. In stylistic terms, she contrasts the bright, daylight shots of Sun City with sombre, impersonal depictions of nursing home and hospital interiors, providing swift changes in atmosphere and mood, from the almost manic good living of the retirement community to the depressing dullness of the depiction of the anonymous hospital rooms.[6]

Subsequent scenes in the film, as we shall see, reinforce the impact that illness and ageing have on both the sufferer and family members. In existential terms, these are the reminders of the physical constraints imposed on the ageing body and the various challenges to achieving a state of transcendence (over a state of immanence).[7] This might concern, for example, being free to initiate new projects and to achieve goals in later life, rather than taking refuge in old habits and routines (Beauvoir 1972: 518), and in the face of death. As Beauvoir notes in *Old Age*: 'life bases itself upon self-transcendence. But this transcendence comes up against death, particularly when a very great age has been reached' (Beauvoir 1972: 414). Remaining wedded to the past poses a threat to achieving self-realisation; increasingly, the elderly person suffers from objectification by society, and is, as Tidd notes, 'no longer viewed by society as a transcendent being' but rather, 'defined by their relationship to death' (Tidd 2009: 143).[8] Beauvoir writes in *Adieux* that Sartre had been keenly aware of this in the latter stages of his life – 'Sartre had always lived with his eyes fixed on the future; he could not live otherwise. Now that he was limited to the present, he looked upon himself as dead' (Beauvoir 1984: 119–20) – as she herself had been in the multiple volumes of her autobiography.

In early scenes in the film, there is ample evidence to support such observations. When Jon and Wendy visit their father at the hospital – the first time they have seen him in years – they confront an elderly man lying on a hospital bed, unable to sit up because of the restraining cuffs around his wrists. The predominant image is one of vulnerability and enforced passivity. A close-up shot of a urine drain bag attached to the bed serves as reminder of his frailty and dependence on others. An advert on the television featuring a brand of washing powder further reinforces the cultural taboo surrounding soiling and staining, and the necessary sanitisation of such evidence. When Lenny is discharged from the hospital subsequently, Wendy confronts the reality of ageing bodies in the form of incontinence (the nurse hands over a pile of adult nappy pads). This embarrassing dependency is highlighted again when the pair take a flight eastwards to join Jon; on the aeroplane Lenny suddenly shouts at his daughter that he needs to visit the bathroom, and on his way up the aisle, we see Wendy's horror as her shuffling father's trousers slowly slide down to his ankles to reveal the nappy underneath, removing all dignity. Mentally also, Lenny remains in the past, sometimes treating his son and daughter as if they were naughty children, sometimes forgetting their identities, mistakenly believing that he is in a hotel, when in fact he is in a nursing home, and suchlike. Thus the spectator is plunged into a context in which ageing has negative, and even frightening, connotations, and where society has dealt with this anxiety in a way that attempts to evacuate its realities.

The circumstances in which Lenny's second wife, Mrs Savage, dies takes the depiction of the ageing body into more darkly humorous territory. In a beauty salon she suddenly keels over onto the manicure table, surrounded by young and beautiful Far Eastern women who provide the manicures for wealthy, white women. Hovering in the background here is the question of the potential exploitation of young foreign women in a wealthy American suburb.[9] However, there is primarily a grotesque aspect to the scene, with the young beautician's inappropriate comments about her client's choice of nail colour being 'sexy' underscoring an abject reality, one in which Mrs Savage is hardly able to speak, let alone be capable of any kind of seductive gambit.

In addition, frank discussions of death seep into the depictions of many other scenes in the film too. These range, for example, from discussion of the rather macabre received wisdom that one of the ways to tell whether death is imminent is to check whether the person's toes have curled, apparently a sign of degeneration, to Jon's outburst on the subject in front of one of the upmarket nursing homes where Wendy has tried, and failed, to find a place for her father. After a difficult interview between the nursing home staff and Lenny, it becomes clear that he has dementia and is not at all suited to the 'independent living' area of the nursing home to which Wendy has applied, despite her best attempts to coach him through the interview. When Jon and Wendy wheel their father out towards the car, the following exchange occurs:

> Jon: Wendy, why are you wasting your time on fantasies?
> …
> Wendy: Ha, ah … I happen to think it's nicer here.
> J: Of course you do, because you're the consumer that they want to target, you're the guilty demographic. The landscaping, the neighbourhoods of care, they're not for the residents, they're for the relatives, people like you and me, who don't want to admit to what's really going on here.
> W: Which is what, Jon?
> J: People are dying, Wendy. Right inside that beautiful building right now, it's a fucking horror show! And, and all this wellness propaganda, and the landscaping, it's just there to obscure the miserable fact that people die …

Jon, particularly in the forceful outburst at the end of their exchange, rails against the ways in which society evades the stark realities of ageing and death. He alerts Wendy to the consumerism and guilt-inducing practices of the 'wellness propaganda' with which they are bombarded. He underlines the fact that our confrontation with mortality is an unavoidable fact, as Beauvoir notes: 'life bases itself upon self-transcendence. But this transcendence comes up against death, particularly when a very great age has been reached' (Beauvoir 1972: 414). The fact of caring for elders, an overwhelmingly universal business, means that most of us are implicated in one way or another. Guilt is a commonly felt response to the handing over of care for elders to a third party or institution, and often goes hand-in-hand with some level of self-deception or what Beauvoir termed '*mauvaise foi*'.[10] Wendy's attempts to alleviate feelings of guilt associated with the fact that her father is in a nursing home will be familiar to many spectators: she provides cosy soft furnishings such as lamps and cushions to personalise the space, even in the face of the evidence that her father is completely oblivious, confused by, and at times actively hostile to such additions. At heart, she berates herself for putting her father into a nursing home ('we are horrible, horrible, horrible people'), and her attempts to lessen the distress caused by those thoughts are portrayed in convincing ways by Jenkins. For Beauvoir, the process of writing *A Very Easy Death* had perhaps served to alleviate guilt, in a different but related way, arising from the circumstances of her mother's death, and to articulate a reconciliation with the mother after her death in a way that had not been possible when she was alive.[11]

Lenny's hostility emerges in other ways too. During a film screening at the nursing home the old man reacts angrily to a domestic scene in the film he is watching; he swears at the male character on the screen, and exclaims that his father always smacked him around.[12] Old memories are revived, and these strong reactions offer a further link to Beauvoirian analysis concerning the cyclical relationship between childhood and old age. Beauvoir remarked in *Old Age* that:

> The child serves a hard apprenticeship to life; he is attacked by complexes that he has to overcome; he has feelings of guilt, shame and anxiety. The unpleasant memories of this time that were repressed in adult life revive in old age.
>
> (Beauvoir 1972: 413)[13]

The child re-emerges at critical moments, and Jenkins pursues this idea of regression to former states in the film. For example, in the interactions between Wendy and Jon, we frequently see the older brother–younger sister dynamic at play, whether in a bar when Jon tells Wendy 'this is not the time to regress', or when he becomes annoyed with her expressions of neediness, suggesting that she is assuming the role of the younger sister requiring to be taken care of. He also becomes irritated by her questioning of his relationship with his Polish girlfriend. The actual processing of childhood trauma also emerges as a theme throughout the film: Wendy's dream of having her play performed – a play based on her childhood experiences and featuring a young boy based on Jon as the central character – is realized at the end.

Death and illness lurk in other parts of the film, beyond the confines of gerontological concerns. Their depictions serve as an example of the ways in which individuals may experience, for different reasons, a generalised existential angst about their mortality, as Beauvoir had explored in depth in her autobiographical writings. Thus Wendy lies to her lover about her recent test results, suggesting that she has received a worrying abnormal result when in fact there is nothing wrong; we learn that she is taking medication for anxiety, and uses herbal remedies as well as availing herself of the drugs belonging to the late Mrs Savage, whilst Jon uses medication to manage high cholesterol. The body therefore also features in the context of what we might call middle-aged, as opposed to end-of-life, maladies. In order to keep the body fit, healthy and beautiful, Wendy follows a keep-fit routine in front of the television, whilst Jon's injury on the squash court which results in his being hooked up to a complex neck harness highlights the ways in which we cannot escape the fact of our embodied selves. The nature of the brother and sister's verbal exchanges about their health also alert us to the fact that they are part of a therapy-savvy generation, familiar with psychoanalytical terminology. More generally, the themes of suffering and illness run as a central thematic strand through the film, even stretching to animal well-being and suffering (Wendy's cat and her lover's dog feature in secondary story lines that highlight the film's central concerns). The themes of mental and physical suffering can also be examined via key intertextual references to the likes of Brecht, Beckett and Genet.[14] The latter, whilst outside the scope of this chapter, offer a cultural 'existential' genealogy in which Beauvoir can be placed.

'Les Belles Images', Time, Space and Situated Selves

The way in which this embodied self is 'managed' offers scope to make connections with other aspects of Beauvoir's oeuvre, and more specifically her 1966 text *Les Belles Images*. In the presentation of end-of-life care it is possible, for example, to trace the ways in which a consumerist ideology connects with a fear of confronting taboos relating to death and ageing. Wendy finds herself poring over the promotional literature for various nursing homes, such as 'Hill Haven' and 'Green Manor'. The promotional film for the latter has recourse to slogans and language designed to elicit guilt in the target audience; the voice-over combines both the euphemistic and the emotive: 'what to do when the parent who took care of you can no longer take care of themselves'. The refrain 'heaven, I'm in heaven' from the Irving Berlin song 'Cheek to Cheek' is heard in the background. Indeed, the residential home functions as simulacrum of a 'heavenly' place, offering the prospect of enduring good health and, perhaps, some promise of immortality. These are the kinds of 'belles images' which Beauvoir's character Laurence in *Les Belles Images* (in her capacity as an advertising copy editor), would spend much of her time creating, and which Beauvoir used as a vehicle in order to denounce, as Blandine Stefanson puts it, 'the transformation of people into things, slogans, images' [my translation] (Stefanson 1980: 60).[15] Laurence's work would involve the creation of fantasy worlds through the language of advertising to sell a product ('I am not selling wooden panels. I am selling security, success and a touch of poetry into the bargain' (Beauvoir 1969b: 20)), just as the brochures and film become the means for Wendy to evade the reality of her father's situation, that he is not in control of his faculties, and is dying.[16] Image and reality are frequently juxtaposed on the screen, and Jenkins' visual effects serve to reinforce her consumerist critique. If we now analyse the significance of time within these various spaces, there is further scope for comparison with Beauvoirian concerns, in particular 'the way in which the aged man inwardly apprehends his relationship with his body, with time, and with the outside world' (Beauvoir 1972: 16).

Jenkins' use of spatial imagery in the film, and in particular her juxtaposing of movement and stasis, is particularly marked. If Beauvoir suggests that elderly people's relationship to time is akin to living in a 'perpetual present' (Beauvoir 1972: 144), which militates against the pursuit of future goals, such ideas also find expression here. In Beauvoir's terms, the forward-looking potential of 'praxis' is replaced by a simple 'exis' of the aged. While Lenny remains for the majority of the film confined to bed, Jon and Wendy are frequently filmed in motion, whether travelling (in cars, planes, trains), walking, running, playing sport or teaching. For Lenny, the days resemble each other, punctuated by the same routines and family visits. His 'perpetual present' is located in an enclosed world, in which the only excursions that take place are not physical but mental shifts into the past, sometimes with unhappy, dramatic consequences (as noted earlier, for example, when he first sees his children at the hospital, and then during the film screening at the nursing home).

The depiction of shifts from present to past is, however, not restricted to the character of Lenny. The scene which presents Wendy travelling by train enables the director to highlight an important time shift from present to past for her also. A right-to-left travelling shot (a useful technique to suggest this type of temporal shift) tracks her journey from the nursing home back to the hotel. Wendy's memories are jogged there when we see her exploring a box containing her father's memorabilia; this includes photos of herself and Jon as children and assorted notes and mementos. She finds herself momentarily in a nostalgic space. The relationship with her father is in a state of limbo, has not been able to develop in the present, and is painful to recollect in the past; indeed, the prospect of re-engaging with someone who is so clearly 'other' to her is a daunting one. The filming of the subsequent phone call with Jon concerning the care of their father further highlights their different situations and perspectives. Wendy is in a warm sunny spot resplendent with blue skies, deluding herself into thinking that her father can be supported in an assisted living residence whereas Jon is in a snowy Baltimore in winter clothes, recommending nursing homes in a more matter-of-fact way, and talking about dementia without baulking. Their approaches to illness differ, and in Beauvoirian terms, Jon approaches the reality of the situation in a more authentic manner than Wendy in his attempts not to shy away from the reality of the situation (although he is not exempt from inauthentic behaviour either; rather, his self-delusion is highlighted in the context of his relationship with his girlfriend).

The film's depiction of old age as discussed thus far has been largely negative; where there are positive depictions, the authenticity of such scenes has been questionable because they are supremely stylised and have an air of artifice about them. Does Jenkins have anything positive to say about the subject? It could be argued that the structure of the film itself functions in a metatextual way as a commentary, not specifically on old age, but on the importance of recognising the value of past cultural artefacts in the present. Jenkins' appreciation and homage to the films, literature and music of past eras is clearly in evidence.[17] Such references are also used within the storyline to highlight, for example, Wendy's *mauvaise foi* or Jon's passion for Brecht.[18] Brechtian theatre is a politically engaged art form which highlights the constructed nature of a play, via what is known as the '*verfremdungseffekt*' (a distancing effect), and intersperses songs to interrupt the action, as is the case in Jenkins' film. The cultural references have a rejuvenating effect, finding a new context in which to operate. Thus, in this more academic way, Jenkins brings the past into the present and thereby halts one potential process of stagnation. This appreciation of the past may function in a tangential way as regards the subject matter of the film, which is a largely bleak account of ageing, yet it does offer some kind of counterpoint nonetheless.

In conclusion, the film, although set in a very specifically contemporary western 'situation' (of a pill-popping, therapy-savvy generation), has at its core universally-recognisable concerns – relationships, ageing and dying – and dramatises existential questions of 'embodied' living and dying that so concerned Simone de Beauvoir.[19] It depicts universal experiences from which few are exempt – dealing with ageing parents and confronting the question of how to care for them. Jenkins shows how the elderly can so easily become objectified and/or marginalized in society, and how their situations affect their offspring. If there is little evidence of a re-evaluation of the positive aspects of age (wisdom, experience), that were acknowledged by Beauvoir,[20] Jenkins, however, by the diverse use of intertextual references in the film skilfully interweaves legacies from the past with the 'ordinary' flow of present-day concerns. Her middle-aged protagonists, Jon and Wendy, are neither idealised nor demonised; they are presented humanely in their efforts to deal with dying. Beauvoir would write at the end of *A Very Easy Death*: 'All men must die: but for every man his death is an accident and, even if he knows it and consents to it, an unjustifiable violation' (Beauvoir 1969a: 92). Jenkins' film explores the potentially hazardous territory of death in film, in particular looking at the subject from the perspective of those who care for the dying, through the eyes of those whom the dead leave behind.

Notes

1. She also won Best Screenplay at the following awards in 2007: Independent Spirit Awards; Los Angeles Film Critics Association; National Society of Film Critics; San Francisco Film Critics Circle. For further biographical and background information on the director, see the *New York Times* directors' archive entry by Nathan Southern, at http://movies.nytimes.com/person/1548287/Tamara-Jenkins/biography (retrieved 2 December 2009).
2. On transgressing taboos in Beauvoir's writings, see Marks (1986), Jardine (1985) and Bainbrigge (2002).
3. Henry Petrie, Philip Wingate and Dick Manning; performed by Peggy Lee.
4. In *Old Age* Beauvoir would make links between age and poverty, quoting for example Margaret S. Gordon, who wrote that 'Poverty among the aged remains one of our most persistent and difficult problems' (Beauvoir 1972: 275).
5. Catriona Mackenzie writes, 'Our bodies define our situation in the world; consciousness is a relation to the world from a particular bodily perspective: "To be present in the world implies strictly that there exists a body which is at once a material thing in the world and a point of view towards this world" (SS 39)', in 'A Certain Lack of Symmetry: Beauvoir on Autonomous Agency and Women's Embodiment' (Evans 1998: 140).
6. After Lenny's death, the scene in which Jon and Wendy return to collect their father's belongings also serves to highlight the impersonality of the space.
7. For definitions of the terms 'transcendence' and 'immanence' as they are used by Beauvoir, see Alex Hughes (1995). On 'transcendence' she writes that 'This notion signifies that potential for ongoing, willed self-(re)construction and self-redefinition, via freely chosen projects, which for Sartre is what marks us out as human. It suggests a kind of forward movement into the future', and on 'immanence', using Moi's analysis: 'A key term in *Le Deuxième Sexe*. Moi states that "most precisely defined as non-transcendence, immanence [...] would seem to include everything from the state of thing-like facticity sought by the for-itself to bad faith and various kinds of unfree situations"' (Moi 1994: 154) in Hughes (1995: 63).
8. She also writes: 'My past is the in-itself that I am in so far as I have been outstripped; in order to possess it I must bind it to existence by a project; if this project consists of

knowing it then I must make it present to myself by means of bringing it back to my memory' (Beauvoir 1972: 402). Beauvoir advises in *Old Age* that, 'There is only one solution if old age is not to be an absurd parody of our former life, and that is to go on pursuing ends that give our existence a meaning – devotion to individuals, to groups or to causes, social, political, intellectual or creative work' (601).

9. It is a society riven by racial inequalities, as we see in the nursing home where black employees look after white residents.

10. 'Bad faith' is a term in existentialist thought which refers to the process by which we hide, consciously or unconsciously, the truth of a situation from ourselves, preferring to behave inauthentically rather than to exercise our freedom to make decisions based on our acceptance of a certain responsibility in the process.

11. This aspect of the text is considered in more detail in my chapter on *A Very Easy Death*, in *Writing Against Death: the Autobiographies of Simone de Beauvoir* (Bainbrigge 2005: 176–78).

12. The film is *The Jazz Singer* (1927).

13. See also Beauvoir's comment: 'It is his childhood above all that returns to haunt the aged man: ever since Freud's time we have known the great importance of the first years in the formation of the individual and his world – an importance already sensed by Montaigne. The impressions received at that time are so deeply imprinted that they can never be effaced' (Beauvoir 1972: 412).

14. For example, Jon is an academic who is working on a book on Bertolt Brecht.

15. 'La transformation des gens en choses, en slogans, en images'.

16. Implicit critiques of consumerism are also evident in the scene in the supermarket in which the camera homes in on ceiling-high shelves of cereals, and in the manner in which the Savages' home is open to potential buyers before Wendy has time to pack up her father's belongings.

17. Jenkins refers to authors Beckett, Brecht and Genet, and features extracts from songs ('I Don't Want to Play in Your Yard'; 'On a Slow Boat to China'; 'Sentimental Lady'; 'Two of a Kind'; 'You Make Me Feel So Young'; 'Cheek to Cheek'; 'Nostalgic Memory'; 'Solomon Song'; 'Soldadi'; 'Sitting by the Riverside'; 'I'm Sticking with You'), and films (*The Big Noise*, *The Blue Angel*, *The Jazz Singer*, *Night and the City*, *All About Eve*).

18. Wendy and her lover discuss their relationship in the context of the 1930 Josef von Sternberg cult German film starring Marlene Dietrich, *The Blue Angel*, for example.

19. The film could be compared with Mike Leigh's very British take on class, ageing and social structures in *High Hopes* (1988).

20. As Tidd notes: 'Old people's marginalization meant that they have never played a consistently determining role in history, although some non-Western societies have historically valued the experience of its aged members, equating their increased age with wisdom and greater experience' (Tidd 2009: 142).

Bibliography

Bainbrigge, S. 2002. '*La Cérémonie des adieux* and *Le Livre brisé*: Situating Sartre in the text', *MLR* 97(4): 835–49.

———. 2005. *Writing Against Death: the Autobiographies of Simone de Beauvoir*. Amsterdam: Rodopi.

Beauvoir, S. de. [1964] 1969a. *Une Mort très douce*. Paris: Gallimard. *A Very Easy Death*, trans. P. O'Brian. Harmondsworth: Penguin.

———. [1966] 1969b. *Les Belles images*. Paris: Gallimard. *Les Belles Images*, trans. P. O'Brian. London: Fontana.

———. [1968] 1969c. *La Femme rompue*. Paris: Gallimard. *The Woman Destroyed*, trans. P. O'Brian. New York: Pantheon.

————. [1970] 1972. *La Vieillesse*. Paris: Gallimard. *Old Age*, trans. P. O'Brian. Harmondsworth: Penguin.

————. [1981] 1984. *La Cérémonie des adieux*. Paris: Gallimard. *Adieux: A Farewell to Sartre*, trans. P. O'Brian. Harmondsworth: Penguin.

Evans, R. (ed.). 1998. *Simone de Beauvoir's* The Second Sex: *New Interdisciplinary Essays*. Manchester: Manchester University Press.

Hughes, A. 1995. *Beauvoir: Le Sang des autres*. Glasgow: University of Glasgow French and German Publications.

Jardine, A. 1985. 'Death Sentences: Writing Couples and Ideology', *Poetics Today* 6: 119–31.

Mackenzie, C. 1998. 'A Certain Lack of Symmetry: Beauvoir on Autonomous Agency and Women's Embodiment', in R. Evans (ed.), *Simone de Beauvoir's* The Second Sex: *New Interdisciplinary Essays*. Manchester: Manchester University Press.

Marks, E. 1986. 'Transgressing the (In)cont(in)ent Boundaries: The Body in Decline', *Yale French Studies* 72: 181–200.

Moi, T. 1994. *Simone de Beauvoir: The Making of an Intellectual Woman*. Cambridge and Oxford: Blackwell.

Pamerleau, W.C. 2009. *Existentialist Cinema*. London: Palgrave Macmillan.

Stefanson, B. (ed.). 1980. *Les Belles Images*. By Simone de Beauvoir. London: Heinemann.

Tarr, C., and B. Rollet. 2001. *Cinema and The Second Sex: Women's Filmmaking in France in the 1980s and 1990s*. New York; London: Continuum.

Tidd, U. 2009. *Simone de Beauvoir*. London: Reaktion Books.

Filmography

Jenkins, T (dir.). 1994. *Family Remains*. Boyfriend Productions Inc. Independent Television Service.

————. 1998. *The Slums of Beverly Hills*. Twentieth Century Fox Film Corporation; South Fork Pictures.

————. 2007. *The Savages*. Fox Searchlight Pictures (www.fox.co.uk).

Leigh, M. (dir.). 1988. *High Hopes*. British Screen Productions; Channel Four Films.

11

FEMINIST PHENOMENOLOGY AND THE FILMS OF SALLY POTTER

Kate Ince

Sally Potter's place in British cinema is uncontested, as a recent retrospective organised by the British Film Institute shows.[1] Since her debut with the half-hour *Thriller* in 1979, she has carved out a place for herself as one of our leading independent filmmakers, but success has often not come easily: the highly crafted experimentalism of *Thriller* met with acclaim, but her similarly styled first feature *The Gold Diggers* (1983) failed to find much appreciation, and she struggled for nine years to be able to complete *Orlando* (1992), her adaptation of Virginia Woolf's 1928 *Orlando: A Biography.*[2] With *Orlando* Potter was carried by the spirit of the shift in women's filmmaking from experimentalism and explicitly political reflection on representation towards narrative pleasure, while still giving an undeniably feminist twist to Woolf's story of time-travel and gender-bending from the seventeenth to the twentieth centuries. The feminist political drive that had marked all her films up to 1992 was maintained by Potter's own performance in the allegory of gender relations built into her next film *The Tango Lesson* (1997), but has been much less evident subsequently, in *The Man Who Cried* (2000) and *Yes* (2005). Other kinds of politics have marked Potter's filmmaking in the 2000s, although in her most recent production *Rage* (2009), anti-capitalism might be said to be just as evident as in *The Gold Diggers*. While feminism may have faded from view in Potter's most recent work, however, it is indispensable to any discussion of her early and 1990s films.

In the context of this volume of essays, Simone de Beauvoir scarcely needs introduction, but it is in her work in feminist phenomenology rather than in existentialist philosophy that a convergence with Potter's filmmaking can be seen. As is now widely accepted, the supporting role to Sartre's philosophical work Beauvoir insistently adopted throughout her life began to be questioned and unpicked in her last years, and she was re-interpreted as a philosopher in her own right by a number of commentators.[3] In most of these books, Beauvoir's identity as a phenomenologist is to the fore, and a key notion securing this for her is Edmund Husserl's concept of the 'lived body'.[4] In France in the 1940s, the primary currency of the concept of the *corps vécu* was via the work of Beauvoir's and Sartre's friend Maurice Merleau-Ponty, who had studied Husserl's unpublished papers in Louvain in the late 1930s, and whose *Phénoménologie de la perception* had been published in 1945, just as Sartre and Beauvoir set up *Les Temps modernes*. The superiority of Beauvoir's deployment of the notion of the lived body over Merleau-Ponty's, as feminist commentators have repeatedly pointed out though, is that it is always particularised in a concrete, historical *situation*: Beauvoir's concept of the body *as* 'situation', developed in her philosophical writings of the 1940s and referred to throughout *The Second Sex*, is distinct from and distinctly more concrete than the parallel concept Sartre developed over the same period. Embodiment is always particular, always different, and the feminist philosophers undertaking the work of re-evaluating Beauvoir draw attention to the direct focus on embodied experience to be found in her novels, stories and autobiographical volumes, as well as in her philosophy. The strength of Beauvoir's thought, they claim, lay in her method, whatever the genre she was writing in, and since the embodied experience described was very often that of women, she could be regarded as the founder of her own mode of political philosophy – feminist phenomenology. By adding sexual difference to the notions of the lived body proposed by Husserl and Merleau-Ponty and developed by Beauvoir in her concept of the (historical) body as situation, feminist phenomenology is born – though in fact it may be regarded as having had other precursors, such as Husserl's student and assistant Edith Stein, and the political philosopher Hannah Arendt.[5]

Amid the re-evaluation of Beauvoir's importance to twentieth-century philosophy during the 1990s, polemic arose over which type of feminist philosophy, or theory, was more relevant to feminist politics. Frustrated by what she saw as the jargon-ridden abstraction of much of the poststructuralist feminist theory written in the 1980s and still influential in the 1990s, Toril Moi – whose 1994 book *Simone de Beauvoir: The Making of an Intellectual Woman* made a vital contribution to the new wave of Beauvoir studies – inserted Beauvoir right back into mainstream feminist theoretical debate, with her 1999 essay 'What is a Woman? Sex, Gender and the Body in Feminist Theory'. Her grounds for so doing were that the usefulness of the sex/gender distinction for feminism had foundered amid the abstruseness of contemporary gender theory, and that poststructuralist philosophy, often critiqued for its perceived remoteness from 'real-life' political situations, had offered feminist theory no usable account of embodied subjectivity:

> I have come to the conclusion that no amount of rethinking of the concepts of sex and gender will produce a good theory of the body or subjectivity. The distinction between sex and gender is simply irrelevant to the task of producing a concrete, historical understanding of what it means to be a woman (or a man) in a given society. No feminist has produced a better theory of the embodied, sexually different human being than Simone de Beauvoir in *The Second Sex*. Because contemporary English-language critics have read Beauvoir's 1949 essay through the lens of the

1960s sex/gender distinction, they have failed to see that her essay provides exactly the kind of non-essentialist, concrete, historical and social understanding of the body that so many contemporary feminists are looking for. In short, Beauvoir's claim that 'one is not born, but rather becomes a woman' has been sorely misunderstood by contemporary feminists. Lacan returned to Freud; it is time for feminist theorists to return to Beauvoir.

(Moi 1999: 4–5)

Moi's argument here is highly convincing, and it is perhaps surprising that her essay was not more widely taken up by feminist critics and theorists of literature and film. Their failure to do so might, however, be explained by the divisiveness of her argument, which drives a wedge between Beauvoirian feminism and the poststructuralist critical approaches to gender and embodiment that held sway following the publication of Judith Butler's *Gender Trouble* (1990) and *Bodies That Matter: the Discursive Limits of 'Sex'* (1993). But although the turn away from the sex/gender distinction called for by Moi may not have been explicitly signalled in literary and film studies, it has been felt, and will be one important element of my exploration of Sally Potter's films. Potter's filmmaking, I shall argue, is an excellent dramatization of the central ideas underpinning feminists' turn toward the phenomenological notion of the 'lived body'. A feminist phenomenological enquiry into film must start from and focus on screen women as embodied subjects of their own experience and desire. Little work linking phenomenology, film and feminism has been done, although one of the few articles to adopt such an approach, by Elena del Rio, focuses on Potter's *Thriller* (del Rio 2004).[6] In my readings of *Orlando* and *The Tango Lesson*, I shall employ a similar blend of methodologies to the one adopted by del Rio,[7] detailing the pleasure women take in movement and bodily action in these films, while also considering the meanings offered by their living, acting bodies, and the symbolic frameworks within which their agency and physical actions take place.

Embodiment, Femininity and Becoming in *Orlando*

In *Orlando*, history – a very selective and English history – is made a theme by the film's structure: Potter treats her protagonist's travels from the Elizabethan age to the twentieth century in six chapters, 1600 Death, 1610 Love, 1650 Poetry, 1750 Society, 1850 Sex and, finally, Birth (date unspecified). The death is that of Queen Elizabeth I, the love Orlando's for Sasha, the daughter of the Muscovite ambassador to England, and the birth that of Orlando's daughter, in one of Potter's few significant changes to Woolf's text, where Orlando's child is a son. The historical moment of this childhood seems to be a mixture of 1928 (the date of Woolf's book) and the 'present day' of the film (1992), in that Orlando rides a vintage 1928-style motorbike with a sidecar through a recognizable early-1990s London of Canary Wharf and Docklands. Orlando is thus always in a well-defined and dated historical situation, even if he/she inexplicably advances as an embodied and situated subject through over three centuries while 'hardly ageing a day', as both text and film state. That Orlando's body is his/her situation is illustrated in at least two ways. First, there is his change of sexed body just before her entry into the society of 1750, upon which follow two scenes emphasising just how objectified and excluded women of the period were. In one, Orlando wanders idly through the sunny, silent long gallery of her country seat to the sole sound of peacocks calling on the lawns outside, adjusting her movement to prevent her voluminous hooped skirts from knocking over pieces of furniture draped in sunlit white dust-sheets. Since Orlando too is clad in brilliant white, the most striking element of this brief scene is her resemblance to the furniture and, hence, the status of woman as property at this period – a prefiguring of how she will be stripped of her inheritance by a lawsuit that begins in the eighteenth century and concludes in the nineteenth. In the second scene, a literary gathering hosted by a countess at which Jonathan Swift, Alexander Pope and Joseph Addison hold court, 'Orlando is immobilized like one elaborate frosted blue cake on a love seat. Complete with an unlikely sculpted headdress, she becomes a porcelain figurine, hampered equally by costume and convention from moving or responding to the routine snubs of the male "wits"' (Pidduck 1997: 176).

The second manner in which *Orlando* envisions history, already anticipated in the scenes described above, is the continuously glorious use it makes of lavish costume. But although the film is often included alongside Jane Campion's *The Piano* (Australia/New Zealand/France 1993) and Julie Dash's *Daughters of the Dust* (U.S. 1991) in a list of what was in 2003 called 'the emerging global feminist reappropriation of costume drama' (Imre 2003: 188), the genre category 'costume drama' suggests a realist treatment of a particular era and set of characters never allowed to develop by the film's restless progress. Rather, as Patricia Mellencamp argues, 'the performative elements (of gesture, glance, pose, costume) are more telling than the narrative. History becomes something to learn from, move through, and get beyond' (Mellencamp 1995: 283). Orlando the character and *Orlando* the film skip energetically through history, or perhaps fly in the manner characteristic of Hélène Cixous's *écriture féminine*,[8] defying history's gravity and territorializing forces. This brings me to the core of the convergence between Potter's envisioning of womanhood and Beauvoir's theorizing of femininity, which I see in the type of energy driving their filmic and philosophical narratives – the positive desire of becoming, and becoming-woman.

In *The Second Sex*, Beauvoir sums up the importance of becoming to her enquiry into womanhood as follows:

> But the definition of man is that he is a being who is not given, who makes himself what he is. As Merleau-Ponty rightly said, man is not a natural species: he is an historical idea. Woman is not a fixed reality but a becoming; she has to be compared to man in her becoming, that is, her *possibilities* have to be defined.
>
> ([DSI 73] SS 46)

This statement, which is both existentialist and feminist, is in no way at odds with the 'sex/gender' feminist theorizing dominant in the humanities and social sciences from the 1960s till the end of the twentieth century: biological sex gives way to cultural/social gender, of which a feminine gender identity is one possible outcome. But Beauvoir's emphasis in her description of woman as a becoming is clearly on history and process rather than identity, and on an unbounded, infinite mode of historical desire and energy. The quotation continues:

> what skews the issues so much is that she is being reduced to what she was, to what she is today, while the question concerns her capacities; the fact is that her capacities manifest themselves clearly only when they have been realised: but the fact is also that when one considers a being who is transcendence and surpassing, it is never possible to close the books.
>
> ([DSI 73] SS 46)

Women's historical possibilities are unlimited, just as men's are. By virtue of its transgendering narrative and passage through nearly four centuries, *Orlando* allows – or, perhaps we should say, gloriously stages – the comparison of woman's becoming to man's Beauvoir speaks of in *The Second Sex*, a narrative drive picked up on by many critics.[9] One aspect of the film on which much critical commentary has focused is the contrast between the universalist androgyny of Woolf's text and the queer postmodern reconstruction of a female genealogy in Potter's film: as Roberta Garrett summarises, 'Woolf's "modernist" project aims to undermine the stability of forms of gender identification, whereas Potter's "postmodern" interpretation posits a "reconstructed" notion of female subjectivity which acts as a locus of resistance to the "master narrative" of British history' (Garrett 1995: 96). The birth of Orlando's daughter and her happiness as a mother despite having been dispossessed of her inheritance would seem to make this digression of film from book unambiguous, and yet Potter has stated that where Orlando's change of sex is concerned, she thought that using the same actor for the male and female character would help 'the idea of individuality' to prevail, and what she has called 'the seamless individuality across the genders' would not be lost (Potter in Degli-Esposti 1996: 88). She may have been wary of making a feminist film – '"feminist" has become a sort of trigger word that closes down thinking rather than opening it up' (Potter in Degli-Esposti 1996: 89) – but ended up with one nonetheless, perhaps because of the thoroughly postmodern sensibility of *Orlando*'s queer, flighty, disrespectful treatment of identity, history and the genre of costume drama. The affirmative energy of becoming-woman spills out of almost every scene of *Orlando*, from its clipped, witty dialogue and protagonist's meaningful looks to camera.

Amid many meticulously performed such looks from Tilda Swinton, in fact, one scene in *Orlando* strikingly stages vision as female, and as embodied. After Orlando tends to Shelmerdine's injured ankle at her country seat, and confesses to the camera that although she feels she is about to faint, she has never felt better in her life, the action cuts to their love-making. Stereotypically gendered bodily postures are reversed here, as Shelmerdine (with his flowing hair and sensuous mouth) lies back to be stroked by Orlando and the camera, in several close-ups on his face. So intense is Orlando's/the camera's gaze upon him that at one moment, he registers embarrassment and perhaps a wish that she relax the attention she is directing at him. The camera then cuts to a tracking shot along a human torso, which is revealed by its curves to be a woman's rather than a man's – but this gentle caress of Swinton's torso is no display of female nudity or objectification of the feminine, and ends instead on a long close-up on Orlando's eye. In addition to privileging the woman's look at this point in the action, the shot reminds us insistently that the look itself is embodied, rather than transcendent and immaterial. Speculatively distinct modes of feminine and masculine desire are undermined by the blurring of gender identities evident throughout Orlando and Shelmerdine's encounter, but there is no confusing their female and male bodies, or disputing that her woman's look is privileged over his.

Perhaps the principal way in which Potter dramatizes the affirmative energy of becoming-woman in *Orlando*, though, is through bodily action. As man and as woman (when she is not constrained by her clothes), Orlando engages in an enormous range of physical activity, from the straightforward (running back to and through Queen Elizabeth's court in '1600 Death', hastening through the maze until she breaks into a run after indignantly refusing the Archduke Harry's offer of marriage) to the sporting – skating on the frozen river Thames, horse riding with Shelmerdine, motorcycling through London with her daughter. On the one hand, this reinforces how Potter's experience as a choreographer is to the fore in her adaptation, whose credited choreographer is Jacky Lansley, the dancer with whom Potter cofounded The Limited Dance Company in 1974 (Fowler 2009: 21), and who performed in *Thriller*, *The Gold Diggers* and *The London Story*. Dance and choreography are drawn on just as extensively in *Orlando* as in *The Tango Lesson*, though displayed more subtly. On the other hand, body comportment, motility and spatiality are the chief concerns of feminist phenomenology, which takes differences between male and female modes of moving and relating to space as the starting point for its enquiry into differentiated embodiment. Beauvoir discusses these issues repeatedly in *The Second Sex*; in Volume I, towards the end of the first, 'Biological Data' chapter, in the second chapter on 'The Psychoanalytical Point of View', and in the first chapter of Part Three on 'Myths'; in Volume II, in the first three chapters of Part One 'Formation' and in the chapter in Part Two on 'The Mother'. In each instance, her framework is the opposition of free, transcendent, unrestricted movement enjoyed by men to the inhibitions of immanence, which can be viewed as thwarting women's motility through menstruation, pregnancy, childbirth and a variety of other phenomena specific to women. Beauvoir rejects the logic of castration intrinsic to psychoanalysis, maintaining that the girl/woman does not experience the absence of a penis as a lack – 'her body is evidently a plenitude for her' (Beauvoir 2009: 297) – but her assessment of women's motility up to 1949 is in other respects famously negative. In *Orlando*, by contrast, Tilda Swinton's lithe, muscular physique is given every opportunity to run, jump and indulge in the sporting activities I have already mentioned: Orlando courts Sasha as they skate elegantly on the Thames, in contrast to Orlando's clumsy fiancée and the self-important English nobleman who insists on having a cloth laid on the ice for him to walk over, and when Shelmerdine is thrown by his horse and twists his ankle after riding out of the mist, she rides them both to safety. In the brief scene of Orlando's pregnancy, she runs frantically across a twentieth-century battlefield at night, stumbles, and falls, but the image cuts to her standing again, and as she moves on, the shelling ebbs away, she rubs her rounded belly, day breaks, and she disappears into the quiet mist, communicating a sense of tranquillity and hope. We do not see her give birth, and generally, as a woman, Orlando appears strong, healthy, and active rather than passive in her love-making and encounters with other bodies, such as her daughter's.

Critics have admired the dynamism and energy of *Orlando*, as I have already indicated, but its sexuate character – how and to what extent the 'voyage of "becoming"' (Pidduck 1997: 172) Potter screens *is* female, feminine or feminist – has only really been touched on by Julianne Pidduck. Drawing on Teresa de Lauretis's essay 'Desire in Narrative' and Mary Ann Doane's extension of a gendered economy of stasis and movement to spatiotemporal patterns of genre, Pidduck proposes that there is 'an explicit play (in both Virginia Woolf's source novel and Potter's film adaptation) upon gendered conventions of movement' (ibid.: 173). By observing that during *Orlando*'s 'utopian feminist voyage of "becoming"', 'the dry theoretical problem of gendered narrative movement becomes an explicitly collective project of social critique' (ibid.), Pidduck opens the door to feminist accounts of embodied subjectivity and motility, but quickly shuts it again by turning to Mikhail Bakhtin (whose 'Forms of Time and Chronotope in the Novel' takes no account of sexual difference) for her account of articulations of time and space within historical literary genres. Although she returns to de Lauretis's 'Desire in Narrative' later in her article, she refers to de Lauretis citing a structuralist narrative theorist called Lotman whose fundamental binary opposition is into mobile and immobile character types, again without reference to differentiated embodiment (although de Lauretis herself adds male and female to the theoretical mix). For Pidduck, finding in *Orlando* the unadulterated dynamism that might seem necessary 'to a feminist journey of becoming' – 'would be manipulating the text to my own ends' (ibid.: 185): she points out that Orlando ends his/her historical peregrinations in the same places he/she began them, and there are all kinds of ways in which his/her actions are not effective and purposeful. In my view these instances of inefficacy pertain mostly to his 150+ years as a man, when as England's Ambassador to an unspecified Eastern country, he fails to match the Khan at drinking and to take up arms in battle. If Pidduck is right to point out that Orlando does not *achieve* much for a narrative that extends over more than 450 years (though I am inclined to argue that independence, motherhood, and success as a writer adds up to a lot), then it should probably be remembered that when assessing the gendered qualities of movement and achievement in *Orlando* or any film, different levels of action must be distinguished, at least analytically. My descriptions of the positivity and dynamism of Swinton's movements remain at the level of performance, whereas for Beauvoirian feminist phenomenology, different analytically separable levels of action are fused: the body is 'our grasp on the world and the outline of our projects' (Beauvoir 2009: 46). It is precisely to counter the deterministic tendencies that arise from building sexual difference into this philosophy of free, transcendent action – as Beauvoir does in *The Second Sex* by emphasising women's historical desire and capacities – that it is worth dwelling on the detail of particular visions and narratives of female embodiment. I shall return to *Orlando* in my conclusion to this chapter, but first, turn to Potter's treatment of female movement and action in *The Tango Lesson*.

The Tango Lesson: Dancing, Bruises and Blisters

Two films compete with one another to produce *The Tango Lesson*: the first is a sumptuously costumed drama about the Paris fashion industry the character Sally (played, of course, by Potter) struggles to write in the opening scenes, the second a 'more personal' project about the Argentinian tango. The first, which proves to have been a real project of Potter's by becoming *Rage* (2009), although it has been transposed to New York as the Hollywood producers Sally meets in *The Tango Lesson* suggested it should be, is in glorious colour, the second in black and white. A step back from the resplendent colour Potter screens so magnificently for the first time in *Orlando*, *The Tango Lesson* nevertheless substitutes for it alternative visual and aural pleasures – memorably melancholy music, a romantic narrative, and many scenes of expert tango dancing by Pablo Veron, Potter herself, and diverse practitioners from the tango halls of Buenos Aires. Although men are seen dancing as much as Potter and the one other woman dancer (Pablo's other partner), the film is, through Sally, just as complex a visualisation of female embodiment as *Orlando*.

By directing and starring in *The Tango Lesson*, as Lucy Fischer points out, Potter joins a distinguished list of other women artists – Maya Deren and Yvonne Rainer among them – who have made experimental films highlighting their status as dancers and filmmakers (Fischer 2004: 46). Fischer's claim that Potter's focus on dance 'links her to the mainstream cinema' is in my view arguable, but she also makes two points wholly supportive of the vision of female embodiment and its capacities I see in *The Tango Lesson*. The first, actually articulated by Beatrice Humbert, is that although tango gives the more spectacular role to the man (vividly illustrated by Pablo's display of wounded narcissism after Sally fails to follow his every move in their one public stage performance), its popularity in Europe at the turn of the twentieth century was in part because it 'opened a venue for women to exhibit sensuality in public …

Tango showed and performed the strong changes in gender roles that were under way at the time' (Fischer 2004: 50). The second is the ambivalent status of dance on film as both visual spectacle and athletic physical performance. Potter trained as a dancer as well as a choreographer in the 1970s, in her twenties, but for *The Tango Lesson* had not only to master an entirely new dance form (albeit one she was obviously passionate about), but regain comparable strength, suppleness and technique in her mid-forties, all while directing herself, other actors, and the entire film. Her physical achievement alone in *The Tango Lesson* is remarkable, though not without obvious effort and fatigue – in a scene where she returns to her Buenos Aires hotel after a night's dancing to find a sheaf of faxes from producers, Sally is seen soaking her aching feet in a hot bath while she starts to phone replies[10] – and if her dancing is not as spectacular as Pablo Veron's, she nonetheless fulfils her intention 'to show, somehow, what dancing *feels* like, rather than what it *looks* like' (Potter, quoted in Guano 2004: 471). The aim of the very physical project she undertook in making this personal, clearly partly autobiographical, film was not to produce visual spectacle her audience could marvel at from a distance, but to communicate the intensely bodily experience of dancing, from her woman's point of view.

It is not only in dance that the type of bodily agency proposed by phenomenology's concept of the 'lived body' is dramatised in *The Tango Lesson*. Vitally for feminist film theory, looking is also seen to be agentic and what defines Sally as a film director – when she tells Pablo, enraged by her lack of compliance during their public tango performance, that he only knows how to be looked *at*, not how to look, and again later, when the film that is *The Tango Lesson* is under way, that it is 'With my eyes. With my work' that she loves him.[11] Looking is every bit as embodied as dancing, a honed, perfected technique. One early scene dramatises this better than any other: as she location-scouts for the abandoned version of *Rage* in the Parc de St Cloud, outside Paris, Sally runs around pacing out the dollies and levels that her camera will need to film the Red Model. As Potter explains in her commentary on the shoot:

> This scene was snatched as the sun went down at the end of a shooting day … We had more or less an hour to do about six set-ups, so we ran from location to location as the shadows got longer. My job as a performer was to look – really look – at the locations in the strange (but to me, natural) way that a director looks at a place: seeing it as it is, and, simultaneously, superimposed, seeing it as it could be onscreen. When I saw the rushes I realised, with a shock, that one rarely sees a woman looking out like that on screen. Normally she is dragging the look towards her, as an invitation.
>
> (Potter 1997: 4)

The sharp, acquisitive look of a woman prospecting for her film is caught on camera in this scene, and shown to be a thoroughly embodied, physical activity. This type of look by a woman is rarely screened, as Potter notes, and it seems to me that a woman director imitating her camera is just as rare a sight. The camera is a cyborg rather than a human body (Sobchack 1992: 163), so by including this scene in *The Tango Lesson* Potter raises many of the same film-philosophical questions about the interrelationship of gender, embodiment and vision as phenomenologically oriented film theorists of the 2000s.

Running against the grain of most film theory written between the 1970s and the early 1990s, phenomenology affirms this bodily gaze both within the filmic frame (and in both *Orlando* and *The Tango Lesson*, in the woman within the frame) and in the spectator, creating the possibility of a meeting or exchange of looks across what Laura Marks so memorably calls 'the skin of the film'. Potter's *Orlando* and *The Tango Lesson* convey women's embodied looking as stylishly and affirmatively as they stage female physicality and historical becoming, envisioning dramas both echoed and elucidated by the feminist existential phenomenology pioneered by Simone de Beauvoir in *The Second Sex*.

Notes

1. The first full career retrospective granted to a British woman filmmaker by the BFI, this series of screenings and events ran from 2 to 28 December 2009.
2. As commentators have pointed out, the dispersal of *Orlando*'s action over more than three centuries makes it better described as an 'elegy' than as a fictional biography or a novel: Woolf wrote it above all as a satire on the very grounded and chronological conventions of the literary biography.
3. Sonia Kruks in *Situation and Human Existence: Freedom, Subjectivity and Society* (Kruks 1990), Kate and Edward Fullbrook in *Simone de Beauvoir and Jean-Paul Sartre: the Remaking of a Twentieth-Century Legend* (Fullbrook and Fullbrook 1993), Karen Vitges in *Philosophy as Passion: The Thinking of Simone de Beauvoir* (Vitges 1996), Debra Bergoffen in *The Philosophy of Simone de Beauvoir: Gendered Phenomenologies, Erotic Generosities* (Bergoffen 1998), and Margaret Simons in various essays collected in *Beauvoir and the Second Sex: Feminism, Race and the Origins of Existentialism* (Simons 1999). This series of studies emphasising Beauvoir's continuing importance for feminist thought continued into the 2000s, with Nancy Bauer's *Simone de Beauvoir, Philosophy and Feminism* (Bauer 2001), Sara Heinamaa's *Towards a Phenomenology of Sexual Difference* (Heinamaa 2003) and Penelope Deutscher's *The Philosophy of Simone de Beauvoir: Ambiguity, Conversion, Resistance* (Deutscher 2008).
4. In French, the *corps vécu*: the (mis)translation of the subtitle of the second volume of *Le deuxième Sexe*, 'L'expérience vécue' as 'Woman's Life Today', is one of H.M. Parshley's most notorious failures to recognise the importance of Beauvoir's phenomenological vocabulary.
5. The first book in English on this new branch of political philosophy was Linda Fisher and Lester Embree's co-edited *Feminist Phenomenology* (2000), which was based on a symposium held in 1994. Perhaps the principal initiator of its contemporary origins was philosopher Iris Marion Young in her essay 'Throwing Like a Girl: A Phenomenology of Feminine Body Comportment, Motility and Spatiality' (Young 1989).
6. Other articles to broach these cross-disciplinary connections are Gaylyn Studlar's 'Reconciling Feminism and Phenomenology: Notes on Problems and Possibilities, Texts and Contexts' (Studlar 1990) and Elizabeth Newton's 'The Phenomenology of Desire: Claire Denis's *Vendredi soir* (2002)' (Newton 2008).

7. While making it clear she is seeking to redress the imbalance created by the semiotic and psychoanalytic preference for a fetishized over a lived female body, del Rio states that she is not entirely rejecting semiotic and psychoanalytic perspectives, but 'combin[ing] these with a phenomenological approach that identifies bodily action as not only inherently significant, but also indivisible from symbolic and discursive structures' (del Rio 2004: 12). The stress on the body as 'a written and a spoken sign' rather than a 'material entity' in feminist film theory of the 1970s to early 1990s, she states, was '[b]orn of urgent necessity', and did not foresee how it 'would relegate the sensual and bodily aspects of female subjectivity to a practically irrelevant status' (del Rio 2004: 11).

8. 'For us the point is not to take possession in order to internalize or manipulate, but rather to dash through and to "fly" (*voler*)' (Cixous 1981: 258). A translator's note to 'fly' on this page explains how in French, Cixous puns on *voler*'s double meaning of 'to fly' and 'to steal' in this and subsequent sentences.

9. '*Orlando* promises the fulfilment of a metaphysical quest where the question concerns what every being is *in potentia* of becoming' (Degli-Esposti 1996: 82); 'I would even go so far as to say that *Orlando* develops a utopian feminist voyage of "becoming" which can delicately "move", inspire or amuse [its dispersed feminist] audience' (Pidduck 1997: 172).

10. 'Bruises and Blisters' is the title of Potter's commentary on the film in *Sight and Sound*'s supplement to the 1997 London Film Festival, where she explains that after rehearsing the 'tango for four' she dances with Pablo and her two Buenos Airean teachers towards the end of the film, 'it took two hours to be eased out of my shoes at the end of the day – a doctor in attendance to lance the blisters' (Potter 1997: 7).

11. See also Guano (2004: 468–70).

Bibliography

Bauer, N. 2001. *Simone de Beauvoir, Philosophy and Feminism*. New York: Columbia University Press.

Beauvoir, S. de. [1949] 2009. *The Second Sex*, trans. C. Borde and S. Malovany-Chevalier. London: Jonathan Cape.

Bergoffen, D. 1998. *The Philosophy of Simone de Beauvoir: Gendered Phenomenologies, Erotic Generosities*. Albany: State University of New York Press.

Butler, J. 1990. *Gender Trouble: Feminism and the Subversion of Identity*. London and New York: Routledge.

———. 1993. *Bodies That Matter: On the Discursive Limits of 'Sex'*. London and New York: Routledge.

Cixous, H. 1981. 'The Laugh of the Medusa', in E. Marks and I. de Courtviron (eds), *New French Feminisms: An Anthology*. Brighton: The Harvester Press Ltd, pp.245–64.

Degli-Esposti, C. 1996. 'Sally Potter's *Orlando* and the Neo-Baroque Scopic Regime', *Cinema Journal* 36(1): 75–93.

Del Rio, E. 2004. 'Rethinking Feminist Film Theory: Counter-Narcissistic Performance in Sally Potter's *Thriller*', *Quarterly Review of Film and Video* 21(1): 11–24.

Deutscher, P. 2008. *The Philosophy of Simone de Beauvoir: Ambiguity, Conversion, Resistance*. Cambridge: Cambridge University Press.

Fischer, L. 2004. '"Dancing through the Minefield": Passion, Pedagogy, Politics and Production in *The Tango Lesson*', *Cinema Journal* 43(3): 42–58.

Fisher, L. and L. Embree (eds). 2000. *Feminist Phenomenology*. Dordrecht: Kluwer Academic Publishers.

Fowler, C. 2009. *Sally Potter*. Urbana and Chicago: University of Illinois Press.

Fullbrook, E. and K. Fullbrook. 1993. *Simone de Beauvoir and Jean-Paul Sartre: the Remaking of a Twentieth-Century Legend*. London: Harvester Wheatsheaf.

Garrett, R. 1995. 'Costume Drama and Counter Memory: Sally Potter's *Orlando*', in J. Dowson and S. Earnshaw (eds), *Postmodern Subjects/Postmodern Texts*. Amsterdam and Atlanta: Rodopi, pp. 89–99.

Guano, E. 2004. 'She Looks at Him with the Eyes of a Camera: Female Visual Pleasures and the Polemic with Fetishism in Sally Potter's *Tango Lesson*', *Third Text* 18(5): 461–74.

Heinamaa, S. 2003. *Towards a Phenomenology of Sexual Difference: Husserl, Merleau-Ponty, Beauvoir*. Lanham: Rowman and Littlefield Publishers, Inc.

Imre, A. 2003. 'Twin Pleasures of Feminism: *Orlando* Meets *My Twentieth Century*', *Camera Obscura* 18(54): 176–211.

Kruks, S. 1990. *Situation and Human Existence: Freedom, Subjectivity and Society*. London and Boston: Unwin Hyman.

Mellencamp, P. 1995. 'What Virginia Woolf Did Tell Sally Potter', in *A Fine Romance – Five Ages of Film Feminism*. Philadelphia: Temple University Press, pp. 281–88.

Moi, T. 1994. *Simone de Beauvoir: the Making of an Intellectual Woman*. Oxford, U.K., and Cambridge, U.S.: Blackwell.

———. 1999. 'What Is a Woman? Sex, Gender and the Body in Feminist Theory', in *What Is a Woman? and Other Essays*. Oxford: Oxford University Press.

Newton, E. 2008. 'The Phenomenology of Desire: Claire Denis's *Vendredi soir* (2002)', *Studies in French Cinema* 8(1): 17–28.

Pidduck, J. 1997. 'Travels with Sally Potter's *Orlando*: Gender, Narrative, Movement', *Screen* 38(2): 172–89.

Potter, S. 1997. 'Bruises and Blisters', *Sight and Sound*, LFF supplement, November: 4–7.

Simons, M. 1999. *Beauvoir and the Second Sex: Feminism, Race and the Origins of Existentialism*. Lanham: Rowman and Littlefield Publishers, Inc.

Sobchack, V. 1992. *The Address of the Eye: A Phenomenology of Film Experience*. Princeton: Princeton University Press.

Studlar, G. 1990. 'Reconciling Feminism and Phenomenology: Notes on Problems and Possibilities, Texts and Contexts', *Quarterly Review of Film and Video* 12(3): 69–78.

Vitges, K. 1996. *Philosophy as Passion: the Thinking of Simone de Beauvoir*. Bloomington: Indiana University Press.

Young, I. M. 1989. 'Throwing Like a Girl: A Phenomenology of Feminine Body Comportment, Motility and Spatiality', in J. Allen and I. M. Young (eds), *The Thinking Muse: Feminism and Modern French Philosophy*. Bloomington: Indiana University Press, pp. 51–70. Originally published in *Human Studies* 3 (1980): 137–56.

Filmography

Potter, S (dir.). 1979. *Thriller*. Sally Potter and the Arts Council of Great Britain.

———. 1983. *The Gold Diggers*. The British Film Institute Production Board and Channel Four.

———. 1986. *The London Story*. Sally Potter, the British Film Institute and Channel Four.

———. 1992. *Orlando*. Adventure Pictures Ltd. Lenfilm. Mikado Film. Rio. Sigma Films. British Screen. European Co-Production Fund (U.K.). European Script Fund. National Film Development Fund.

———. 1997. *The Tango Lesson*. Adventure Pictures. OKCO Films. PIE. Nippon Film Development and Finance. Imagica. Pandora Filmproduktion. Sigma Films. Arts Council of England. European Co-Production Fund (U.K.). Sales Company. Eurimages Conseil de l'Europe. Medien-und-Filmgesellschaft Baden-Würtemberg. NPS Televisie. Stichting Co-Productiefonds Binnenlandse Omroep. National Lottery through the Arts Council of England.

———. 2000. *The Man Who Cried*. Gypsy Films Ltd. Working Title Films. Adventure Pictures. Studio Canal. Universal Pictures.

———. 2005. *Yes*. Greenestreet Films. U.K. Film Council. Adventure Pictures. Studio Fierberg. National Lottery.

———. 2009. *Rage*. Adventure Pictures. Vox3 Films.

NOTES ON CONTRIBUTORS

Susan Bainbrigge is Senior Lecturer in French at the University of Edinburgh. Her research focuses on twentieth-century and contemporary French literature and autobiography studies, especially in relation to Simone de Beauvoir. More recent research has taken her into the field of Belgian francophone literature. She is the author of *Writing against Death: the Autobiographies of Simone de Beauvoir* (2005), *Culture and Identity in Belgian Francophone Writing: Dialogue, Diversity and Displacement* (2009) and co-editor, with Jeanette den Toonder, of *Amélie Nothomb: Authorship, Identity and Narrative Practice* (2003) and, with Joy Charnley and Caroline Verdier, of *Francographies: Identité et altérité dans les espaces francophones européens* (2010).

Jean-Pierre Boulé is Professor of Contemporary French Studies at Nottingham Trent University and the author of a number of books, notably on Sartre, including *Sartre médiatique* (1992) and *Sartre, Self-Formation and Masculinities* (2005). He is the co-founder of the U.K. Sartre Society and executive editor of *Sartre Studies International*. He has given papers at conferences on Simone de Beauvoir in Italy and the U.S. and has published in *Simone de Beauvoir Studies*. His most recent books include *Jean-Paul Sartre: Mind and Body, Word and Deed*, co-edited with Benedict O'Donohoe (2011) and a companion volume to the present one, *Existentialism and Contemporary Cinema: A Sartrean Perspective*, co-edited with Enda McCaffrey (2011).

Oliver Davis teaches in the Department of French Studies at Warwick University, U.K. In 2006 he published *Age Rage and Going Gently: Stories of the Senescent Subject in Twentieth-Century French Writing*. His more recent research has taken him well away from ageing and is focused mainly on the leading contemporary continental philosopher of equality, Jacques Rancière. He published a comprehensive critical introduction to Rancière in 2010 with Polity Press in their Key Contemporary Thinkers series and is currently working on a volume of new critical essays on Rancière, which is scheduled for publication by Polity in 2013.

Claire Humphrey has recently completed a Ph.D. at the University of Manchester. Her doctoral thesis draws on Beauvoir's feminist phenomenology to analyse contemporary representations of 'Parisienne' subjectivities in film, literature, photography and street art. An article on femininity and counter-culture in the work of graffiti artists Miss.Tic and Princess Hijab will be published in *French Cultural Studies* in August 2012.

Kate Ince is Reader in French Film and Gender Studies in the School of Languages, Cultures, Art History and Music at the University of Birmingham. Her work in film includes a monograph on *Georges Franju* (2005) and an edited book of essays on European francophone auteur directors, *Five Directors: Auteurism from Assayas to Ozon* (2008). She is currently editing a themed issue of *Studies in European Cinema* on women's film-making in France in the 2000s and beginning a book on female subjectivity in French and British films of the 1990s and 2000s.

Constance L. Mui is Youree Watson S.J. Professor of Philosophy at Loyola University New Orleans, where she teaches philosophy and women's studies, and is co-founder of its Women's Studies Program. She specialises in continental philosophy, with research interests in Sartre, Beauvoir, pheno-menology and feminist theory. Her publications include *Gender Struggles: Recent Essays in Feminist Philosophy* (co-editor, with J. Murphy, 2002), 'Shattering of the Self: Analyzing Trauma Through Sartre's Ontology of Person' in *Remembering Sartre, 1905–1980* (2007), 'Willing the Freedom of Others After 9–11' in *Feminist Philosophy and the Problem of Evil* (2007, with J. Murphy) and 'A Feminist-Sartrean Approach to Understanding Rape Trauma' in *Sartre Today: A Centenary Celebration* (2005).

Julien S. Murphy is Professor and Chair of Philosophy at the University of Southern Maine. She teaches graduate and undergraduate courses in applied ethics and continental philosophy. She is the author of *The Constructed Body: AIDS, Reproductive Technology and Ethics* (1995), editor of *Feminist Interpretations of Jean-Paul Sartre* (1999) and co-editor (with Constance Mui) of *Gender Struggles: Recent Writings in Feminist Philosophy* (2002). Her publications include articles on Beauvoir and the Algerian war, Sartre and American Racism, Sartrean freedom after 9/11 (with Constance Mui) and rural bioethics. Her research interests currently are in Sartrean social democracy and in digital pedagogies.

Michelle Royer was educated in France and is now a Senior Lecturer in the Department of French Studies at the University of Sydney where she lectures in contemporary French cinema. Her major research interests are in the field of contemporary cinema and the work of French writer and filmmaker Marguerite Duras. She has published several books (*Repenser les processus créateurs*, 2001; *L'Ecran de la Passion*, 1997) and recently several chapters and articles on French cinema and on the work of Marguerite Duras. Her current research focuses on senescence in World Cinema.

Linnell Secomb has taught in Australian and U.K. universities and is currently Head of Social, Political and Cultural Studies at the University of Greenwich (U.K.). She has published extensively in journals and edited collections and is the author of *Philosophy and Love: From Plato to Popular Culture* (2007). Linnell has presented papers at conferences in Europe, the U.K., the U.S. and Australasia. Her current research projects are on 'Emotional Economies' and 'Culture, Community and Identity'.

Bradley Stephens is Lecturer in French at the University of Bristol. His research interests lie in receptions of French Romanticism from the early nineteenth century to the present day, with a particular focus on literary and visual culture. In addition to various articles and book chapters on this subject, he is the author of *Victor Hugo, Jean-Paul Sartre and the Liability of Liberty* (2011) and co-editor of *Transmissions: Essays in French Literature, Thought and Cinema* (2007). He is currently working on a study of the tensions between literary grandeur and masculinity in nineteenth-century France, as well as a joint project on the 150-year legacy of *Les Misérables*.

Ursula Tidd is Senior Lecturer in French Studies at the University of Manchester, U.K. She is the author of three monographs: *Simone de Beauvoir, Gender and Testimony* (1999), *Simone de Beauvoir*, Routledge 'Critical Thinkers' series (2004) and *Simone de Beauvoir*, Reaktion 'Critical Lives' series (2009) as well as articles and chapters on Beauvoir's autobiographies, fiction and philosophy. She has given papers at conferences on Simone de Beauvoir in France, Sweden, Germany, China, the U.S., Canada and the U.K. Her current major project is writing a monograph on the Francophone Spanish Holocaust writer Jorge Semprún (forthcoming with Legenda/MHRA 2013) supported by a Leverhulme Trust Research Fellowship.

Emma Wilson is Professor of French Literature and the Visual Arts at the University of Cambridge and a Fellow of Corpus Christi College. Her publications include: *Sexuality and the Reading Encounter: Identity and Desire in Proust, Duras, Tournier and Cixous* (1996), *French Cinema since 1950: Personal Histories* (1999), *Memory and Survival: The French Cinema of Krzysztof Kieślowski* (2000), *Cinema's Missing Children* (2003), *Alain Resnais* (2006) and *Atom Egoyan* (2009). Her latest book, *Love, Mortality and the Moving Image*, appeared in 2012.

Index